Counselor Licensure: Issues and Perspectives

A Book of Readings

Richard W. Warner, Jr.
David K. Brooks, Jr.
Jean A. Thompson
EDITORS

American Personnel and Guidance Association
Two Skyline Place, Suite 400
5203 Leesburg Pike
Falls Church, Virginia 22041

Copyright © 1980 American Personnel and Guidance Association

Dedication

This book is dedicated to the pioneering work in counselor licensure of individuals such as Tom Sweeney, Carl Swanson, and Harold Cottingham and to the literally hundreds of individuals who have spent and are spending tremendous amounts of time and energy in the pursuit of the licensing of professional counselors.

RWW
DKB
JAT

About The Editors

RICHARD W. WARNER, JR., is Dean of the School of Education, East Carolina University, Greenville, North Carolina, and is serving as Chair of the American Personnel and Guidance Association (APGA) Preparation and Standards Committee. He is also a Certified Clinical Mental Health Counselor.

DAVID K. BROOKS, JR., is past Chair of the American School Counselor Association (ASCA) Licensure Committee and is presently serving as Chair of the American Personnel and Guidance Association (APGA) Licensure Committee.

JEAN A. THOMPSON, is on special assignment from DeKalb Community College, Clarkston, Georgia, to serve as President of the American School Counselor Association (ASCA).

Table of Contents

v PREFACE

1 INTRODUCTION AND BRIEF HISTORY

PART I: THE COUNSELOR LICENSURE MOVEMENT

9 Licensure in the Helping Professions: Anatomy of an Issue
Thomas J. Sweeney and *Alan D. Sturdevant*

16 Recent Licensure Developments: Implications for Counselor Education
Harold F. Cottingham and *Carl D. Swanson*

31 Counseling and Professional Psychology: A Dialogue
Rodney K. Goodyear and *Gordon F. Derner*

37 Attention Students: Be Advised . . .
Steven P. Lindenberg

42 Who Says You're a Counselor?
Thomas J. Sweeney and *J. Melvin Witmer*

47 APGA and Counselor Licensure: A Status Report
Harold F. Cottingham and *Richard W. Warner, Jr.*

52 Professional Disclosure in Licensure
J. Melvin Witmer

56 The Politics of Licensure: Questions Legislators are Asking
J. Melvin Witmer

PART II: CREDENTIALING: ACCREDITATION, CERTIFICATION/REGISTRY, AND STANDARDS

63 An Introduction to the Standards for the Preparation of Counselors and Other Personnel Services Specialists
Jerald R. Forster

70 Guidelines for Doctoral Preparation in Counselor Education
Association for Counselor Education and Supervision

75 Standards and Accreditation in Counselor Education: A Proposal
Robert O. Stripling

80 Toward a New Professionalism: Certification and Accreditation
Daniel C. McAlees and *Brockman Schumacher*

87 The History of Rehabilitation Counselor Certification
Roger Livingston

103 Why Establish a Certification System for Professional Counselors? A Rationale
James J. Messina

118 Toward Performance-Based Counselor Certification
Stan Bernknopf, John L. Shultz, and William B. Ware

129 The Coming Exclusion of Counselors from the Mental Health Care System
Janet K. Asher

APPENDIX A

138 Copies of the Alabama, Arkansas, and Virginia Licensure Laws

APPENDIX B

170 Chronological Bibliography of Certification, Credentialing, and Registry
Sylvia Nisenoff

Preface

This book concerns an important professional issue in the mental health field. The crux of the issue is whether the mental health needs of this nation can or even should be met by a relatively small band of professionals or whether the needs can be better met with a broad spectrum of mental health professionals. Professional counselors have never objected to psychiatrists, psychologists, and social workers providing to clients whatever services they are qualified to provide. We simply believe that counselors are also qualified to provide important services to clients, and the articles in this book support this belief.

The purpose of this book is to provide an overview of the licensure issue and a brief introduction to the related issues of accreditation, registry, and preparation and standards.

Introduction and Brief History

The current concern with counselor licensure and related credentialing issues is a result of forces both internal and external to the profession of counseling. The internal influences center on professional identity, role and function, preparation and standards, and self-regulation of the profession. Counseling journals have carried articles dealing with these issues for the past 25 years. Indeed, counseling professionals have revealed in introspective debate, asking such questions as, Who are we? What is it that we *should* be doing? How do we know that we can do what we say we do? What makes us different from psychologists? How should we police our own ranks?

While this internal debate has been going on, external forces related to conflicts with state psychology boards, eligibility for third-party insurance reimbursements, rendering of "services psychological in nature," and job security materialized in the 1970s. Before this, counselors trained at the doctoral level rarely had difficulty becoming licensed as psychologists. The practice of counseling was usually limited to schools, colleges, and a few agencies that dealt with vocational assessment and job placement. Economic recession, the declining birthrate, changes in government priorities, and expanding demand dramatically changed the delivery of counseling services. School counselor certification was no longer an all-purpose credential. The lack of credentialing in the emerging settings has put counselors in a disadvantaged position as compared with psychologists and social workers when all three compete for the same job.

In 1972, in the case of *Weldon* v. *Board of Psychologist Examiners,* a Virginia court recognized counseling as a profession separate from psychology but stated that because counseling used the tools of psychology and there was no statutory regulation of the profession of counseling, the plaintiff, John I. Weldon, was enjoined from practicing as a counselor. This was the first in a chain of events that eventually resulted in organized legislative activity by professional counselors. By the fall of 1979, Virginia, Arkansas, and Alabama had passed counselor licensure laws (see Appendix A at the end of this book). Eighteen state branches of APGA introduced counselor licensure bills in 1979 alone, and there were active counselor licensure committees functioning in most other states. A brief outline of events occurring between a losing court case and intense political activity seven years later is presented in the next section.

May 1974—"Licensure in the Helping Professions: Anatomy of an Issue" (Sweeney and Sturdevant) appeared in the *Personnel and Guidance Journal.*

July 1974—APGA Board of Directors adopted a position paper, "Licensure in the Helping Professions," which called for licensure legislative efforts in every state. The APGA Licensure Commission established the following objectives:

1. To formulate and disseminate model legislation on licensure for counselors.
2. To establish procedures for state and regional leadership workshops on licensure.
3. To help initiate and maintain liaison and dialogue with associations in the counseling related professions (e.g., psychology, psychiatry, social work, marriage and family).
4. To testify on federal legislation having implications for professionals trained in counselor education programs.
5. To identify for the membership nonlegislative activities having implications for the counseling profession (e.g., importance of liaison with related state professional groups in psychology and social work and with mental health insurance companies, when appropriate).
6. To consider other alternatives or avenues to earning recognition for counseling as a profession (e.g., academy of diplomates and/or national registry of persons qualified to offer specialized counseling services to the public for a fee).
7. To encourage cooperative efforts between the various divisions, state branches, affiliates, and subgroups of APGA in the area of licensure.
8. To encourage research and innovations on traditional methods of licensure including possible use of more performance-based criteria and unified administrative boards for all counseling-related professions.
9. To identify test cases where evidence of discrimination against qualified members takes place by boards of related professions.

October 1974—Southern Association for Counselor Education and Supervision (ACES) adopted a position in support of counselor licensure efforts and established a licensure committee.

March 1975—APGA Senate affirmed the Board of Directors' July 1974 action and approved the personnel of the APGA Licensure Commission (now Committee); Tom Sweeney of Ohio was appointed first chairperson.

August 1975—*State of Ohio* v. *Culbreth B. Cook:* The defendant, an APGA member, was arrested and sued by the Ohio Psychologists Licensure Board for practicing psychology without a license. Cook did not represent himself as a psychologist but as a private consultant dealing with mental assessment of children in academic difficulty. In a directed verdict, the court found Cook not guilty.

January 1976—APGA Licensure Commission, now chaired by Carl Swanson of Virginia, issued a draft of a model state counselor licensure bill. A doctoral degree in counseling was recommended as the educational requirement for licensure.

April 1976—The Governor of Virginia signed into law the first state counselor licensure bill. The law passed after prolonged educational and lobbying efforts by the Virginia Personnel and Guidance Association. The effort began as a direct result of the Weldon case of 1972.

January 1977—APGA Licensure Commission, now chaired by Harold Cottingham of Florida, adopted the contents of the APGA Licensure Commission Action Packet. Included in the packet was revised legislative language that set the master's degree with appropriate supervised experience, rather than the doctorate, as the minimum recommended academic standard for counselor licensure.

**January –
March 1977**—The ACES Licensure Commission, chaired by Richard Warner, conducted a nationwide survey of ACES members in relation to a National Registry for Counselors. On the basis of that data, an individual plan for a registry for professional counselors was presented at the Dallas Convention in March 1977.

March, 1977—The ASCA Delegate Assembly adopted a resolution setting licensure as a priority to which extensive time, effort, personnel, and finances should be committed.

May, 1977—In line with Delegate Assembly action, eight ASCA Regional Licensure Consultants were trained at a special workshop in Madison, Wisconsin. Plans were made to coordinate educational efforts with the APGA Licensure Committee.

July, 1977—APGA Board of Directors approved appointment of a special commission to study credentialing issues. Past President Bruce Shertzer was appointed to head the commission.

**September –
November 1977**—APGA Licensure Committee, now chaired by Richard Warner of Alabama, in conjunction with the ASCA Licensure Consultants, conducted licensure workshops in the four regional branch assembly sessions held during this time. A nationwide licensure network, made up of state licensure representatives, was also set up.

November 1977—Shertzer Commission completed its report, which was adopted by the APGA Board of Directors at its December meeting. The commission recommended a four-fold thrust in credentialing activities described in more detail below.

March 1978—APGA Licensure Committee issued the revised Action Packet. It was announced at the APGA Convention in Washington, D.C., that 42 states had functioning licensure committees and that counselor licensure bills had been introduced in 10 states. Virginia remained the only state with a licensure law enacted.

July 1978—APGA Board of Directors approved plans of action for Preparation and Standards,Licensure, and Registry Committees. ACES was directed to proceed with preparations for counselor education program accreditation.

November 1978—ACES conducted five regional training sessions to prepare individuals to serve as members of program accreditation teams.

February 1979—The first administration of a national examination to prospective members of the National Academy of Certified Clinical Mental Health Counselors occurred. This body was established through the efforts of the American Mental Health Counselors Association (AMHCA), APGA's newest division, to certify counselors in community mental health agencies, other agency settings, and private practice. Academy procedures were designed to meet the standards of the National Commission of Health Certifying Agencies.

March 1979—The Governor of Arkansas signed the second counselor licensure law in the nation.

April 1979—Continuing high level of state licensure activity was reported at APGA Convention in Las Vegas, Nevada. Counselor licensure bills were introduced in 18 states in 1979.

July 1, 1979—National Academy of Certified Clinical Mental Health Counselors officially came into existence. More than 1,800 injuries had been received about the certification process in the previous five months.

July 26, 1979—The Governor of Alabama signed counselor licensure law, making Alabama the third state to achieve counselor licensure.

What began in 1974 as a tentative step toward professional credibility has indeed become a national movement involving almost all of APGA's state branches and at least half of its divisions. Counselor licensure efforts have been the most visible components of this movement, which also encompasses preparation and standards, accreditation, and registry. This four-fold credentialing thrust was recommended by the Shertzer Commission Report, which was adopted by the APGA Board of Directors in December 1977. In addition, two divisions have promoted professional certification as an alternative means of endorsing professional competency.

This book attempts to provide the reader with the most comprehensive overview of the licensure movement. The major focus is on counselor licensure, but the second section deals briefly with the related issues of accreditation, registry, certification, and standards.

Part I traces the evolution of the counselor licensure movement by presenting several classic articles that deal with the critical issues involved during the various phases of development. Thus, we begin by presenting the classic article by Sweeney, which appeared at a time when most of us were not even aware there was a problem. From there we move to an examination of training implications. The next four articles deal with various issues related to counselor licensure and reflect the evolution of the movement from strictly a question that concerned only doctoral-level counselors to one that concerned all counselors, including paraprofessionals. The final two articles in Part I present a view of the current situation.

Appendix B, at the end of this book, is an annotated bibliography developed by Sylvia Nisenoff, APGA's Professional Reference Librarian. This is an exhaustive listing of available material related to licensure. It should be very helpful to readers who want to go beyond this book of readings.

As stated earlier, Part II focuses on licensure issues. It follows a format similar to Part I by providing what we believe are the best statements about the issues involved. Our hope is that after completing this text the reader will have a sound understanding of the basic issues involved in credentialing. As the Shertzer Commission Report states, "Now is the time to get on with the task of credentialing professional counselors."

PART I

The Counselor Licensure Movement

This article by Tom Sweeney and Alan Sturdevant is the classic publication in the history of the counselor licensure movement. The article is an excellent beginning point for this text because it not only provides a clear picture of how naive we were but also offers some clear recommendations for action, which we are still attempting to implement. Thus, it is both a historical document and a map for the future.

[From: *Personnel and Guidance Journal,* Vol. 52, No. 9]

Licensure in the helping professions: anatomy of an issue

THOMAS J. SWEENEY

ALAN D. STURDEVANT

The licensing of psychologists is not generally a concern of counselors, counselor educators, or supervisors. However, with the enactment of new licensing laws such as the one described here, an issue is emerging that members of the counseling professions should not leave unattended. Through ignorance or complacency, we may contribute to the demise of the counseling professions as self-regulating groups. The authors examine this matter here and offer some recommendations for action.

Licensure in the helping professions is a topic relatively unfamiliar to most counselors and counselor educators (Scott 1971). For those of us who are members of both APA (American Psychological Association) and APGA, there may have been, during the 1950s and '60s, a growing awareness of and support for the psychologists' efforts to protect the public from persons who operate beyond the bounds of responsible practice. Yet for most of us, legislation has not been the focus of our attention. Recent developments in licensure, however, deserve careful study by members of APGA.

Most persons with training and experience in education are familiar with certification laws. A certification law controls the use of a professional title by persons offering services to the public. Licensure, unlike certification, regulates both the practice and title of a profession. Previously some laws licensing psychologists were no more than certification laws under a misnomer. There is now a tendency among psychologists and legislators to clarify this distinction, particularly as new or revised laws are formulated. The result is far more powerful and broad-reaching legislation.

LEGISLATIVE GUIDE

The report of the APA Committee on Legislation (American Psychological Association 1967) is increasingly guiding state psychological groups in the formulation of new laws. Cognizant of the struggle that psychology still experiences to some degree for equal status among related mental health professions, the committee cautioned:

Psychology believes it undesirable to attempt to control the practice of all psychological functions by restricting them to members of any single profession *except insofar as it can be clearly demonstrated that such restriction is necessary for the protection of the public.* Psychology, therefore, does not favor narrowly restrictive legislation, which provides that only psychologists (or teachers, or physicians, etc.) may engage in certain applications of psychological knowledge and techniques [p. 1098].

More recently the *APA Monitor* (Psychology briefs 1973) noted with satisfaction that the American Psychiatric Association Task Force on Inter-

---

THOMAS J. SWEENEY is Program Coordinator and Professor of Guidance and Student Personnel, Ohio University, Athens. ALAN D. STURDEVANT is a doctoral student and NDEA fellow, Ohio University.

professional Relations also had declared that "there should no longer be divisive wedges between professions striving toward a common goal...." and that "no profession should attempt to define the functions and responsibilities of any other profession.... Complaints against other professionals should be directed to the responsible authorities of the profession concerned [p. 7]."

With such strong, affirmative positions stated and approved by the governing bodies of two of the major psychological associations, how could problems develop? The answer is relatively simple. Functions, like terminology, are difficult to define. Interpretations of what is intended are revised not only by professional organizations but by legislatures and ultimately by boards of psychology and the courts. So long as what some term as "liberal" laws are enacted (Pennsylvania implements... 1973), relatively few persons become unduly alarmed. More recently, however, the enactment, the attempted enactment, and the interpretation of the laws in some states have been more restrictive (Asher 1973). In point of fact, the APA committee referred to earlier recommended the following:

Legislation regulating the practice of psychology should be restricted to one level, requiring the doctoral degree from an accredited university or college in a program that is primarily psychological, and no less than 2 years of supervised experience, one of which is subsequent to the granting of the doctoral degree [American Psychological Association 1967, p. 1099].

A CASE IN POINT

Ohio is one state that has enacted for psychologists and school psychologists a licensing law that follows closely the recommendations of the APA Committee on Legislation. The legislation became effective in September 1972, but many persons in the counseling professions were (and still are) unaware of its implications. Some thought that it pertained only to persons in private practice; others thought that it applied only to persons who considered themselves to be psychologists; and still others were not even aware that legislation was pending. Most of these persons now wish they had had an opportunity to study the law before it was enacted.

The Legislation

The State of Ohio Board of Psychology created under the new legislation (Licensing law ... 1972) derives executive power directly from the governor, who is instructed to select representatives from lists of names tendered by the Ohio Psychological Association (OPA) and the Ohio School Psychologists Association (OSPA). The Board also acquires quasi-legislative power. Privileged to "make such rules as are necessary to conduct its business," the Board has developed the "State of Ohio Board of Psychology Rules and Regulations" (1973), which are tantamount to law. Included among these rules are APA's ethical standards for psychologists. Thus, the psychologists' standards acquire both ethical *and* legal ramifications with a viable means of enforcement. OPA and OSPA, therefore, have acquired considerable power. They establish the criteria for membership in their own associations and select nominees for the Board. The Board in turn has the power to determine who needs a license to practice, what ethical practice is, and under what circumstances to issue, deny, or revoke a license.

If the rights and duties of psychologists were clearly different from those of persons in any other profession, this closed circle of power would not be problematic. In Section 4732.01 (c) of the Ohio Revised Code, however, the definition of "psychological procedures" states that such procedures

include but are not restricted to application of principles, methods, or procedures of understanding, predicting, or influencing behavior, such as principles pertaining to learning, conditioning, perception, motivation, thinking, emotions, or interpersonal relationships; the methods or procedures of verbal interaction, interviewing, counseling, behavior modification, environmental manipulation, group process, psychological psychotherapy, or hypnosis; and the methods or procedures of administering or interpreting tests of mental abilities, aptitudes, interests, attitudes, personality characteristics, emotions, or motivation [p. 2].

As defined here, operations of interest to the Board can include, but are not restricted to, procedures specific to clinical and counseling psychologists as well as deans of students, personnel officers, reading specialists, high school teachers of psychology, and—most emphatically—members of the counseling professions. Although the Board is permitting many persons educated in areas other than psychology to be licensed under a grandfather clause, the president of the board has indicated that in the future persons will be required to prove not only that their nonpsychology department courses were psychological in nature but also that any of their teachers who were not licensed were adequately trained in psychology as well. For those seeking licensure in the future, this may mean their providing transcripts for themselves and for their unlicensed professors who are from departments other than psychology.

Also of significance are the specifications that (a) only licensed psychologists may supervise practicum and intern students; (b) these students must be registered with the Board by their supervisor; and (c) appropriate written records of these students' progress must be kept, in the event that the Board wishes to review them.

Effects of the Legislation

Although the above are matters of immediate concern, the long-range implications can be of even greater significance. Consider, for example, the following:

- Student programs will require planning according to content and experience needed to meet licensing expectations, including successful completion of the Board examinations.

- Employment of new teaching staff will require determining in advance whether an individual can be licensed or at least meet Board criteria for teaching courses of a psychological nature.

- Accountability for laboratory, practicum, and intern experiences of students now takes on ethical *and* legal ramifications, with the State Board as a significant source of criteria and judgment.

- Membership in psychological associations—previously considered a voluntary, professionally responsible choice—may seem an economical and professional requisite for job mobility and credibility.

- Implicit in this process is the implication that persons trained as psychologists are preferred to those not trained as psychologists, particularly in circumstances involving the supervision of others who use psychological processes.

- Academic advisors, deans of students, and similar professionals may safely perform their functions so long as they neither hold themselves out to be psychologists nor use psychological procedures that the State of Ohio Board of Psychology "judges by uniform rule . . . to be a serious hazard to mental health and to require professional expertise in psychology." With no definitions of these terms yet available, the full significance of this regulation is unclear. Anyone who engages in counseling functions, however, will potentially come under the influence of the Board's rulings.

- School counselors appear protected under the certification laws in performing their normal functions so long as they do not hold themselves out as psychologists or receive personal remuneration for special services of a psychological nature. One might interpret this to include potential prohibition from administering college entrance examinations on weekends for pay or performing similar activities that may have been common in the past.

The real threat to school counselors under the new law is directed, by inference, at their comparative status in the professional order rather than their right to practice. The school counselor is certified as a teacher; the school psychologist is now explicitly certified under the same section of the Revised Code as the school counselor *and licensed* by the State of Ohio Board of Psychology. This latter distinction not only affords the school psychologist a professional posture unavailable to the school counselor; it also allows the school psychologist's constituents privileged communication—a protection not available through the school counselor. There are 16 states that afford privileged communication to constituents of school counselors at the present time, but Ohio is not one of them (Maine counselors . . . 1973; Privileged communication 1973).

The confidentiality distinction is important. The professional posture of counselors in the helping professions can be crucial. In Ohio, the right for school counselors to practice at all is being challenged. An independent, self-appointed Commission on Public School Personnel Policies in Ohio (1973) makes clear a strong bias in favor of the school psychologist by urging school districts to ask: "Is the preparation for guidance counseling adequate for the difficult counseling situations or do these problems require the type of training that a school psychologist should have [p. 23]?" They recommend that school districts "re-examine the need for guidance counselors [p. 38]." The new law may further reinforce the Commission's bias and, out of ignorance or complacency, counselor educators and supervisors may have unwittingly contributed to the demise of those whom they train.

IMPLICATIONS FOR THE COUNSELING PROFESSION

There are many in the ranks of counseling who, like the writers, will feel that their professional prerogatives may be violated by more restrictive laws for psychologists. On the other hand, are we prepared legislatively to establish regulatory guidelines and standards for those who practice under the title of "counselor"? There are alleged abuses not only by persons with little or no training but also by those whose training did not include supervised experience in private and clinical therapeutic practice. While there are ways to demonstrate competence other than through graduate credits earned, a credibility gap with the other helping professions will grow unless we help to see that our publics are protected. If we do not assume responsibility for such actions, we have little choice but to accept the leadership of other professional groups.

PROPOSED ALTERNATIVES

For those who prefer that counseling be subsumed and delimited under psychology, the new laws will be welcomed. Some alternatives follow, however, for those who wish to maintain the counseling profession's identity under another heading. Some readers may discount these proposals as high-minded rhetoric without a chance of enactment or acceptance. Others may question their justification. For these reasons we have cited, after each proposal, events relevant to licensure that have already transpired. Many of these evidence optimistic trends; others are alarming and thus further attest to the need for immediate action.

ALTERNATIVE 1: *In states without licensure laws for psychologists, counselor associations may wish to propose legislation independently or jointly with the state psychological associations for licensure of counselors and psychologists. In states with "liberal" licensure laws for psychologists, counselor associations may wish to study the existing law for possible amendments or separate legislation that would recognize the counseling profession as an equal partner. School psychology has this distinction in Ohio and other states.*

Counselors in several states have initiated efforts to obtain licensure for counselors. Through personal correspondence, we have learned that the Virginia Personnel and Guidance Association has proposed an amendment to the Code of Virginia that would license professional counselors and that this action has garnered support from the Virginia Psychological Association.

An organization's numerical strength is of vital interest to legislatures. APGA has over 34,000 members. Aggressive lobbying efforts, even by smaller groups, can be similarly influential. An organization as small as the Ohio School Psychologists Association lobbied effectively enough in 1971 to block passage of a licensing bill that excluded them. APGA, now with 11 divisions representing wide yet common interests, not only has great inherent strength but also has access to countless parents and professionals who constitute a potentially very powerful lobbying force. Counselors, other educators, and parents have already experienced significant gains in legislation through cooperative effort. Recent funding for elementary school guidance in Florida (They came, they saw . . . 1972) is a case in point.

ALTERNATIVE 2: *Where licensing of counselors is already under psychology, APGA members may seek means of gaining representation on the state boards and examining committees.*

Some members of APGA also hold membership in state and national psychological associations. Such persons have occasion to serve on committees or in offices of these organizations. In states that license counselors as psychologists, a purposeful and open effort to gain a berth on these licensing boards should be encouraged. We know that this has been possible in at least one state.

ALTERNATIVE 3: *In states where licensure is apparently discriminatory, test cases may be developed to revise or clarify the interpretation of the law.*

Unknown to most counselors is the fact that some of their colleagues are presently being sued for violating psychologists' licensing laws. In other cases, persons who have applied for licensure have been denied a license and now have recourse only through legal channels. Liability insurance notwithstanding, the limits of an individual member's resources can be tested severely in these cases. For this reason, counselor associations would do well to consider collectively challenging the limits of other professions in order to define the counselor's field of practice. With the membership we have available to develop financial and related resources, the counseling professions can be influential.

ALTERNATIVE 4: *In states where privileged communication is not afforded clients of counselors, efforts to do so may be undertaken through advisement with members in states that have such statutes.*

Sixteen states have obtained privileged communication statutes for school counselors, and the *APGA Guidepost* (Maine counselors . . . 1973) noted that "several other states are working on getting them through the legislatures this year [p. 5]."

This marks an admirable contrast to an earlier report (Pietrofesa & Vriend 1971) that found this protection available in only two states. It also attests to the influence counseling groups can exert when their goals are clearly in the interest of the publics they serve.

ALTERNATIVE 5: In light of recent trends toward competence-based counselor training programs and certification, APGA members may wish to develop strategies for licensure in other than the traditional mode.

The state of Washington has already instituted for school counselors a certification plan based on performance criteria (Brammer & Springer 1971). This (or similar plans) could be used as a model for developing nontraditional licensure laws.

CONCLUSION

As noted earlier, most counselors have not focused their attention on legislation regulating practice in the helping professions. Primary reasons for this have been the assumptions—now apparently incorrect—that such legislation pertained only to persons who were engaged in private practice or who considered themselves to be psychologists. Even counselor educators, one-third of whom hold joint membership in APA and APGA, previously tended to identify themselves as "educators" and reject the title of "psychologist" (Scott 1971). The issue, however, is being forced by the enactment of laws such as the one described earlier. Are counselors, counselor educators, and supervisors bona fide professional groups unto themselves under the general title of counselors, or must they be psychologists who function in educational, community, or related settings? Individually and collectively, we must answer this question.

Obviously, there are many facets to an issue such as this one. It seems clear, however, that responsible action by APGA members is necessary to help prevent or resolve the problems that can result from legislation touching on the very essence of the counseling professions. ■

REFERENCES

American Psychological Association. A model for state legislation affecting the practice of psychology 1967: Report of APA Committee on Legislation. *American Psychologist,* 1967, *22*, 1095–1103.

Asher, J. Opposition wins latest round in fight over New York licensing bill. *APA Monitor,* 1973, *4*(6), 1.

Brammer, L. M., & Springer, H. C. A radical change in counselor education and certification. *Personnel and Guidance Journal,* 1971, *49*, 803–808.

Commission on Public School Personnel Policies in Ohio. School Leadership. Report Number Seven. Cleveland, Ohio: Author, 1973.

Licensing law for psychologists and school psychologists in Ohio. Sections 4732.01 to 4732.25 and Section 4732.99 of the Revised Code. Columbus, Ohio: State of Ohio Board of Psychology, 1972.

Maine counselors: Privilege statute. *APGA Guidepost,* 1973, *16* (Extra), 5.

Pennsylvania implements liberal licensing law. *APA Monitor,* 1973, *4*(6), 12.

Pietrofesa, J. J., & Vriend, J. *The school counselor as a professional.* Itasca, Ill.: F. E. Peacock, 1971.

Privileged communication. *APGA Guidepost,* 1973, *16*(3), 6.

Psychology briefs. *APA Monitor,* 1973, *4*(5), 7.

Scott, C. W. Characteristics of counselor educators. *Counselor Education and Supervision,* 1971, *10*, 99–111.

State of Ohio Board of Psychology. State of Ohio Board of Psychology rules and regulations. Revised version. Columbus, Ohio: Author, 1973. (mimeo)

They came, they saw, they funded. *APGA Guidepost,* 1972, *15* (Extra), 1.

This 1976 article by two former chairpersons of the APGA Licensure Committee is an excellent review of the licensure movement at that time. Of particular importance is the section dealing with implications for counselor education programs. These implications in many ways are still in need of attention, although APGA's efforts in accreditation and standards are addressing some of the issues. The article is also a reflection of the times in which it was written because it is primarily concerned with licensure of doctoral-level individuals.

[From: *Counselor Education and Supervision,* Vol. 16, No. 2]

Recent Licensure Developments: Implications for Counselor Education

HAROLD F. COTTINGHAM
CARL D. SWANSON

> This article describes several current developments in the licensing of helping professionals, and it identifies problems in the definition and preparation of qualified behavioral science practitioners. It also lists implications for certain aspects of counselor education, including educational orientation, advisement practices, curriculum development, and professional leadership. Specific concerns are noted in each of the four areas.

The demand for qualified helping professionals, illustrated by the inclusion of mental health services in pending comprehensive national health insurance coverage and by freedom-of-choice legislation, has direct implications for the field of counselor education (Wachtel 1973). As each specialty area within the helping professions has expanded, it has also tried to establish its own identity and to receive recognition for the unique services it offers. The concepts and practices of psychology as a behavioral science are employed by a variety of specialties in the helping professions. Such areas as criminology, social work, and rehabilitation services rely heavily on psychological assumptions and skills. Students in counselor education departments whose programs emphasize training in counseling psychology represent one particular professional specialty group. Particular problems arise, however, when those individuals seek licensing, an important credential in private practice.

BACKGROUND—COUNSELING PSYCHOLOGY AS A SPECIALTY

The problem of identity for counseling psychology as a sub-field of psychology is about three decades old, reaching back to the period after World

Harold F. Cottingham is Professor of Counseling and Human Systems, Florida State University, Tallahassee; Carl D. Swanson is Professor of Psychology, Madison College, Harrisonburg, Virginia.

War II in the late 1940s and early 1950s. Division 17 of APA was renamed Counseling Psychology in 1951; the following year, the Veteran's Administration created the Civil Service position of Counseling Psychologist, and, in 1955, the *Journal of Counseling Psychology* was founded. Counseling psychology as a concept and a function emerged as a response to the post-World War II need for vocational and educational counseling for veterans. It also reflected the professional advancement and integration of vocational guidance, psychometrics, and personality development (APA 1956).

Essentially, counseling psychology is concerned with mental health services as they relate to educational and vocational problems of normal individuals. Professionals holding the title of counseling psychologist provide a variety of assessment, as well as counseling or therapeutic, functions. Their job settings are usually found in university or college counseling centers, government agencies, hospitals, clinics, and in private practice. The professional competencies of a counseling psychologist rest on the basic knowledge required of other psychologists, but they differ in application, focusing on helping services and career and educational decision making. Counseling psychologists see their clients as total persons seeking optimal fulfillment and positive growth, rather than as problem-centered individuals needing intensive therapeutic intervention.

Identity problems have also arisen in comparing counseling psychology with clinical psychology and with counseling provided in educational settings. Generally, clinical psychology is concerned with processes of personality change that take place in institutional or medical settings through intensive therapeutic involvement with persons having relatively severe personal dysfunctions. Clinical psychology appears to have greater prestige among psychologists than does counseling psychology (Brigante, Haefner & Woodson 1962). However, similarities in counseling and clinical training components were reported at the Greystone Conference (Thompson & Super 1964). Later, Chin (1967) indicated that counseling and clinical psychology had evolved sufficiently from their respective educational and medical backgrounds and that their rapprochment was possible, necessary, and desirable.

Counseling psychology has also had close connections with education. There is an overlap of function between the two. That is, both psychologists and educational counselors offer counseling functions, and they both rely on psychological principles and techniques for appraisal, intervention, or therapeutic growth. An estimated 10 of 20 APA-approved doctoral-level training programs are based in nonpsychology departments, jointly with psychology, in educational psychology, or in counseling and guidance departments (APA 1974a). In a recently published study on the status of training in counseling psychology, 32 program directors reported the following departmental affiliations: Psychology—11, Education—9, the program itself a department—6, Educational Psychology—4, and combined Psychology/Education—2 (Banikiotes 1975). With respect to relationships with other programs, overlap of "very much" or "a good deal" with counselor education was reported by 15 program directors; of the 14 counselor education programs with which there was "very much" overlap, 10 were identical with the counseling psychology programs. Overlap with clinical psychology of "very much" and "a great deal" was indicated by eight program coordinators (Banikiotes 1975). In one sample of the membership of the Division of Counseling Psychology (Division 17) of APA, 70 percent had PhDs and 30 percent, EdDs. It is estimated that approximately half of the PhD counseling psychologists in Division 17 hold a PhD in education (Weeks 1975).

Although earlier counseling psychology training followed a traditional, academic scientist-practitioner model, the need for a more relevant approach is now discernible. At the recent 1973 Vail Conference on levels and patterns of professional training in psychology, a number of significant recommendations were made, among them being that "The development of psychological science has sufficiently matured to justify creation of explicit professional programs, in addition to programs for training scientists and scientist-professionals" (Ivey & Leppaluoto 1975, p. 750). This professional training model for a basic service orientation was suggested *"without* abandoning comprehensive psychological science as a substantive and methodological root of any educational or training enterprise in the field of psychology, and *without* depreciating the value of scientist or scientist-professional training programs for certain specific objectives" (Korman 1974, p. 442).

The identity of the counseling psychologist as being unique in training, function, and orientation has also been brought into question by studies of occupational affiliation and training program characteristics. Krauskopf, Thoreson, and McAleer's (1973) study of the characteristics of doctoral graduate counselors and counseling psychologists suggests the existence of at least two or possibly three subgroups within the specialty. These researchers concluded that there are three somewhat distinct groups of counseling psychology professionals: (a) a student personnel group that carries out educational/administrative functions, (b) a subgroup of professional psychologists that has moved from the scientist/professional role to a practitioner's role, and (c) a subgroup that has assumed the traditional, academic role of social and behavioral scientists. With regard to the training of counselors at the doctoral level, Fretz (1975) examined the psychology course offerings of both APA- and non-APA-approved programs; he concluded that there is more homogeneity of preparation of counseling psychologists with respect to counseling courses than with respect to general psychology courses. This clearly indicates a lack of agreement on a common core of counseling psychology, and it directly relates to the issue of professional identity.

THE QUESTION OF LICENSING AND CERTIFICATION

Historically, licensing and certification have been developed by certain professions offering a unique and definite service, in order to guard the public health, safety, and welfare; the right for this control stemmed from the state's police power to protect the public from quackery and malpractice (McCully 1961). Medicine and psychiatry, by virtue of their priority, established licensing boards much earlier than psychology, which emerged as a discipline only in the early part of the 20th century. As of 1955, for example, only nine states had passed laws regulating the practice of psychology. The current difficulties in instituting legal control over counseling as a public service are due essentially to three conditions: (a) many helping professionals representing a variety of disciplines, job settings, and titles provide some type of counseling service; (b) psychology, following medicine and psychiatry, initiated the first state legislation, thus preempting regulation of a wide range of helping functions, many of which are now carried out by counseling personnel who are not psychologists; and (c) counseling professionals come from diverse training programs with varied levels of preparation in academic settings other than psychology departments.

Licensing or certification laws provide two services to the public: They identify individuals who have been recognized as qualified to offer psychological services to the public, and they define the services and responsibilities of the psychologist. The psychology profession also benefits from these laws since licensing provides a means by which practitioners of demonstrated competence can offer their professional services to the public.

Early state legislation made no distinction between licensing and certification. However, there is an important difference between the two today. Initial certification laws identified those persons who were qualified to call themselves psychologists but made no attempt to delineate the nature of psychological practices. Current laws in most states, frequently called licensing laws, also define the practice of psychology regardless of what the professionals call themselves. Integral to any licensing act is a definition of the practice of psychology in terms broad enough to cover all activities of psychologists. For example, the APA (1967) model for state legislation, as well as the proposed draft revision for 1975, defines the practice of psychology as the application of principles pertaining to learning, interpersonal relationships, interviewing, education and vocational counseling, prevention of adjustment problems, planning for effective work situations, and "the resolution of interpersonal and social conflicts" (p. 1099). Such a broad definition allows the boards of psychologist examiners to gain legal control over operations and services provided by many helping professionals offering counseling (Cottingham 1975; Sweeney & Sturdevant 1974). Thus, without their own licensing legislation, counselor education graduates could be violating the law if they performed these psychological functions or assumed the title of psychologist. In accordance with the fact that many helping professionals "do work of a psychological nature," most licensing laws include an exemption provision that permits qualified members of other professions to do psychological work as long as they do not present themselves to the public using a title or description with the words *psychological, psychologist,* or *psychology* in it. Varying interpretations of these legal provisions by state boards are widespread.

As psychology boards have become more restrictive and have further defined the practice of psychology, limiting it to licensed psychologists, court cases have arisen. In the *City of Cleveland, Ohio v. Cook 1975* case, the defendant, C. Cook, was arrested "on a charge of offering or rendering services as a Psychologist, otherwise engaged in the practice of Psychology for compensation or other personal gain, while not a licensed Psychologist." The prosecution stated ". . .we will grant that on occasions, he (Dr. Cook) has in fact helped people. . . . We don't think that is an issue." The issue was that Cook, who held a degree in counseling but was not licensed as a psychologist, was offering services that were "psychological in nature." In fact, he had not claimed to be a psychologist but instead was offering counseling and testing services.

The defense attorney moved for a directed verdict for Cook, arguing ". . .your Honor. . . , one (witness) said (Dr. Cook was) counseling only. That is what he received. . .counseling. The other (witness) said counseling and testing. . . . It would appear that when the witness (for the prosecution from The Board of Psychology) Dr. McMcPherson said, 'this is the exclusive prerogative of the Psychologist, and therefore, no other individual can avail of themselves of that use,' I say, your Honor, it's either totally unconstitutional or something is radically wrong when somebody is capable, might avail themselves of the tools of other individuals."

After hearing these arguments by both the prosecuting and defense attorneys, Judge Gaines granted the motion on behalf of the defendant for a directed verdict (*City of Cleveland, Ohio v. Cook 1975*). This signifies that the prosecution had not presented a case warranting further deliberation.

Another line of cases has delved into the issues of levels of training and grandfathering. A U.S. Court of Appeals in the *Berger v. Board of Education of Psychologist Examiners* case (1975), in reversing a trial court opinion, ordered the psychology licensing board to permit Berger to take the examination even though he lacked the required degrees. The court stated:

. . .the very reason psychology has not been regulated before is that it has been and remains an amorphous, inexact and even mysterious discipline. Possession of a graduate degree in psychology does not signify the absorption of a corpus of knowledge as does a medical, engineering or law degree; rather it is simply a convenient line for legislatures to draw, on the brave assumption that whatever is taught in the varied graduate curricula of university psychology departments must make one a competent psychologist, or at least competent enough to be allowed to take a licensing examination. (p. 1056-1057)

The court here eloquently addresses both the subject of competency as opposed to "hours" and the question of degrees coming from psychology departments and the variations therein. One may argue that competency could just as well come from counselor education departments even though certain state psychology boards refuse to recognize graduates from such departments as "equivalent" and, therefore, deny them the right to take the psychology examination (Weeks 1975).

Another significant condition in the state licensing/certification issue is the lack of any national roster of professional psychologists whose qualifications are known to third party reimbursers, such as insurance companies. These organizations are unwilling in most cases to accept the varying state licensing standards for psychologists (rather than clinicians) as interpreted by state boards, and thus they will not reimburse psychologists directly for services. In response to this situation and the possible advent of national health insurance, a National Register of Health Service Providers in Psychology was established in 1974 (Asher 1975) that will offer to agencies, insurance companies, and consumer groups the names of over 7,000 psychologists who are qualified to provide mental health services. One requirement for being in the register is certification or licensing by a state psychology examining board.

DEFINING A "QUALIFIED" HELPING PROFESSIONAL

The difficulty of defining a qualified helping professional is compounded by several factors. Psychology licensing legislation in all states is broadly written and includes psychological activities actually carried out by helping professionals in a variety of disciplines other than psychology. Such legislation, which stems from models proposed by APA, follows a somewhat common form but is subject to individualized state policies and interpretations that vary widely and differ from time to time. APA has also developed an approved set of "standards for providers of psychological services" that also applies to the consumers and sanctioners of services (APA 1974b). In 1947, APA supported the creation of the American Board of Professional Psychologists (ABPP), whose function is to award the diplomate title in four areas of psychology, including counseling. Again, however, one must be licensed in a state to become eligible for the diplomate examination. The National Register of Health Service Providers in Psychology operates independently under the auspices of ABPP and APA; it was developed primarily to establish the identity of psychology as an independent health services field.

The proliferation of individuals from various disciplines who perform counseling functions in different settings further complicates defining a qualified professional. These practitioners come from disparate training programs and educational levels, and their degrees range from PhD to EdD and PsyD. In addition, no national body certifies or licenses psychologists because certification and licensing are state concerns; thus, these functions are carried out by boards that follow widely differing policies and persuasions. No performance or competency system for state regulation or psychologists exists; approval is almost always attained by written and oral examination and credential review.

This situation has become more crucial as potential counseling psychologists in some states have been denied access to licensing or certification processes by state boards, usually because of the specific degree held by the applicant or because of the department that has awarded it. In this connection, however, it has been suggested that the quality of counseling psychology programs is related to the qualifications of the psychologists who teach in them, not necessarily to the university division that offers the program (APA 1975). Although state laws are reasonably flexible, state board interpretations of them have been criticized as being unduly restrictive. Such action not only denies a psychologist the right to practice but also deprives the citizen of psychological services and may lower the quality of services available to the public, as well as increase costs to the public. These and related concerns of one segment of APA appear in a position statement prepared by an Ad Hoc Committee on Human Rights and Social Issues of Division 17, the Division of Counseling Psychology (APA 1975).

In assessing the applicants for licensing, most state boards review transcripts and educational experiences to determine if the applicants' programs were "primarily psychological in nature" (APA 1974b). Since no national or association criteria exist as guidelines for interpreting this standard, much inconsistency is found in the review of applicants. Thus, the issue centers around the legal and ethical propriety of denying licensure to individuals who consider themselves eligible.

THE LICENSURE OF COUNSELORS—AN EMERGING CONCEPT

Professionals in fields other than counseling have been ahead of counselors in understanding and foreseeing new roles. A 1971 Iowa Law Review reference article points out this trend "in the expansion and redefinition of the counselor's role from that of educational-vocational counseling to personal problem counseling" ("Note, Testimonial Privileges and the Student-Counselor Relationship in Secondary Schools" 1971). In arguing for privileged communication, the author sees a further shift due to "the increasing numbers, quality and roles of school counselors indicating the potential importance of counselors as sources of aid for students with personal problems." The article goes on to say that the "primary, if not the sole function of school counseling is to help students better understand themselves and their environment." This the author views as "personal problem counseling [which] encompasses the whole spectrum of personal difficulties which students encounter" (p. 1324). A 1972 court decision held "that the profession of personnel and guidance counseling is a separate profession (from psychology) and should be so recognized" (*Weldon v. Board of Psychologists Examiners* 1972). This was the first case that recognized counseling as a profession.

Counselors themselves have had difficulty defining their role and practice. Various definitions are now emerging as licensure laws are enacted or being sought. It is of interest to compare the terminology used in counseling certification/licensure laws in Virginia, both of which passed the General Assembly and were signed by the Governor during the 1975 and 1976 sessions. The 1975 law, Chapter 5.2 § 54-102.15 (Code of Virginia 1950), states, "Guidance and Personnel Counseling means the application of those principles of guidance and personnel functions which focus on the developmental process of a person in relation to educational and social progress, and occupational and career goals." In March 1976, the General Assembly enacted Chapter 28 Article 2 (Code of Virginia) entitled, "Professional Counselors." Under §54-932 a., the following definition was given: "Professional counselor shall mean a person trained in counseling and guidance services with emphasis on individual and group counseling designed to assist individuals in achieving more effective personal, social, educational and career development and adjustment." Further, the legislature stated in §54-932 d. (11) that practice is defined to include "Counseling which means assisting an individual through the counseling relationship, to develop understanding of personal problems, to define goals, and to plan action reflecting his interest, abilities, aptitudes, and needs as these are related to educational progress occupations and careers, and personal-social concerns."

Other states with legislation pending define counseling in different ways. In Ohio's present Substitute HB. No. 1043, Section 4755.01(A), introduced in March 1976, " 'counseling' means. . . the application of counseling procedures to help in learning how to solve problems or make decisions related to careers, personal growth, marriage, family or other interpersonal or intra-personal concerns. . . . 'counseling procedures' include but are not restricted to the use of counseling methods and techniques, both verbal and nonverbal, which contribute to self-understanding, desired personal behavior change, or more effective interpersonal behavior. . . ." Counseling has also been defined in the United States Congress (HR 3270, 1975 session, 94th B Congress) as ". . .The process through which a trained counselor assists an individual or group to make satisfying and responsible decisions concerning personal, educational, and career development."

From these varied definitions, one can see the profession of counseling emerging in the eyes of the law, and one is able for the first time to define its function. As the profession develops, counselors can more clearly define their role. In licensure, political realities will continue to have a great effect on what counselors may claim as function or role, which will depend on what has or has not been legally reserved for another profession.

A possible solution in the defining of functions of the various behavioral sciences at the state level may lie in the creation of a comprehensive behavioral science board. The Virginia General Assembly created such a board, which includes subprofessional boards of professional counselors, psychologists (school and clinical), and social workers. In establishing the Behavioral Science Board, the legislature stated:

It is declared to be the policy of the Commonwealth of Virginia that the activities of those persons who render services to the public in the behavioral science area be regulated to ensure the protection of the public health, safety and welfare. The Commonwealth also recognizes the fact that the many professions offering these services overlap and intertwine to a substantial degree. This fact results in the need for those professions to work in close harmony with each other to maintain quality service to the citizens and to prevent infringement on the rights of practitioners to engage in their lawful professions, which infringements may harm the public. The system of regulation established herein is intended to provide professional responsibility for the public and harmony among the professions. (Chapter 28, Article 1,§54-923, Code of Virginia)

This approach to the overlapping functions of those practitioners in the behavioral sciences can eliminate jurisdictional squabbles, court suits between professionals, and confusion in the mind of the public. Thus, at this time, the possibility of licensing counselors, as distinct from psychologists, appears to be a workable alternative for some states. Such a regulatory policy could protect the public, control the quality of services, and legitimize the counseling functions of helping professionals in public service.

IMPLICATIONS FOR COUNSELOR EDUCATION

Philosophy and Orientation

Current licensing developments pose a number of problems for counselor educators and for counselor education departments. One implicit issue concerns the counselor educators' attitudes toward licensing. Some may support present laws that permit licensing of only psychologists; others may reject this as too limited to serve the public. This difference of opinion may prevent a united position in program design or objectives. A related concern may be a lack of interest in licensing problems, with the attitude that it is an unimportant factor in graduate education. Such a viewpoint suggests that the faculty member has not realized that counselor education graduates must qualify for psychology board examinations if licensing is a prerequisite to an occupational goal.

Of more individual than group importance is the professional allegiance of individual faculty members, that is, whether they identify with psychology or education. A professor's endorsement of students for APA membership or licensing is a practical as well as a philosophical matter. Professors can endorse graduate students for APA membership only if they are themselves APA members. Similarly, licensing applications require endorsements from licensed psychologists. The problem of getting endorsements from APA members of licensed psychologists is aggravated as new faculty members are employed and as more students seek credentials for private practice work. Staff development and postdoctoral work in psychology may be the only solution for faculty members seeking eligibility for APA membership or board examinations. In some states, approval of licensure applications depends on course work taught by faculty members who are also members of APA.

Program Development and Content

Curriculum content and organization should reflect an awareness of current licensure practices. Faculty agreement on alternate programs should permit students to seek psychology licensing either within or outside of the counselor education framework. For example, a student may be allowed to elect a heavy psychology program in lieu of the standard courses in education. State boards appear to be sensitive to such factors as course content, course prefixes, location of program department (education or psychology), and type of degree. Another problem pertains to the extent to which collaborative arrangements have been made with applied psychology faculty members for service courses (e.g., admission of nonpsychology majors and counselor education students who wish to strengthen their background in psychology). The frequency or availability of these courses is also important.

One problem associated with the counselor education program may be the variety of curriculum options it offers to students. Naturally, this depends on a number of variables, including where the program is located and the faculty philosophy. Alternate course plans would permit students to pursue counseling psychology, school counseling, human services work, or a student personnel management program. Students seeking private practice as a vocational goal would thus have the maximum chance to prepare for licensing requirements, while others not so inclined could follow a different route. Available course patterns in relation to potential job opportunities should be made clear to beginning students. If no clear curriculum track is designated or available, student access to course experiences permitting licensing should be explained to them. The type of degree awarded could also be a factor in obtaining licensing with some state boards. For example, an EdD or PhD in education is seen by some boards as a disqualification.

Within the curriculum or program itself, certain provisions ought to be made if current licensing in psychology for private practice is an objective. Among other experiences, there should be an opportunity for appropriate supervisory work in both practicum and internship settings. This would require arranging for suitable placement as well as supervision by APA faculty, a significant factor for getting licensed in some states. Beyond this, courses in the ethical, legal, and professional aspects of private practice should be scheduled. Such offerings should also cover referral systems, interprofessional relationships, and the operational aspects of private practice. Finally, as licensing requirements change in the various states, such standards for eligibility and examination should be reflected in departmental curriculum modifications. Graduate students should be thoroughly informed as to the experiences, skills, and academic relationships that are integral to the licensing process.

Another possibility open to some institutions is that of seeking APA approval as a counseling psychology program. A precedent has been set in light of APA action in this respect. For example, at present, about half of the APA-approved doctoral training programs in counseling psychology are not based in traditional academic departments of psychology (APA 1974a). Such an approval process would undoubtedly be facilitated if the counselor preparation work was contained within the department of psychology or if it was arranged jointly through psychology or an allied department, such as educational psychology. Other factors that would also have to be seriously considered include APA membership of faculty, nature of required and recommended courses, available psychology offerings, and academic qualifications of the faculty in the discipline of psychology.

Student Placement and Advisement

Due to the highly varying licensing practices in different states, student advising takes on a greater significance. The key phrase—"primarily psychological in nature"—holds considerable weight in the licensing process as graduate credentials are reviewed by state boards of psychology. Since no specific criteria exist nationally for interpreting this standard, each state board of examiners in psychology develops its own policies. Students should be informed of current state practices in licensing; state laws, guidelines, or regulations should be on file for faculty and student use. Course planning based on this type of information is even more important for counselor education majors whose programs are not located in departments of psychology or educational psychology.

These same conditions will also affect graduate programs that must be tailored to the individual seeking licensing in one or several states. This advisory process, which may result in more flexible student choices, places a much greater burden on graduate advisors. Students themselves may not be aware of state requirements or institutional options. Certainly, if the licensing requirements are altered and counselor education majors become eligible for licensing by a title other than "psychologist," such changes will affect the advisory process. The possibility of eventual modifications in licensing laws requires that advisors and counselor education faculty members be aware of related legal and policy developments in different states. When placing students in different job settings, faculty advisors should be aware of the extent to which licensing is a factor in initial and continuing employment.

Professional and Interdisciplinary Relationships

On this level, counselor educators have a number of responsibilities. Such activity is not only a reflection of one's own professional interest, but it is almost a necessity if students are to be informed, advised, and placed effectively in assignments requiring some form of licensing. The bulk of a professor's efforts can be directed toward liberalizing licensing laws or, in the interim, toward assisting other professionals and students to qualify for psychology licensing.

Although there is less than complete agreement on how present licensing laws or policies must be modified, there appears to be a consensus among several types of helping professionals that some broadening is needed. Counselor educators must be concerned with this movement since their graduates are frequently ineligible for psychology licensing under present regulations. Their involvement could take the form of developing better relationships between educators and psychology groups as changes are proposed. This process could be initiated at the local, state, or national levels through cooperation with ad hoc committees or assignment to special commissions; if such an opportunity is not proffered, some initiative may be required.

When liberalizing developments are in immediate prospect, the counselor educator could work directly with psychology board members to consider methods by which qualified counselor educators may be appointed to the psychology board. Counselor educators may have to work with state legislative committees responsible for instigating changes in licensing procedures or regulations. In order to establish an ongoing professional relationship, faculty members with education backgrounds need to develop interdisciplinary contacts with psychologists, particularly those in applied areas. This connection could be achieved by their participating in state psychological meetings, serving on doctoral committees, or developing informal contacts with those representing psychological organizations. Currently, most state legislators are only interested in changes in the law that represent collaborative interests of a number of interdisciplinary professional groups.

Beyond these functions, faculty members responsible for teaching counselor preparation courses have other obligations. In addition to being informed on licensing regulations and private practice conditions, faculty members should themselves be models of professional behavior by being licensed and personally knowledgeable about private practice. Part of this role requires assuming responsibility for developing higher standards of competency and recognition. This effort could result in diplomate status with the American Board of Professional Psychology or membership on the National Register of Health Service Providers in Psychology. Counselor educators might also seek to be approved for psychological consultation services by such state agencies as vocational rehabilitation, state employment services, and the Veteran's Administration,

With respect to field settings and contact with counseling professionals, the counselor educator has certain leadership opportunities. Those in school or community college positions may have to explain the merits of licensing, as well as the requirements for registration or certification, if states have the option of accepting applicants with lower credentials. If qualified in the psychological sciences, faculty members may be called on to offer course work related to eligibility for licensing or certification. Such courses, however, may not be creditable unless they are offered by psychology departments or at least are part of a graduate program that is primarily psychological in nature. Faculty members in counselor education who are credentialled, might offer to teach field courses for psychology departments, thus reinforcing their status as academically qualified instructors for in-service psychological education purposes. In any case, those in higher education and, particularly, in counselor preparation can provide a variety of services for counseling and helping professionals in the field.

This article has identified a number of aspects of the counselor licensing process that may be of concern to counselor educators. Their orientation, advisory practices, curriculum efforts, and professional leadership are important factors in meeting their licensing responsibilities as advisors and as professionals. However, the real issue is how they respond to these problems individually and institutionally.

REFERENCES

American Psychological Association, Division of Counseling Psychology Committee on Definitions. Counseling psychology as a specialty. *American Psychologist*, 1956, *11*(6), 282-285.

American Psychological Association. A model for state legislation affecting the practice of psychology, 1967: Report of APA Committee on Legislation. *American Psychologist*, 1967, *22*(12), 1095-1103.

American Psychological Association. APA-approved doctoral programs in clinical, counseling, and school psychology. *American Psychologist*, 1974, *29*(11), 844-855. (a)

American Psychological Association. *Standards for Providers of Psychological Services*. Washington, D.C.: Author, 1974. (b)

American Psychological Association. The licensing and certification of psychologists. A position statement by the Division of Counseling Psychology of the American Psychological Association. *Counseling Psychologist*, 1975, *5*(3), 135.

Asher, J. First edition of National Register due: 7,000 psychologists to be included. *APA Monitor*, 1975, *6*(5), 1.

Banikiotes, P. G. The status of training in counseling psychology. *Counseling Psychologist*, 1975, *5*(4), 106-108.

Berger v. Board of Education of Psychologist Examiners, 521 F. 2d 1056 (U.S. C.A., D.C. Circuit, 1975).

Brigante, T. R.; Haefner, D. P.; & Woodson, W. B. Clinical and counseling psychologists' perceptions of their specialties. *Journal of Counseling Psychology*, 1962, *9*(3), 225-231.

Chin, A. H. New perceptions on the relationship between clinical and counseling psychology. *Journal of Counseling Psychology*, 1967, *14*(4), 374-381.

City of Cleveland, Ohio v. Cook, Municipal Court, Criminal Division, No. 75-CRB 11478, August 12, 1975. (Transcript dated August 19, 1975)

Code of Virginia, 1950, as amended, Chapters 5 & 28. Charlottesville, Va.: The Mitchie Company.

Cottingham, H. F. School Counselors face the issue of licensing. *School Counselor*, 1975, *12*(4), 225-258.

Fretz, B. R. Psychology in counseling psychology: Wither or wither? *Journal of Counseling Psychology*, 1975, *22*(3), 238-242.

Ivey, A. E., & Leppaluoto, J. R. Changes ahead. Implications of the Vail Conference. *Personnel and Guidance Journal*, 1975, *53*(10), 1747-1752.

Korman, M. National conference on levels and patterns of professional training in psychology. *American Psychologist*, 1974, *29*(6), 441-449.

Krauskopf, C. E.; Thorenson, W. W.; & McAleer, C. A. Counseling psychology: The who, what and where of our profession. *Journal of Counseling Psychology*, 1973, *20*(4), 2370-2374.

McCully, C. H. A rationale for counselor certification. *Counselor Education and Supervision*, 1961, *1*(1), 3.

Note, Testimonial privileges and the student counselor relationship in secondary schools. 56 *Iowa L. Rev. 1323*, 1971.

Sweeney, T. J., & Sturdevant, A. D. Licensure in the helping professions: Anatomy of an issue. *Personnel and Guidance Journal*, 1974, *52*(9), 575-580.

Thompson, A., & Super, D. E. (Eds.). *The professional preparation of counseling psychologists: Report of the Greystone Conference*, New York: Bureau of Publications, Columbia University Teacher's College, 1964.

Watchel, M. M. Summaries of National Health Insurance Bills. *APA Monitor*, 1973, *4*(5), 10-11.

Weeks, J. *Position statement, Div. 17, APA*. Unpublished paper presented at the American Psychological Association Convention, Chicago, August 30, 1975.

Weldon v. Board of Psychologists Examiners, Corporation Court Opinion, Newport News, Va., October 4, 1972. (Court Order)

A basic problem from the beginning of the counselor licensure movement has been the varying degrees of opposition from our counterparts in "traditional psychology" and other mental health professions. This 1978 article is a reflection of some of the basic issues involved in the struggle between counseling and psychology. It also reflects the concern held by some about the licensing of master's-level practitioners. It should be pointed out that the APGA licensure committee did not support master's-level licensure until 1977. Up until that time the suggested licensure bill called for doctoral-level licensing only. Since that time, the suggested legislative language in the APGA Licensure Committee Action Packet has called for licensing of individuals with a master's degree who have completed at least three years of supervised experience.

[From: *Personnel and Guidance Journal*, Vol. 56, No. 10]

Counseling and Professional Psychology: A Dialogue

The primary concern of this special feature is how the counselor is to be established as a competent, autonomous professional. Most discussions of this topic have been written by counselors for other counselors. Counseling does not exist in a social vacuum, however, and its sister professions will inevitably have some impact on the manner in which counseling is defined. It is imperative that counselors have input from persons in related professions if they are to adequately understand the question of professional identity now confronting the counseling profession. The following dialogue provides such input from an influential clinical psychologist.

Clinical psychology fought difficult battles of its own in order to earn a place as a recognized mental health profession. Now counseling is engaged in such a struggle and clinical psychology is often seen as one of the opposing forces. It is particularly important for counselors to understand the nature of that opposition.

Gordon F. Derner, who describes himself as a "company man for psychology," is strongly opposed to the concept that master's level counselors might function as mental health professionals. His credentials are such that counselors cannot simply ignore him. Gordon is dean of the Institute of Advanced Psychological Studies at Adelphi University and is quite active in the American Psychological Association (APA). He has served as president of its Divisions of Clinical Psychology, Consulting Psychology, and Psychotherapy and was a candidate for the APA presidency in 1977. He is currently president of the National Council of Schools of Professional Psychology.

By contrast, I refer to myself as a counselor or as a psychologist with equal ease and have maintained loyalties to both APA and APGA. I have been distressed by psychology's tendency to define itself so narrowly that counselors are generally excluded from that definition; I have been even more upset by psychology's efforts to constrain counselors' activities as mental health professionals, for I believe many counselors deserve recognition for their competence in that area. I remain consistent with that belief by specializing at Kansas State in the training of both MS- and PhD-level counselors for community agency settings. I have also been an active and enthusiastic supporter of the fledgling American Mental Health Counselors Association.

The dialogue began with private comments between Gordon and myself about the appropriate role of counselors. We soon realized that the issues we were discussing had important implications for the counseling profession and that counselors might like to be aware of them. A dialogue seemed a useful vehicle for highlighting those issues.

Rodney K. Goodyear is a member of the Kansas State University Counseling and Student Personnel faculty. He is also a part-time psychologist at the Sunflower Mental Health Center in Corcordia, Kansas, and a trainee in the Menninger Foundation's family therapy program. Concerned with counseling's increasing professionalism, Rod chairs the Professional Education Committee of the American Mental Health Counselors Association and recently served on the ACES Commission on Community Counseling.

Gordon F. Derner is Dean and Professor of Psychology at the Institute of Advanced Psychological Studies (IAPS) at Adelphi University. He is co-director of IAPS and Franklin General Hospital Biofeedback Clinic and Research Laboratory. He is a former president of the American Psychological Association divisions of consulting psychology, psychotherapy, and clinical psychology. He is a Diplomate in Clinical Psychology of the American Board of Professional Psychology and recipient of the 1977 Distinguished Psychologist Award of the APA Division of Psychotherapy.

Credentialing Dialogue

After coping with the difficulties of busy schedules, tight deadlines, and the considerable distance between New York and Kansas, we are each satisfied the article serves its purpose.

We would like to thank Dave Myers for his ideas and technical support during the writing of this article. In the following dialogue, Gordon and I share our respective views about the nature of counseling and about its relationship to professional psychology. —Rod Goodyear.

MA Counselors and Mental Health Settings

Gordon: First of all, Rod, let me point out that I have no question at all about a profession called "counseling" or about a group of people called "guidance counselors" who work in schools. I find, however, that counselors do not want to do vocational or academic counseling only. They want to do psychotherapy. I am very concerned that counselors have aspirations to be something for which they do not have adequate training and experience.

Rod: I am curious, then, how we should distinguish counseling from psychotherapy. With the exception of vocational counseling, I find it virtually impossible to differentiate the two, for they share the same processes, goals, and techniques. In fact, students of clinical psychology and of counseling are taught the same helping models. Although counseling and psychotherapy are often distinguished by the settings and populations they serve, I do not think that is a really substantive differentiation.

Gordon: You are right. It is tough to separate counseling and psychotherapy except at their extremes and numerous national conferences have struggled to define them. You are also correct that the clearest differentiation can be made by setting and population. Psychotherapy is more frequently related to emotional, personal, and behavioral disorders and to work with more dysfunctional populations. Counseling is frequently related to the daily choices of living, including academic and vocational choices, life-style planning, and help in thinking through personal dilemmas or conflicts.

Regardless of how we define those terms, we are left with a crucial issue: Is it possible to work into a one- or two-year program sufficient skills training for the counselor to handle the problems with which he or she will be confronted? I would think they could only if those problems are of a very carefully delimited nature.

Rarely would a new clinical psychology PhD be prepared to go into private practice—I would say *never*. He or she can handle certain kinds of patients because they have had such experience, but it is inappropriate for them to take on a full range of responsibilities. Now if I feel that about PhDs, I certainly have doubts about the competency range of the MA level counselor.

Rod: I am puzzled that MA counselors frequently run into this sort of argument while MSW social workers find ready acceptance as mental health professionals. Psychology does not seem to have questions about them. I personally suspect that this is because MSWs have been able to define and grab their piece of the turf and have developed the power to maintain it. I have trouble believing that the typical MSW is a significantly better helper than the typical MA counselor, especially since counselor education programs have geared up in the past few years to train mental health counselors.

Gordon: Social workers have managed to define their professional area of competence and have developed the structure to maintain it. Social workers run social work agencies and these have become increasingly more concerned with the psychological problems of their clients than with monetary and other concrete problems. It used to be that social workers concerned themselves with such things as getting coal and winter clothes to needy families during the winter. Social work clients are now all defined by their psychological problems: The child has behavior problems; mother has made three suicide attempts, etc. These agencies have all become, in effect, psychology agencies. I am not saying they belong to the profession of psychology, but to its discipline. They deal with people's thoughts, feelings, attitudes, and awarenesses.

You alluded to MSW training. I would say most of it is very job-oriented. They spend essentially half of their two years of training in very thoroughly supervised clinical practice. The other half is in taking courses of a very practical nature, such as what the Social Security laws are all about.

Incidentally, I should note here that I have no objection to nondoctoral people working in clinics. I think, however, that their work has to be done under supervision, and I do not mean the nominal supervision which is so prevalent. Also, the authority to make disposition of cases should be through someone who is more qualified, such as a psychologist or psychiatrist who is a fully trained clinical practitioner. One of the reasons I would support social workers doing psychotherapy in a clinic is that they have so many controls through a very well-developed supervisory system.

So there are jobs that can be done by nondoctorates. However, their functions ought to be circumscribed, with someone who has broader training and experiences making such determinations.

Rod: What I am understanding now is that you would have no quarrel with counselors working in mental health facilities if they were tightly controlled through adequate supervision and through checks on their intake procedures.

Gordon: Yes, if we start with the premise that they are qualified by relevant training and experience obtained in the academic program and in their clinical activities. There is another aspect to consider, however. Most of us feel that we can do more than we can and counselors are no exception. As MA counselors are accepted into mental health, their ambition is not to work under somebody else's supervision but on their own. The technicians who make false teeth, for example, are obviously quite capable of making false teeth—that is how dentists use them. But their goal is frequently to make false teeth on their own referral and many of them probably could do it all on their own. They are not allowed to practice independently because they lack the dentists' training in such areas as mouth pathology. Nevertheless, they are constantly fighting to do so. The same is true of counselors: They are not content to have what they have come to view as second-class professional status.

If universities would follow what I think is the appropriate model, they would train mental health counselors at only the bachelor's level (Derner 1976). Just as medical assistants do not presume to have physicians' skills, the BA–level counselor would not be tempted into assuming competencies he or she does not have. They could also then be licensed because they would have received specialized, circumscribed training and would be in positions where they would necessarily have adequate supervision. Parenthetically, it is important not to give people a license that gives them the impression they have more professional prerogatives than they really have.

Are Doctors More Effective?

Rod: Your argument, Gordon, is based on the assumption that those with doctorates are somehow more effective practitioners than those without. I do not know of any research that would support that position. In fact, there is evidence for a quite different conclusion, that academic degrees may correlate at only low levels with therapeutic effectiveness.

An entire generation of research suggests that a therapist's success is determined more by his or her personality and interpersonal skills than by any specific technical training. What is even more important, it is now pretty clear that some therapists are not merely ineffective, they are actually destructive influences on their clients. This destructiveness is related to the absence of those same interpersonal skills. It is significant that these studies have yielded similar results whether done with doctoral or nondoctoral therapists.

From another direction, we have to acknowledge the tremendous acceptance that paraprofessionals have received in mental health during the past decade. In fact, some human services, such as drug abuse treatment, are staffed almost exclusively by paraprofessionals who generally work without the very close and intense supervision of which you speak.

As a final point, I might add that highly trained mental health professionals are actually among the last to be sought out when people are hurting. In fact, physicians and clergy seem to be the most frequently sought helpers. And I have been quite interested that Vanderbilt University's Psychotherapy Research Project recently found no differences in the success rates of highly experienced therapists and of professors chosen for their warmth when these two groups worked with college students. It may be that there are a lot of natural helpers among us who are providing effective helping services even without training. Given all this, I cannot help but wonder if psychology's efforts to restrict professional status to doctorates is not merely self-serving.

Gordon: Well, Rod, let us easily agree that psychologists and psychiatrists are not the major source of mental health care, just as physicians are not the major source of health care. If a person has a headache, he or she is most likely to take an aspirin and not call a physician. Most of our health care is done by absolute laymen. Just because they are caregivers, however, does not make them professionals.

Yes, there clearly are natural healers, and many of them might function well without going through any program at all. Also, there is no guarantee that a person who goes through a given program will be a healer. I do not, for example, think the surgeon who went through a surgical residency is necessarily excellent. If I had some surgery done, however, I would rather have that surgeon than a physician who did not take the extra surgical training. Similarly, if I were seeking psychotherapy for myself or for someone close to me, I think I would pick the person with credentials. I would assume that he or she is more likely to be competent than if I took a chance on someone with lesser credentials who, if I am lucky, might even be a better helper.

Now although there is no evidence for the superiority of doctoral therapists, the reverse is also true: There is no evidence that they are not superior. I do not think it is possible yet to adequately research psychotherapy and to reach such conclusions. There is still, for example, some controversy over whether psychotherapy works at all, and Eysenck thinks we are wasting our time as therapists. There is no way yet to disprove him, although no therapist of any consequence would believe psychotherapy is ineffective.

I do agree with you that the therapeutic tool is the therapist and that his or her personality is a crucial factor. But technical tools are also imperative. Therefore, good training would be that in which students' personality and interpersonal skills are considered during selection and in which the tools of treatment are imparted. The technical training is necessarily lengthy.

Vail Conference Recommendations

Rod: I am aware that your position is at variance with that endorsed by participants at the Vail Conference. They took the stance that the MA is the appropriate degree for journeyman-level entry into professional psychology. Vail was the most recent APA-sponsored conference on the training of professional psychologists, so I have wondered why the recommendations made there have been so largely ignored.

Gordon: The Vail recommendations have not had a very substantial impact in psychology generally. The argument for the MA as the "journeyman's degree" grew out of the aggressive equalitarianism of the conference participants, who felt that by lowering the entrance requirements into the profession, groups that had limited participation in the profession would be thus accommodated. Generally the lowering of standards is not viewed favorably by any professional group, and the APA Council of Representatives, the legislative body of APA, has consistently maintained the doctorate as the recommended level of training. Thus the Vail recommendation has not had much effect.

Rod: I was recently surprised to find that 490 counselor education programs are producing 19,000 MA-level counselors per year. I doubt that more than a minority of them are likely to be-

Credentialing Dialogue

come employed as school guidance personnel. Therefore, you will likely be finding a rather sizeable number of MA-level counselors fighting for professional recognition during the coming years.

The MA counselor, however, is not the only one to experience problems with the psychology establishment. As you may know, a substantial portion of those with counseling doctorates in APA and in APGA received their degrees in schools and colleges of education rather than in departments of psychology. Even so, many of these people consider themselves psychologists because their programs were psychological in nature, if not in name. Although some of us have obtained certification or licensure as psychologists, others have been denied that credentialing, and the decision about who is to be accepted as a psychologist has often seemed very arbitrary.

Who is a Psychologist?

Gordon: Well, it makes no difference at all where counseling psychologists are trained as long as they are trained as psychologists. APA has recognized this issue and has stated criteria for what constitutes a psychology program. It seems to me that if a program adheres to those criteria and gains APA recognition, there is no question that its graduates are psychologists, regardless of the department in which the program is housed.

Incidentally, I know it is common to talk of a program being "psychological in nature," but I am not at all clear what that means. Nursing, psychiatry, psychology, social work, and education all apply psychological knowledge and science, so they are all "psychological in nature." What is really needed is a precise definition of what a psychologist is. Without that, there will continually be people saying, "How about my program in such-and-such? It was psychological in nature," and we will have continuing confusion. For purposes of clarity we need as precise a definition as possible. APA is developing such a set of standards at this very time.

An analogy may make my point clearer. In our community a child can start kindergarten if his or her birthday is prior to December 1. But what if the child were born on December 2? I would hate to have to argue that he or she is more immature than the one born on November 30, but we have to set a benchmark. So is someone qualified to be a psychologist if he or she has not adhered to all the APA criteria? Quite possibly. But we have to draw a line somewhere and say this person is a psychologist and this one is not.

Rod: It seems to me that if counselors are excluded from psychology then they will define themselves as a distinct professional group and will develop their own power base. In fact, such a movement is already under way. Counselors are now talking of developing their own program accreditation process, their own national registry, and their own licensure, such as that already in effect in Virginia. If psychology is so concerned with client care, it seems to me that it would be in a much better position to monitor counselors' behavior by having counselors within its ranks.

Gordon: We had school psychology within the APA structure, but a group of them decided against APA. When APA continued to endorse its standards of professionalism, those opposed to the standards broke away and formed their own organization. So I think it is inevitable that counselors too will form their own organization. The development of an independent organization is likely to happen whether counselors meet APA membership standards or not.

It is all right for counselors to fight for things they want. However, as long as I am involved professionally, I will be active in advocating a certain standard of training for anyone who does what is essentially psychotherapy. I do not believe you can attain that standard in an MA program.

The crucial issue is the type, quality, and extent of practitioners' academic training as well as the relevance and intensity of their supervised clinical experience. We assume an enormous responsibility for a person's well-being when we engage him or her in psychotherapy. Our ethical values should determine who can properly offer such services to the public. Some activities can be done by BA-level technicians under supervision but psychotherapy requires extensive training. Nothing, including self-interest, should lead us from demanding less than the very highest standards for entrance into the field. Also, there should be societal control through licensure and peer review of the individual's practice.

Rod: Few of us could argue that our concern for clients' well-being is not paramount. Where we are at odds is over the implications that has for professional preparation—just as psychiatry has often argued with psychology over that very issue. It seems to me, in fact, that psychology's stance toward counselors is very similar to that which psychiatry has maintained toward psychology.

Gordon: Certainly the effects may be the same, but psychology's motivations are quite different. Psychiatry was motivated in part by issues of power and prestige, and in part by financial concerns; they saw psychologists as competitors for patients. They are now, for example, concerned that we will get into national health insurance and compete with them. The argument they gave was that medical school was necessary training for psychotherapeutic practice. I think what has helped our relationship with psychiatry is that they now have a better understanding of what psychologists' training is.

Rod: Psychiatry argued that medical training is necessary for psychotherapeutic practice. Psychology seems to be taking the analogous tack of insisting on training in psychology.

Gordon: Yes, but they were not arguing that you had to have medical school as such. They were arguing that it was the attitudinal training that was vital, the frame of reference that they are responsible for life and death. Although all health professionals should have feelings of responsibility for their patients, physicians have done so to the extent that they are almost arrogant about it.

What I am saying, then, is that the parallel is not exact. The level and intensity of professional preparation is the major issue for psychology, not any sense of financial threat from counselors. There are enough clients to go around. And I should add that psychology is in a better position to comment on counselors' training than psychiatry was to comment on psychology training, for our two professions are closely related and there is considerable overlap among our members—people such as yourself—so that we do know something of counselors' training.

Rod: As you know, this issue of the *Personnel and Guidance Journal* deals extensively with the issue of counseling licensure. Many counselors have viewed their inability to get licensed as psychologists as an example of psychologists' guild-like self-protectiveness. Licensure—and particularly psychology's posture toward it—is a big concern for most counselors.

Gordon: First of all, licensure is for public protection and is not for the chauvinistic enhancement of a given group. Physicians, for example, are not given medical licenses so they can make $100,000 a year. That is a consequence, not its purpose. Where medicine has been exclusionary has been in not allowing medical schools to develop. They put the barrier in earlier than the licensing stage by not allowing people to get the education.

I think clinical psychology can feel rather better about that issue, although we still turn away huge numbers of highly qualified applicants. As an example, at Adelphi we get about 700 applicants for our PhD program every year and select 25. Many of the other 675 do get into other schools, but a number of excellent people do not get picked for training. There is, however, no evidence that psychology is trying to keep people out—just be aware of the new schools of professional psychology during recent years. Incidentally, many of those who do not get into any clinical psychology program seem to take a back-door route through counseling programs.

Licensure does set standards for practice, including a definition of what is to constitute minimal training. I think all professionals, including counselors, should be licensed. My major concern is that the person who is offering a service be prepared to do it. Therefore, I would be very concerned about persons with less than appropriate doctoral training obtaining a license that allows them to conduct psychotherapy, particularly as private practitioners. Therefore, I do think counselors should be licensed. I worry only about what the license will permit them to do.

The crucial issue on which psychology, and particularly clinical psychology, has taken a strong stand is that a person who wishes to qualify in the mental health field should be properly trained through academic and supervised practice experience to assume such responsibility. It is questionable whether a person can have the quality of training necessary to do a first-rate professional job without an extensive amount of pertinent training. If counseling educators wish to expand the training of their students to make them mental health professionals with training comparable to that of doctoral-level psychologists and psychiatrists, they must demonstrate to the public that such training demands are required for professional service. There are a variety of tasks that can be done in helping people that are not psychotherapy as such.

Persons qualified as counselors, or by any other name, to serve persons with these needs should be permitted, in fact encouraged, to practice, but even as we expect a dentist to have dental training school and physicians to have medical school, we should expect psychotherapists to have the same high standards of professional preparation. Clinical psychology has developed such professional programs. We believe it is ethically responsible to insist that the public welfare is more crucial than self-interest. Therefore, all persons who have the doctorate in psychology are not considered competent to do psychotherapy even though they possess the doctorate. In like manner, we do not think every person who has training in counseling can be judged to be a psychotherapist simply because he or she chooses to use the words "counseling" and "psychotherapy" interchangeably. There is no particular animosity on the part of psychology toward counseling as a profession but rather an appeal for a commitment to high standards for prescribed services.

I am aware that my part of the dialogue with Gordon often had something of a "yes, but . . ." reactive quality to it. I consciously used that mode as a means of raising issues to which he could respond. As I think about it, it seems almost as if my interactions with Gordon were a metaphor for how counseling typically relates to psychology. That is, counseling seems often to experience itself in a reactive, one-down position toward psychology. This position is partly a function of the real differences in power and prestige between the two professions. Much of it, however, stems from counseling's attitude toward itself. My hope is that this posture will change. P&G

Reference

Derner, G. F. The education for the profession of clinical psychology and the psychology technician. *Clinical Psychologist*, 1976, 29, 1–2.

In this article, Steve Lindenberg, a former member of the APGA Licensure Committee and one of the prime movers in the development of the American Mental Health Counselors Division of APGA, takes a look down the road. His not so tongue-in-cheek future view raises some very good questions that are still pertinent: The article reflects the concern of many students of counseling who choose counseling as a profession because they are committed to its approach as opposed to a medical or clinical model.

[From: *Personnel and Guidance Journal,* Vol. 55, No. 1]

Attention Students: Be Advised . . .

A post-1984 vision of counselor certification and licensure. Attention counselors: Be advised . . .

Steven P. Lindenberg, a doctoral candidate at the University of Georgia, won honorable mention in the National Rehabilitation Association's Graduate Literary Awards Contest in 1975. Currently he is occupied with writing, professional standards, action therapies, and group work. He is a member of the APGA Commission on Counselor Licensure, for which he is presently conducting a pilot study regarding certification, licensure, and registry of professional counselors.

On occasion, there presses to the fore an issue that appears to be of concern to only a small segment of a professional body. Such is the issue of counselor certification and licensure. In reality, this issue holds a far greater significance and implication for the entire profession and touches even the rationale for the existence of that profession as a viable entity.

Sweeney and Sturdevant (1974) cited legislation enacted in Ohio in 1972 that, if interpreted to its limits, would have far-reaching implications for the future of counselor education and the counseling profession, as evidenced in the case of the *State of Ohio vs. Culbreth B. Cook, Ed.D.* on August 12, 1975. Dr. Cook allegedly engaged in *psychological testing* in violation of Ohio state laws governing the practice of psychology. Dr. Cook's lawyer, Philip Lustig, argued that counseling and testing, as a means of assessing the work of a person, should not be considered the exclusive prerogative of the psychologist in view of Dr. Cook's background and knowledge. He concluded that to prevent "somebody who is capable" from availing "themselves of the tools of other individuals" must be "either totally unconstitutional" or "radically wrong" (p. 4).

Although Dr. Cook was acquitted, the decision was not based on legal recognition of counseling as a profession; primarily it was because he had not held himself out to the public as a psychologist. However, such action does seem to imply that the domain of the psychologist is not sacrosanct.

Earlier, in a letter dated October 4, 1972, regarding the case of *John I. Weldon vs. Virginia State Board of Psychologist Examiners,* Judge Douglas H. Smith of the Corporation Court, Newport News, Virginia, stated: "I . . . feel that the profession of personnel and guidance counseling is a separate profession and should be so recognized. However I further feel that this profession does utilize the tools of the psychologist . . . .

"It appears now that the General Assembly has said that even if it is true that you are in another profession which uses to some degree the tools of psychology that there must be a regulatory body to govern this profession.

"I feel therefore that I am bound by this statute and since there is no regulatory body governing the profession of guidance and counseling, I must uphold the Virginia State Board of Psychologist Examiners and deny that he [Weldon] may practice this profession as a private practitioner open to the public." (pp. 1–2)

There appear to be three points to be made regarding these two cases: (a) counseling as a profession has been established by a legal precedent even though the profession avails itself of psychological "tools"; (b) counseling needs to establish certification and legislative criteria for regulation as a profession; and (c) with regard to the future, counseling is either on the threshold of autonomy or on the threshold of dissolution as a separate and *equal* profession compatible with all of the helping professions.

Dr. Thomas J. Sweeney (Ohio University) and Dr. Carl Swanson (Madison College, Virginia) have been responsible for much of the energy and direction given to the issue of certification and licensure. Although piecemeal successes have been achieved, much work remains to be done as our profession's viability is being eroded by the restrictive practices of some psychological boards in states across the nation. In addition, the certification/licensure issue is compounded by the consumer's call for accountability and minimal competencies in regard to the delivery of all services, particularly medical and mental health services. The controversy brewing over the proposed National Health Insurance Act is fostering the pragmatic and capitalistic question: Who shall be entitled to collect fees for the delivery of health services? And there appears the philosophical issue: Who can legislate which profession is exclusively authorized to perform *therapy?*

With these points in mind, one can envision the future of our profession as it might appear to the observer, should the charge of the American Personnel and Guidance Association Commission on Counselor Licensure not be fulfilled. The date is May 5, 1985.

Memo

Date: May 5, 1985
To: Mr. Calvin Murdock Ed.S., Counselor
From: Dr. Howard McCoy, Director of Human Development Services
Subject: Certification of Counselors

Dear Mr. Murdock:
The issue of counselor accountability

assessed via student outcomes has recently been debated in our State Legislature. Governor Steng has signed Senate Bill 9024 into law. As you know, this bill requires all people functioning as counselors to be American Psychological Association Certified (APAC) and carry the initials "APAC" after their names. Furthermore, only those persons so certified may perform therapeutic intervention as described by the American Psychological Association position paper dated October 1, 1982.

As Director of Human Development Services, I have been reviewing the records of all staff members in order to implement the law by the beginning of the 1985–86 school year. There is no "grandfather" clause in this law, and while this issue is being contested in the courts, final adjudication may take five years or more. Thus, the State Attorney General has advised all Public School Superintendents to detail a procedure for implementation of this law in writing by June 1, 1985, to take effect in September, 1985. In the process of our review, it has come to our attention that Dr. Henry Markley, a member of your committee, was not APA certified nor APA licensable making the Counselor Education program there nonaccredited.

Unless you can prepare an affidavit contesting the above statement, it is my unpleasant task to inform you that you will not be able to function as a counselor during the next academic year. You will be restricted to performing pupil personnel services. You will continue to receive your base salary, plus a meritorious increment based on your 1984–85 job position and Behavioral Outcomes Ratio (BOR) as computed by Educational Research Services (ERS). However, beginning with the 1986–87 school year, your salary will be computed on Behavioral Outcomes Ratio Step 13 (BOR–S–13) instead of BOR–S–15, as therapy will no longer be considered in the Behavioral Outcome Intervention Criterion (BOIC) in computing your meritorious increment.

A written response is requested no later than May 18, 1985; otherwise, it will be assumed that you fully understand and concur with the above, and this information will then be coded for the computer program for staff contracts. I am sympathetic toward your regrettable position, but I must call for your complete cooperation in this matter.

Sincerely,
Dr. Howard McCoy
Director of Human Development Services

HM/rl
cc: Superintendent's Office
pc: School Board Computer Control
2A4-03

Even though I knew this was coming, I still find it difficult to believe. I remember McCoy talking about the "APAC" after his PhD when he first got here in '81. He said, "Cal, you'd better get your credentials together and check out your instructors' backgrounds to see if they're APA certifiable and that your department is APA accredited. The handwriting is on the wall." I just assumed that Franklin State would take care of all that. Apparently they haven't. At forty and with all my responsibilities, I can't possibly change jobs. Because of this ruling I'd probably have to move to another state anyhow, assuming they haven't passed similar laws. Besides, I haven't had my Computer Language Update since '83, and I can't switch jobs without a one semester update and demographic reapportionment, which isn't scheduled until 1987.

I guess I really should have paid more attention to what was happening in the profession. When I received my Specialist in Education degree from Franklin State in 1979, Henry assured me that all anticipated criteria for counseling in the public schools would be satisfied. I don't think that he intentionally misled me. . . . Now that I think about it, I vaguely remember discussing the certification/licensure issue in a course called CSN 419—Accountability by Outcomes under Dr. Drake. Let's see . . . the Sweeney and Sturdevant article in 1974 . . . Sweeney, Chairperson, APGA Commission on Counselor Certification and Licensure . . . Florida . . . Ohio . . . Virginia . . . Swanson, 1975, Commission Co-chairperson . . . Cook vs. Ohio, 1975. . . . Then there was the funds crisis in APGA that forced discontinuation of the APGA Commission on Counselor Licensure in 1977 and the landmark case of the *American Psychological Association vs. Ohio Personnel and Guidance Association* in 1978.

Even my friend Al Regaf in Mechanicsburg Public Schools told me about the problems with accountability and student outcomes back in 1975 and how administrators were moving toward the Behavioral Outcome Ratios. Then, when the National Health Insurance Act (NHI) was signed into law in 1980, it became mandatory that anyone in the mental health services engaged in private practice or consultation or employed by any governmental agency be accredited by a bona fide professional organization recognized in the NHI–Index–4A. This action was designed to insure that mental health workers would have minimum uniform competencies and increased accountability in the delivery of services. Within six months, APGA membership fell to 50 percent of its 1979 level, retaining primarily counselor educators, public school counselors, and student personnel workers. By 1981, APGA had been amalgamated into Division 17 of APA because of financial insolvency. I remember that at that time it was understood that public school counselors could belong to Division 17 without certification because of the unique circumstances surrounding the jointure.

But the clincher was the position paper of October 1, 1982, entitled "Qualifications of Therapists." This paper was incorporated into NHI policy IV, Section 2, paragraph B, as I recall. I didn't pay much attention when it appeared as an article in the Division 17 *Guidepost*, since it didn't affect public education. As I remember, it was in September 1984 that a release was mailed to all teachers in our state informing us of the Elementary and Secondary Education Act (ESEA) guidelines that set the precedent for McCoy's memo.

McCoy told me then that I could get APA certified if I took 15 semester hours at an APA-accredited institution and a one-semester internship under the supervision of an APAC diplomate. But the nearest school was 150 miles away and the nearest APAC diplomate was Folson at the State Hospital in Northview. Besides, I had no funds and had used up my ESEA Subsidized Education Socioeconomic Apportionment.

I guess another thing that prompted this whole issue was the Supreme Court's ruling in February 1985 on the case of *Culbertson vs. The State of California Board of Regents* in which Culbertson accused his high school counselor of malpractice for attempting to intervene therapeutically when he was not APA certified. The plaintiff alleged that as a result of this intervention he became thoroughly irrational and guilt ridden about his homosexuality and attempted suicide, permanently crippling him from the waist down and causing irreparable damage to his mental health and personal life.

As I recall, the Supreme Court ruled in favor of Culbertson and awarded him token damages, despite the difficulty in determining the influence of other

Attention Students

variables in the deterioration of the plaintiff's mental health and the somewhat vague interpretation of "therapeutic intervention" cited in the October 1982 APA position paper. In deciding for the plaintiff, the court handed down the opinion that, since the counselor involved was not certified by "the professional body representing mental health services personnel," the Board of Regents was accountable for the delivery of less than ideal services to the distraught plaintiff in the form of a counselor, particularly when certified applicants had been passed over by the respective school district. Related legislation spread like wildfire because of the implications of this ruling. Insurance companies doubled their malpractice insurance rates to school districts, and for several months, students nationwide had to be referred to APA-certified therapists for mental health services. The insurance companies issued a joint communique stating that malpractice rates would be returned to 1984 levels when the staff of each respective school district consisted of counselors who were APAC's and only if there was no "grandfather" clause. That's when I knew that it was only a matter of time until something like this memo was coming. Back in '75, I never dreamed anything like this could happen. The certification question never seemed to be an issue because it didn't seem to pertain to my becoming a counselor.

My dilemma is the end result of our profession's failure to set up uniform certification standards in the mid-seventies. But I'll have to think more about this later. The kids are plugging in, and the 9:00 Computed Electrical Upsurge tone has sounded. I guess I'd better go to the office and utilize the State Career Compatability Network before my 10:30 terminus if I'm to place some of my matriculated upper-levels. Hey, what's this new sign on my door?

"ATTENTION STUDENTS:
BE ADVISED . . ." P&G

References

Cook wins psychology licensure case. *Guidepost*, September 25, 1975, p. 1.

John I. Weldon vs. Virginia State Board of Psychological Examiners. September 28, 1972.

Smith, D. H. Corporation Court, Newport News, Virginia. Letter dated October 4, 1972.

State of Ohio vs. Culbreth B. Cook, Ed.D. August 12, 1975.

Sweeney, T. J., & Sturdevant, A. D. Licensure in the helping professions: Anatomy of an issue. *Personnel and Guidance Journal*, 1974, *52*(9), 575—581.

Three years after the publication of his classic article, which appears at the beginning of this book, Tom Sweeney, first chairperson of the APGA Licensure Committee, teamed with Mel Witmer, a current member of the committee, to write another classic piece. This article very carefully examines legislative and nonlegislative factors that affect the counseling profession. If counseling is to be a legitimate profession, we must respond to the factors outlined by Sweeney and Witmer.

[From: *Personnel and Guidance Journal,* Vol. 55, No. 10]

Who Says You're A Counselor?

So you want to be a counselor! Tell you what I'm going to do! Step right up and sign on the dotted line. Three days of intensive training and you will receive a genuine blue ribbon gold sealed certificate!

This offer sounds pretty wild to someone who had to meet graduate faculty, state department, or employer criteria in order to earn the title "counselor." Although a fictitious example, it is not far removed from reports received from APGA members in two states. On the other hand, we have a report of counselor positions in one statewide agency being eliminated on the proviso that only psychologists or social workers may perform these functions in the future. In addition, at least two separate federal agencies have policies that preclude master or doctoral trained counselors from acquiring positions with them. In a recent survey, 70 members of the Association for Counselor Education and Supervision (ACES) reported that they were denied employment as unlicensed professional counselors in a clinic or agency because of medicaid or other insurance coverage requirements (Carroll & Halligan 1976).

Unfortunately, credentialing problems are becoming more numerous and more complex. The senior author identified some potential problems related to licensure about three years ago (Sweeney & Sturdevant 1974). Since that time there has been a rapid escalation of activity in response to these problems. APGA adopted a position "in favor of vigorous, responsible action to establish provisions for the licensure of professional counselors in the various states" (APGA 1975). Following its charge, the APGA Commission on Counselor Licensure: (a) developed tentative guidelines for licensure legislation, (b) responded to hundreds of inquiries concerning the predicaments of members affected by state and federal legislation or regulations, (c) conducted workshops and (d) prepared educative materials for the membership.

More than 20 states have indicated a desire to develop legislation for credentialing counselors apart from that already available to school counselors. So far, only the Virginia legislature has passed a "professional counselor" licensure law for persons desiring to practice outside of public school settings. In addition, members in several states report that new legislation will be introduced in the coming year.

Other developments include four court cases that have implications for counselors. First, a district court judge ruled that counseling and guidance is a separate profession, i.e., requiring regulation separate from psychology (*Weldon* v. *Virginia State Board of Psychologists Examiners*). Second, a judge reaffirmed the rights of competent counselors when he dismissed the charges of a board of psychology brought against a trained person who was not a licensed psychologist (*Ohio State Board of Psychology* v. *Cook* 1975).

A third case still under appeal by

Thomas J. Sweeney is a Professor and Director of the School of Applied Behavioral Sciences and Educational Leadership in the College of Education at Ohio University in Athens. Currently he is president of the Association for Counselor Education and Supervision. He was largely responsible for initiating action that led to the establishment of the APGA Commission on Counselor Licensure, was its first chairman, and continues to be active as a consultant in counselor licensure and credentialing efforts throughout the country. Besides a long-standing commitment to the quality of counselor education and the competency of counselors, he is interested in career guidance, Adlerian counseling, and parent education.

J. Melvin Witmer is a Professor in the School of Applied Behavioral Sciences and Educational Leadership in the College of Education, Ohio University in Athens. For the past two years he has been active in drafting counselor licensure legislation in Ohio and in organizing a coalition of counseling groups to support such legislation. He has been interested in educational and community approaches to improving mental health, particularly through effective education, and parent education. Currently he is interested in biofeedback, self-control, and the management of stress as ways for improving the quality of living.

the Board of Examiners in Psychology in Mississippi concerns their denial of a doctoral trained person in counseling to take the state examination. The Court directed the Board to license the person without examination because of inconsistencies in the Board's practices. Another reversal of Board action took place in the District of Columbia. The Court directed the Board to grandfather license a person who was previously denied. In this case the Court offered the following opinion:

> The very reason psychology has not been regulated before is that it has been and remains an amorphous, inexact, and even mysterious discipline. Possession of a graduate degree in psychology does not signify the absorption of a corpus of knowledge as does a medical, engineering, or law degree; rather it is simply a convenient line for legislatures to draw, on the brave assumption that whatever is taught in the varied graduate curricula of university psychology departments must make a competent psychologist at the least. (*Berger v. Board of Psychologists Examiners 1975*).

The lessons to be learned from the preceding cases are at least threefold. First, counselors are being discriminated against in a manner that also deprives the public of services that it needs. Second, the unjust or indiscriminate enforcement of licensure laws can be corrected. Unfortunately, this requires great personal courage and legal expenses to those who choose to fight an injustice. Third, counseling as a profession can expect to confront many of the same problems of psychologists if our legislation and efforts are primarily designed to protect "our" interests. There are legislative and non-legislative activities in which we must engage, however, if counseling is to do more than just survive.

Legislative Factors

The legislative factors most affecting counseling are primarily located at the state level. They include (a) psychologists' licensing boards and their professional associations' opposition in some states to counselor licensure, (b) counselors' lack of unity organizationally or operationally, (c) the concern of nonacademically trained community workers who use the title "counselor" and (d) the need for financial resources to sustain legislative efforts.

Psychologists' Impact. State laws to license psychologists have been the most troublesome, particularly to persons without at least a doctorate and to persons who received their training or degrees in education rather than a department of psychology. While certification concerns the title of an occupation, licensure tends to regulate the practice of an occupation as well. Because psychologists' laws define their practice to include everything that counselors do, even doctoral trained counselors become subject to a fine and possible jail sentence for violating the law.

Psychologists have been developing legislation for more than 20 years so that today 49 states have some form of legislation. In recent years the dominant forces among psychologists have seemed to believe that only doctoral trained psychologists should be allowed to provide nonmedical mental health services. There are some compelling reasons for adopting such a position. First, there have been thousands of persons educated in general and experimental psychology with bachelor's and master's as well as doctoral degrees. Many of these persons have had little or no education in psychological counseling or supervised experience in providing psychological services. In point of fact, 56 percent of the PhD graduates in psychology in 1971 were in areas other than personality, clinical, counseling, and school psychology (Kose 1972). There is concern, therefore, that potentially a large pool of individuals would become licensable for private practice or practice in a state, federal, or private agency if the qualifications were changed.

Second, psychologists continue to struggle for equity with psychiatrists and physicians as mental health providers. They wish to qualify for insurance payments from private and state agencies and potentially qualify for national health insurance. Psychologists have succeeded in establishing such equity in more than a dozen states already. They believe that the doctorate is more prestigious and defensible as a training level with insurance carriers. With a carefully identified, limited number of highly academically trained persons to provide mental health services, psychologists argue that they are minimizing the risk to the public.

On the other hand, licensure laws have come under attack as an elitist guildism that works contrary to the publics' best interest (Shimberg et al. 1972). The new head of the federal antitrust division called for "thorough outside scrutiny" of licensing groups "to insure that they are necessary." He said his division will be "watchful" for attempts to use state regulatory methods as a "convenient cover under which private parties develop, maintain, and enforce fundamental competitive restraints, restraints which deprive consumers of choices and information" (*Wall Street Journal* September 6, 1976).

The actions of some boards of psychology have been questioned as noted earlier. In addition, psychologists' efforts to lobby against counselor legislation in some states raises similar questions about their motivation. Counselors also must be reflective and careful to define their motives if they are to pass the test of legislative and public scrutiny.

Counselor Unity. The problems that counselors face in developing their own legislation, however, do not come from psychologists alone. Counselors, at least at the state level, are years behind the psychologists in political sophistication, organizational effectiveness, and commitment of resources to political action. Educating and informing ourselves as to the critical issues in counselor licensure is a staggering task, but an essential step in mobilizing the profession.

Before any legislature is going to give a hearing to a bill licensing counselors, counselor groups must agree among themselves on how best to regulate the profession. When one considers the many specialties and settings of counselors, the term "counselor" takes on a "many splintered" cast. Consider, for example, the following: career counselor, mental health counselor, school counselor, marriage and family counselor, sex counselor, Adlerian counselor, transactional analysis counselor, ad infinitum. Unknown to many APGA members, alcohol and drug workers have been receiving federal funds at the state level to establish competency and experience based credentialing. Indications are that they will subsequently seek statuatory recognition.

To further compound the legislative efforts for credentialing, social workers and marriage and family counselors are pursuing separate licensure legislation in a number of states. For example, seven states already have legislation that license or certify marriage and family counselors. Whether these groups will support, join, or oppose counselor licensure efforts will depend upon conditions in each of the states. A corollary of this parade of groups seeking licensure is the growing reluctance of legislatures to continue licensing all the occupational groups that think statutory credentialing is the royal road to professionalism.

Community Workers. Another large and significant group of persons who are concerned and very vocal with legislators are those who work in neighborhood social service programs. Literally hundreds of small organizations function in every state to provide a variety of human and social services. Many church and community action organizations utilize volunteer and paid employees who use the title "counselor." State licensure planning committees must determine how their proposed legislation will affect these community programs and where justified, make provision for these programs to continue providing much needed services.

Financial Resources. The effort and expense necessary to develop, pass, and implement legislation is considerable. Virginia is the first and only state to have counselor licensure. The omnibus type act includes all counselor groups as well as related behavioral sciences. More than $7,000 and two years of concentrated work were expended by the counselor groups to pass the legislation. In another state more than $7,000 has been spent in two years as they prepare to introduce a bill for the second time. On the other hand, legal expenses cost one counselor more than $20,000 to fight a state psychology board decision. A coalition of well-organized state counseling organizations is a more effective and efficient approach to coping with problems that go beyond the interests of counselors alone.

Nonlegislative Factors

There are a number of nonlegislative factors that are affecting the future of counseling. To be discussed here are (a) third-party payment, (b) national credentialing and (c) state and federal classification systems.

Third-Party Payments. This refers to payments by insurance companies or, in the event of national health insurance, government payment of fees for insured persons receiving counseling or other mental health services. In addition to psychologists and psychiatrists, drug, alcohol, marriage and family counselors, for example, wish to be eligible for reimbursement. Many rehabilitation and community agencies have established eligibility for third-party payments. They often require that the professionals they employ be licensed or licensable.

While many citizen and professional groups will argue for the passage of national health insurance and further expansion of mental health coverage, the potential for abuse economically and otherwise could be appalling (Meltzer 1975). As a consequence, a defensible set of criteria is absolutely necessary to determine eligibility and conditions for receiving third-party payments as a mental health provider. The impetus for licensure and related professional standards comes in part from this realization.

National Credentialing. There already exists at least six means by which counselors can receive a form of credentialing without state or federal legislation, although only a small minority would be eligible by these means. One is the American Association for Marriage and Family Counselors (AAMFC) whose standards require 1,000 hours of experience and 200 hours of supervision in marriage and family counseling for clinical members. AAMFC clinical members seem to have the confidence of at least some insurance carriers.

Second, in the absence of state or federal legislation, rehabilitation counselors have established a national certification process. The Commission on Rehabilitation Counselor Certification administers a practice-based examination for competency and uses supervisor and peer evaluations to supplement the examination. There are also minimum academic and years of rehabilitation counseling experience requirements. Accreditation of counselor training is also a function of this Commission.

Two other means for counselors to attain a form of national certification are through the American Association of Sex Educators and Counselors (AASEC) and the International Transactional Analysis Association (ITAA). Both have established certification criteria and the ITAA has its own training program. Most counselors, however, would not qualify without additional training and experience required by these groups.

Fifth, a national register can be used as a form of credentialing. Psychologists now have two ways for nonlegislative credentialing. One is through the National Register of Health Service Providers in Psychology. This Register, which is a listing of those who are qualified according to the criteria established by the administrative board, is designed to help insurance carriers know who is qualified to provide mental health services. The Register is primarily a list of doctoral trained psychologists (now more than 8,000) who are licensed or certified for the independent practice of psychology, have been trained in a program essentially psychological in nature, and have supervised experience in mental health services. There is some evidence that even doctoral trained persons from departments of counseling (PhD and EdD) are having difficulty being considered eligible for this register.

Another means of recognition within psychology is the diplomate, which is intended for persons who desire special recognition for expertise in a specific area such as clinical or counseling psychology. The number of persons who choose to pursue the diplomate is relatively small and the number receiving it is smaller. For the majority of those whose training has been in counseling rather than psychology, neither of the above means is remotely available to them.

A sixth form of national credentialing is a plan proposed by the Department of Health, Education, and Welfare (US Department of HEW 1976). The proposal presents a national nonfederal system of credentialing for health manpower, including counselors. This credentialing body would transcend the morass of standards that have evolved through state legislation and efforts such as those previously described. The operation of such a plan would be through national certification bodies such as the previously mentioned specialty groups that meet national standards as a certifying agency. Such a system could supersede state licensing as a means of identifying health providers. In the absence of counselors having an acceptable national certification body, they would have difficulty securing positions in many agencies that require insurance payments to sustain the services of the organization.

State and Federal Classification Systems. While agency counselors have known it for years, school and college counselors have been generally unaware of how state and federal classification systems affect the counseling services to which the public has access. The Civil Service and state classification systems identify titles, training, and experience required for positions within these respective systems.

In most states, only employment and rehabilitation counselors are listed in these job classifications. They are determined and approved by a state agency charged with this responsibility. These classified positions are frequently sub-

(Continued on page 594)

Who Says

(Continued from page 591)
ject to change in contrast to the more fixed occupational identifications through legislation. Counselors in Michigan succeeded in having the new classification standards list and describe the requirements for vocational and mental health counselors for the first time in its history. In many states, however, counselors must be employed under titles as assistant psychologists, psychological examiners, case workers, or other euphemisms.

Legislative and nonlegislative events are rapidly shaping the form and destiny of counseling. The efforts of psychologists, various counseling groups, state legislatures, national credentialing bodies, and federal and state agencies are a reflection of the problem that faces counselors as they attempt to bring order out of chaos in defining who is a counselor.

Next Steps

Our next steps will shape the future of counseling as a profession. We believe that our purposes should be clear and our efforts designed to insure accountability to those whom we serve. The authors can support the concept of counselor licensure as a next step for the following reasons:

1. Potentially more counseling services can be made available at less cost to the public.
2. More counseling services can be available in geographical areas not typically served by other counseling related professions.
3. Different areas of social need not typically served by other professions (e.g., mid-life career or retirement counseling) can be served by professional counselors.
4. Qualified counselors will be employable for areas in which they have special competence without hindrance by statutes of other professional groups.
5. Questionable practices of persons allegedly qualified to offer counseling services to the public will be investigated and the persons stopped from practicing if necessary.

For our purposes to be realized, we believe that the next steps for the APGA membership include:

1. Passage of state licensure statutes designed to regulate those who wish to identify themselves as professional counselors. Such statutes must be defensible in the courts as nondiscriminatory and yet permit enforcement against incompetence.
2. Implementation of counselor training program accreditation to insure a more careful recruitment, selection, training and retraining of counselors. Without this as a concurrent step, other legislative and nonlegislative thrusts could be inconsequential at the least and potentially damaging to the public and profession at its worst.
3. Development of a national counselor register to provide a means of recognizing qualified mental health providers and potentially other counselor classifications. As noted previously, national credentialing of health manpower is a likely development in the next few years. Even if it is not, many members whose states do not enact counselor licensure will be interested in a credentialing alternative.
4. Nonlegislative efforts to have counselor positions listed in state and federal classification systems. Employability is more than having training and experience. In the absence of titles and job descriptions within the classification systems, counselors will continue to be unemployable or underemployed for positions that they might otherwise be qualified to fill. As mentioned previously, Michigan counselors succeeded in modifying the mental health classification system after they realized that counselors were not eligible for state employment.
5. Mobilization of greater political and legal support. APGA has more than 42,000 members and is growing. We are influencing national legislation, and members have lobbied effectively in some states on various issues including concerns for children, juveniles, the aging, and other special groups. We can be even more effective if we develop coalitions with other counselor associations sharing similar interests. For example, there are 30,000 school counselors in the National Education Association, the majority of whom do not belong to APGA (N = 14,000). In addition, there are an estimated 14,000 community mental health counselors who do not affiliate with APGA. Our efforts should continue to be directed toward humanizing the institutions and services through which we work in addition to our licensure efforts.
When necessary, state associations also should test the discrimination of other professional groups against counselors. In some carefully selected cases, this may require filing legal statements in support of a member.
6. Establishing a financial basis necessary to carry out the preceding steps. Other professional groups have raised dues, solicited tax deductible donations and sponsored fund raising activities. We must face this need for resources squarely and establish a sound, equitable means of developing the funds needed to carry out the work effectively.

Conclusion

The issues and problems that we face are complex. No solutions will be permanent or perfect. Lindenberg's (1976) vivid portrayal of a future year when even the school counselor is displaced for lack of the proper credentials need never happen.

If we were incapable of establishing a legitimate place for counselors, then our efforts to insure a place for others through career counseling would be folly. We are capable and we have the resources. We only need to educate ourselves and to act responsibly through our professional associations. P&G

References

American Personnel and Guidance Association. Position Statement on Counselor Licensure. APGA, Washington, D.C., 1975.
Berger v. Bd. of Psychologists Examiners, 521 F. St., 1056 (District of Columbia) U.S. Court of Appeals, District of Columbia Circuit, October 28, 1975.
Carroll, M. R., & Halligan, F. G. Current status and opinionnaire of ACES members concerning licensure requirements. ACES, Washington, D.C., 1976.
Lindenberg, S. P. Attention students: Be advised . . . *Personnel and Guidance Journal,* 1976, *55,* 34 – 36.
Meltzer, M. L. Insurance reimbursement: A mixed blessing. *American Psychologist,* 1975, *30,* 1150 – 64.
Ohio State Board of Psychology v. Culbreth B. Cook. Cook wins psychology licensure case. *Guidepost,* September 25, 1975, p. 1.
Rose, R. M. Supply and demand for psychology Ph.D.'s in graduate departments of psychology: 1970 and 1971 compared. *American Psychologist,* 1972, *27,* 415 – 421.
Shimberg, B.; Esser, B. F.; & Kruger, D. H. *Occupational licensing and public policy.* Princeton, N.J.: Educational Testing Service, 1972.
Sweeney, T. J., & Sturdevant, A. D. Licensure in the helping professions: Anatomy of an issue. *Personnel and Guidance Journal,* 1974, *52,* 575 – 581.
U. S. Department of Health, Education, and Welfare. A proposal for credentialing health manpower. Public Health Service, Health Resources Administration, June, 1976.
Wall Street Journal. Reexamination of state licensing boards urged by new head of antitrust division. September 6, 1976.
Weldon v. Virginia State Board of Psychologists Examiners. Corporation Court, Newport News, Virginia, 1972.

Following on the heels of the preceding article is this 1978 article by two people who have chaired the APGA Licensure Committee. Although the article was a status report, its most important contribution was a close examination of the internal (intraprofessional) and external (interprofessional) factors that brought about the creation of the original licensure commission and continue to be important reasons for its existence.

[From: *Personnel and Guidance Journal,* Vol. 56, No. 10]

APGA and Counselor Licensure: A Status Report

On July 14, 1974, the Board of Directors of APGA adopted "a position in favor of vigorous, responsible action to establish provisions for the licensure of professional counselors in the various states" (*Licensure in the Helping Professions* 1975). This same resolution was adopted by the APGA Senate on March 26, 1975. As a result of this action, the first APGA Licensure Commission was appointed.

The Licensure Commission was initially formed to give APGA a sense of direct responsibility and leadership in reacting to increasing concerns about credentialing and licensure, stemming from many conditions both within and outside the association. Its task was essentially threefold.

1. To collect and disseminate information about licensure developments at the state and national level.
2. To assist members and state groups to resolve licensure problems at the legislative, professional, or examining board level.
3. To provide national leadership on counselor licensure needs by seeking active relationships with other professional organizations, state and local government agencies, and state legislative bodies.

The basic philosophy underlying the policies of the Licensure Commission has been one of gradual change from a reactive to an active position through a broad range of services and activities. The purpose of this article is, first, to examine the internal and external pressures that brought about the creation of the Commission. It is important, not so much in a historical sense, but because many of these pressures still exist. Second, the article will trace some important events that have occurred at least in part because of the APGA Licensure Commission. Finally, the article will discuss the active focus of the current APGA Licensure Committee.

Bases for Licensure Concerns

External Pressures. Most of the external pressures emanated from state boards of examiners in psychology operating under state laws designed to regulate the practice of psychology. In several states counselors were told to discontinue their practice because they were in violation of the state's psychology licensure law, even though they were not calling themselves psychologists. The basis for this action by the state boards came from the fact that most state psychology licensure laws had incorporated in them the following definition of the practice of psychology:

> Within the meaning of this act (psychology) is defined as rendering to individuals, groups, organizations, or the public any psychological service involving the application of principles, methods, and procedures of understanding, predicting, and influencing behavior, such as the principles pertaining to learning, perception, motivation, thinking, emotions, and interpersonal relationships; the methods and procedures of interviewing, counseling, and psychotherapy, of constructing, administering, and interpreting tests of mental abilities, aptitudes, interests, attitudes, personality characteristics, emotion, and motivation; and of assessing public opinion.
>
> The application of said principles and methods includes, but is not restricted to: diagnoses, prevention, and amelioration of adjustment problems and emotional and mental disorders of individuals and groups; hypnosis; educational and vocational counseling . . . and the resolution of interpersonal and social conflict. (American Psychological Association 1967, pp. 1,098–1,099).

Harold F. Cottingham is a former APGA president who has been involved with licensure issues since 1973. He was a member of the Southern ACES Committee on Licensure and in 1975 was appointed to the then newly formed APGA Commission on Licensure, which he chaired from November 1976 through June 1977. His contributions to the counselor licensure effort include published articles, workshop assignments, convention programs, and liaison work with other professional organizations. He has written publications on elementary guidance, psychological education, and counselor accountability.

Richard W. Warner, Jr., is Associate Dean, School of Education and a Professor of Counselor Education, Auburn University. He is currently chairperson of the APGA Licensure Committee and is a former chairperson and member of the ACES Licensure Commission. He has written several texts, monographs and articles in the area of individual and group counseling and research and evaluation procedures. He is editor of the state counselors' association journal and past editor and contributor of a research column in the P&G Journal.

Quite obviously, this definition includes the kinds of activities that most counselors, as well as other helping professionals, perform. Yet this definition was used (and is still used) to prohibit counselors from performing such activities.

Related to pressure from state boards was the pressure resulting from the publication of "Standards for the Providers of Psychological Services" (1974).

> The Standards would seem to apply to virtually every group or facility offering psychological services which is not regulated by another legislatively recognized profession. One possible outcome is that counselors not certified, licensed, or otherwise accepted members of psychological groups eventually may be supervised by licensed psychologists. (Licensure in the Helping Professions 1975)

Another provision of the Standards calls for the supervision of all unlicensed persons in schools, colleges, community, or government agencies by a licensed psychologist. Because counselors and counseling have little, if any, legal status, except for school certification, outside the state of Virginia, the Standards place them in a second-class citizen category. If counselors are to be subject to their own control, rather than the control of other professions, counseling must develop some form of legislative recognition.

State boards and the Standards were two of the main external pressures causing the creation of the APGA Licensure Commission headed by Tom Sweeney. In the intervening years, these pressures have not lessened; they have increased and new pressures have been added. In addition to issuing cease and desist orders, state boards have also increasingly refused to permit individuals trained outside departments of psychology to even take the state licensure examination. In some states, there is a move to change the wording of the state licensure law so that only those trained in psychology departments, regardless of the nature of the degree, could take the examination. Such a move would exclude many individuals who are trained in counseling psychology programs located within schools or colleges of education. The licensure commission is currently aware of 27 states where counselors have received cease and desist orders or where individuals have been denied the right to take the examination.

The Council for the National Register of Health Service Providers in Psychology has changed one of its criteria for membership. Before January 1, 1978, the Council required a doctoral degree from a regionally accredited university. As of January 1, 1978, this criteria was changed to read: "A doctorate degree in psychology from a regionally accredited educational institution" (Council for the National Register 1977, p. 4). This new criterion would appear to close the register to anyone trained outside a department of psychology.

The Veterans Administration began a move in late 1976 to require all individuals employed as psychologists in VA hospitals to be licensed by state boards of psychology. Many of these individuals are counseling psychologists who, under current board practices in many states, would not be eligible to take the examination. Although the VA has not as yet implemented that plan, there is every indication they may do so in the near future.

At the federal level, HEW issued a 1977 report dealing with the credentialing of health manpower; it is a follow-up to similar reports in 1971 and 1976. The report calls for national certification of health professionals and the establishment of national standards for professional training. Certain recommendations would limit federal reimbursement to those professionals who are licensed by state boards having national standards. If these recommendations are implemented, the counseling profession could be excluded from all federal programs. It is impossible to tell how many counselors might lose their jobs under such circumstances. One example of the scope of the problem can be seen in a recent survey by Carroll, Halligan, and Griggs (1977). In their survey, 70 members of ACES reported that they had been denied employment in a clinic or agency because of Medicaid and other insurance requirements.

Internal Pressures. The external pressures in and of themselves are important enough reasons for the counseling profession to move toward licensure, but they may not be the most important. "For more than 25 years counselors and educators have been attempting to define counseling within the fields of psychology and guidance" (Carroll, Halligan & Griggs 1977, p. 577). An examination of almost any introductory text in the field will demonstrate that we still have not come to substantial agreement among ourselves as to what counseling is. How can we tell others what we do if we can't agree among ourselves? The licensure movement is forcing us to deal with this dilemma as we attempt to define counseling for legislative purposes.

A second internal problem is our general failure to implement standards for the preparation of counselors at the master's and doctoral levels in counselor training programs. The licensure movement may facilitate this process by writing standards approved by ASCA and ACES into counselor licensing laws.

A third internal problem is that, currently, counselors have little national visibility and no national register that would tell the public that counselors are a professional, legally authorized group of practitioners with professional skills. We do have a professional organization, but this gains us little recognition as long as we follow a policy of letting almost anyone belong to the organization who has the money for the dues. Many of our related professional groups require that individuals meet certain training or experience requirements before they can become members. The National Association of Social Workers, the American Association of Marriage and Family Counselors, and the American Psychological Association are three such organizations. The very fact that these organizations have some standards for membership gives them greater credibility in the eyes of the public and in the eyes of those who establish state and federal policy.

Although the scope of this article prohibits listing all the external and internal forces impinging on the counseling profession, it should be clear that many "events are rapidly shaping the form and destiny of counseling. The efforts of psychologists, various counseling groups, state legislatures, national credentialing bodies, and federal and state agencies are a reflection of the problem that faces counselors . . ." (Sweeney & Witmer 1977, p. 594). In the eyes of the law and of the public, counselors desperately need a national identity, with some form of a national registry, and the legal rights that licensing legislation in the various states might provide. It is to this problem that the APGA Licensure Committee has addressed itself since its inception in 1975. Progress has been slow, but under the direction of Tom Sweeney and Carl Swanson the licensure commission has made some improvement in our situation.

Licensure Developments 1975-1977

Legal Cases. It is estimated that legal grievance procedures involving

Status Report

counseling professionals either as plaintiffs or defendants have been filed in at least 20 states. In a number of those cases which have reached the courts thus far, decisions were handed down that acted to legally define counseling and guidance as a profession (Cottingham & Swanson 1976). Illustrative of these court cases are the Coxe case in Mississippi and the Berger case in Washington, D.C., where the issue centered on the applicant's right to take the examination from the board of examiners in psychology. The Cook case in Ohio centered on the state psychology board, which alleged that a counselor was not qualified to serve the public. The board lost their case on a directed verdict from the court. In Iowa a similar case is now in process.

Although court cases are important because they have given counseling some legal definition as a profession, they are extremely costly. There is no way of telling how many counselors have backed away from taking their case to court because of the economic burden of such action. Yet it is clear that there are those who will seek to remove counselors from practice by either actually bringing a court action or threatening to do so. The senior author, while writing this article, has received phone calls from counselors in two more states where counselors have been threatened with court action unless they cease and desist.

Legislative Action

In 1976 the state of Virginia passed the only professional counselor licensure law yet on record. This legislation created a behavioral sciences board, with separate subboards for counselors, psychologists (clinical and school), and social workers. In turn, the counselor licensure subboard licenses several types of professional counselors and certifies alcoholism and drug counselors. VPGA and APGA were the leaders in this successful licensure effort. Other states where strong efforts to license counselors have been mounted are Ohio, Texas, and Alabama. Although these states have a two-to-three-year history of intense legislative activity, Utah, Arkansas, and Idaho have embarked on attempts to license professional counselors only recently.

Prospects for enactment of the bills in Ohio and Alabama look very good for the next legislative session. The APGA Licensure Committee, the state APGA branches or divisions, and other groups are very active in pushing for the bills in these states. Florida is taking a different tack. Lobbying groups there have been pushing for legal changes to broaden the present psychology licensing law to include marriage counselors and clinical social workers.

In a related development, several states have passed "sunset laws." These acts hold all occupational boards accountable for evaluating their own effectiveness. Legislators are always asking for conclusive evidence that licensing practices do indeed benefit the public. Counselors in states that have enacted sunset laws should not overlook the possibilities such laws create if they believe that their state's current board of examiners in psychology is not operating in a fashion that benefits the public. A word of caution to those who follow this course. By discrediting the idea of a board of examiners in psychology, you may discredit the idea of any board designed to control the broad area of behavioral sciences. Not only are state legislators raising questions about occupational boards in general, but organizations such as the Federal Trade Commission and Educational Testing Service are also raising questions about the monopolistic practices of state psychology boards.

APGA and Other Professional Organizations

One of the main objectives of the APGA Licensure Committee has been to establish dialogues on credentialing and licensure with other professional organizations. To that end, positive communication has been established with the National Association of Social Workers, American Association of Marriage and Family Counselors, American Mental Health Counselors Association, and Division 17 of the American Psychological Association.

Because many APGA members are also members of APA, communication with this organization has been critical. The leadership of APA appears to be sensitive to the complaints of unfair psychology licensure practices at the doctoral level. They are not anxious to license MA-level psychology applicants but appear to accept the licensing of counselors by other organizations or bodies, such as state counselor licensing boards. Because the licensure of helping professionals affects both APA and APGA members, dialogue between the associations has been continuing for some time. At the 1975 and the 1976 APA conventions and at the 1977 APGA convention, programs on licensure were jointly conducted by representatives of both APGA and APA.

Division 17 of APA has taken a very active role in the licensure problem. In 1974–75, their Committee on Human Rights and Social Issues produced a position paper setting forth the key issues in licensure (Weeks 1974). More recently, a blue-ribbon committee composed of past and present officers has worked with both the APGA Licensure Committee and the American Association of State Psychology Boards (AASPB) to develop policy guidelines for examining boards to consider ("Guidelines for Credentialing Set" 1977). In addition, an Ad Hoc Committee on Licensure and Certification has been persistently attacking the same problems by communicating with the current officers and the Division 17 blue-ribbon Committee.

The primary goal of the Ad Hoc Committee has been to seek more positive action from Division 17 leadership to change the repressive practices of some state boards. Finally, the recent Vail conference on levels and patterns of professional training in psychology recognized the need for practitioners who are qualified through a professional training model as well as for traditional academic psychologists (Ivey & Leppaluoto 1975).

Recent Developments and Current Action

Divisional Activities. Interest in licensure among APGA members began with the formation of a committee in Southern ACES in 1974. In subsequent years, ACES organized a similar committee which has been highly active. The results of these vigorous efforts were shown in the "Proposal for a National Registry of Professional Counselors" (*ACES Licensure Committee Report* 1977) and in the ACES survey on licensure (Carroll, Griggs, & Halligan 1977). Both of these reports demonstrated a high level of interest among ACES members in the establishment of state licensure and a national register for counselors.

Recently, ASCA has decided to invest both money and personpower in the licensure movement. At a workshop in Madison, Wisconsin, in May 1977, eight regional ASCA licensure consultants were trained to provide direct assistance to states in their regions. An educational packet for members was also developed at the workshop, which was sponsored by ASCA and co-led by leaders of ASCA and the APGA Licensure Committee. As a direct result of this workshop, several state workshops have been held and licensure workshops co-led by an APGA Licensure Committee member and two

49

ASCA regional licensure consultants have been conducted at all four APGA Regional Branch Assemblies. Although other divisions of APGA have not been as active in the licensure movement, many, such as ACPA, ARCA, ASGW, and ANWC, are becoming more involved.

APGA Licensure Commission

The APGA Licensure Commission, with assistance from the central staff of APGA is currently moving on several fronts. Special projects are underway on a national registry, a third-party payment bill, a national licensure network, regional and state workshops, revision of the licensure action packet, establishment of a procedure for handling complaints, and continuation of dialogue with such groups as NRA, NASW, ABBP, APA, AAMFC, FTC, and the VA.

Registry. A special subcommittee of the licensure committee has taken the basic work of the ACES Licensure Commission on a national registry and is further developing the plan for a national registry for counselors. The subcommittee hopes to have a reasonably complete plan for consideration by members by the end of the current year. The licensure commission, supported by data from two surveys (ACES Licensure Committee Report 1977; Carroll, Griggs & Halligan 1977), feels that APGA must move in this direction. The licensure commission believes that the establishment of a registry that would recognize the many varieties and types of counselors is essential for APGA because of the following reasons.

1. Any professional group seeking the highest level of professional recognition and legislative status first needs to demonstrate its willingness and ability to govern and regulate its own house.

2. Licensure, while ultimately important to the entire profession of counseling, directly affects only a small percentage of our membership. A national registry would have many more immediate benefits to the entire membership while assisting the licensure movement.

3. All other major professional groups similar to ours currently have established either a formal registry system or, at the least, strict criteria have been set for membership. These include APA, NASW, AAMFC, and one of our own divisions, ARCA.

4. A national registry with criteria for listing would facilitate the implementation of our current approved standards for the preparation of counselors at the master's level and our pending doctoral-level standards.

5. A national registry would facilitate understanding of our professional preparation and our qualifications by the consumers of our services.

6. A national registry would make public the credentials of professional counselors to institutions, government agencies, and other interested parties.

7. Although the registry could not assure its users about competent practice, the information provided, the training and experience of those listed, would present a point of departure from which the user could make decisions.

Third-Party Payment. The licensure commission is currently developing a third-party payment (vendorship) bill for submission to Congress. It appears that we may be the only major helping services professional group that does not now have such a bill in Congress.

National Network. The establishment of a national licensure network has been a top priority this year. Currently, 37 states have named a state licensure representative. Another important link in this network is the establishment of ASCA's regional licensure consultants. The network is already facilitating communication among state and regional groups and national headquarters. Some of the fruits of the network have been the licensure workshops at all four APGA regional meetings, some state workshops, and a procedure for responding to member concerns from the field.

Complaint Procedure. The licensure commission has developed a formal procedure for handling member complaints about unfair actions by state boards. The procedure will facilitate the gathering of data related to a complaint and will provide a guide as to the best course of action to be taken by the committee and the appropriate state branch or division. The format for this procedure will be published in the revised action packet.

Action Packet. The publication of the action packet by the licensure commission was a significant step in 1976. This project began as an attempt to assist state professional groups who sought to expand the scope of psychology boards or to create boards for the licensure of professional counselors. Although it was originally designed to offer model legislation, the factors inherent in legislative change suggested the appropriateness of the term "guidelines."

The balance of the packet offered some suggested legislative procedures, background information on the Licensure Commission, comments on the nature of legislative change, and ways to use the guidelines with local educational groups. A general updating of material in the Action Packet is now under way. Included in this new edition will be material suggested from division feedback, an organizational chart, the complaint procedure, a professional disclosure section, and a new reference and materials section.

Summary

It is clear that the licensure movement is rapidly gaining momentum across the country. After much effort, more and more counselors understand the basic issues involved in counselor licensure. Counseling as a profession has little legal status and without such status our existence as a profession is in the hands of others. As a professional group we have matured to the point where we are saying we wish to control our own ranks, and, further, by virtue of our training we have the right to provide quality services to the public. We must not, we cannot afford to lose the momentum toward licensure. We are at a critical juncture that requires the efforts of every APGA member. P&G

References

ACES Licensure Committee. *Report.* Presented at the meeting of the American Personnel and Guidance Association, Dallas, March 1977.

American Psychological Association. A model for state legislation affecting the practice of psychology: 1967 report of APA Committee on Legislation. *American Psychologist,* 1967, 22, 1,095–1,103.

Carroll, M. R.; Halligan, F. G.; & Griggs, S. A. The licensure issue: How real is it? *Personnel and Guidance Journal,* 1977, 55, 577–580.

Cottingham, H. F., & Swanson, C. Recent licensure developments: Implications for counselor educators. *Counselor Education and Supervision,* 1976, 16, 84–97.

Council for the National Register of Health Service Providers in Psychology. *Application form.* Washington, D.C.: Author, 1977.

Guidelines for credentialing set. *Guidepost,* September 22, 1977, p. 1; 12.

Ivey, H. E., & Leppaluoto, J. R. Changes ahead: Implications of the Vail conference. *Personnel and Guidance Journal,* 1975, 53, 1,747–1,752.

Sweeney, T. J. Licensure in the helping professions: A position paper. Washington, D.C.: APGA, 1974.

Sweeney, T. J., & Witmer, J. M. Who says you're a counselor? *Personnel and Guidance Journal,* 1977, 55, 589–594.

Weeks, J. Position statement, Division 17 Committee on Human Rights and Social Issues. *Counseling Psychologist,* 1974, 5, 135.

The following article on professional disclosure is included as an example of a possible alternative to licensure, but most importantly as a concept that we believe should be incorporated in all counselor licensure bills. The concept is part of the suggested legislative package of the APGA Licensure Committee.

[From: *Counselor Education and Supervision,* Vol. 18, No. 1]

ACES corner

Professional Disclosure in Licensure

J. MELVIN WITMER

In a special issue of *The Personnel and Guidance Journal,* Gross (1977) proposed professional disclosure as an alternative to licensure and certification of counselors. This concept, as discussed by Gross, is based on the belief that the best protection is self-protection. Consumers have the ability and the responsibility to protect themselves. They can do so with accurate and sufficient information. To make informed decisions, the consumers of counseling services not only need but have the right to information that describes the nature and cost of the service as well as the credentials of the person providing the service. One of the goals of consumer-protection groups is honest labeling of products and services offered to the public.

Efforts to provide consumers with accurate information have generally focused on products such as hard goods, foods, and medicines. Consumer-interest groups are now looking at professional services provided by physicians, attorneys, and therapists. For example, Winborn (1977) argued for honest labeling and other procedures for the protection of consumers of counseling. What can be done individually and professionally to clear up confusion about the nature of counseling and psychotherapy and to label our services honestly so that consumers can make informed choices when they seek counseling?

Although professional disclosure for the protection of the public has much merit, it does not seem very realistic as an alternative to licensure in today's professional and legislative world. For example, counselors in several states are having to defend the right to practice and in some instances have been seriously restrained in their practice because of conflicts with the psychology-licensing boards. This problem has occurred because counselors outside school settings have no legal status regulating who may identify themselves as professional counselors (Sweeney & Witmer 1977). Federal and state funds for human and social services also require some form of credential for the personnel delivering those services. In making third-party payments, insurance companies require credentialing of the persons delivering the service.

Although professional disclosure alone would not be sufficient, it offers some desirable features as a part of counselor licensure and certification. This article briefly describes the pur-

J. Melvin Witmer is a Professor in the College of Education, Ohio University, Athens.

pose of professional disclosure and suggests how it might be included in counselor-licensure statutes.

Rationale

Purpose and justification. Professional disclosure may be justified from the perspective of the public and the professionals who serve the public. As indicated previously, the public has a right to relevant information before electing a human or social service and, when informed, is capable of making wise decisions if adequate information is available.

When viewed from the consumer's perspective two things are evident. First, there are monopolistic practices and restraint of trade through nonpublic disclosure of such matters as the services professionals are competent to provide, cost of services, and a means for handling dissatisfaction or complaints regarding the services. When the means are available, it is often after the services have been provided rather than before the client has made a decision. Second, there is no legal or ethical requirement that the professional make relevant information available to the individual seeking the service before delivery of that service.

Public and professional benefits. Given the conditions discussed thus far, the purpose of professional disclosure is to provide quality services to the public at fees that are reasonable for the services provided. More specifically, such a provision in counselor licensure would result in

1. Helping ensure the welfare of the public through informed self-protection and responsibility. With increased self-responsibility there are likely to be more positive expectations accompanied by a stronger belief in the services, which will increase the probability of change or improvement.

2. Education of the public regarding the services available, their nature, and costs.

3. Greater counselor accountability to the client for services provided through honest and adequate labeling of qualifications, the nature of counseling, fees, and a recourse for complaints that cannot be resolved by the client and counselor.

4. More appropriate professional referrals being made when such information is available to practitioners in counseling and other professions.

Implementation

The provisions for professional disclosure could be required through licensure legislation in the form of a written statement given to each client before the delivery of any services or displayed in a conspicuous location at the place of service. For example, the statement might include name, business address and telephone number, philosophy of counseling, formal education and training, areas of competence, continuing education, fee schedule, and the name, address, and telephone number of the state government agency regulating the practice of counseling. Winborn (1977) included some of these areas in his example of consumer information for clients. Implementation of these provisions based on suggestions by Gross (1977) would be accomplished by

1. Including a professional-disclosure statement in the application for counselor licensure each time the license is renewed and whenever a change in the statement is indicated.

2. Disclosing the information to prospective clients before providing any counseling service for which a fee is charged. The statement should be prepared in understandable language, in printed form for the client, and

posted conspicuously in the office setting.

3. Stating that disclosure to clients is required, including information about the state government agency that is responsible for licensure so that a complainant would know to whom a complaint could be made.

4. Including in the statute provisions for denial, suspension, or revocation of licensure, or reprimanding the counselor for willful failure to file or for willful filing of a false or incomplete professional disclosure statement.

Professional disclosure has been included in the Ohio counselor-licensure bill introduced in the 112th General Assembly (1977–79). Ohio legislators received this provision quite favorably.

Taking such steps to help ensure consumer protection and counselor accountability may establish a precedent among professions. Then counseling will, in the long run, contribute to making quality services available to more people. It was not the intent of this article to deal with the emerging professional issue of advertising services offered by the media of newspaper, radio, and television. If we as professionals do not become more open in our professional relationships, however, it may fall to the Federal Trade Commission and the federal courts to determine whether we are violating antitrust laws. A professional-disclosure provision in counselor licensure has promise as a reasonable approach to providing sufficient information to aid the consumer to make informed judgments and choices.

References

Gross, S. J. Professional disclosure: An alternative to licensure. *Personnel and Guidance Journal,* 1977, 55, 586–588.

Sweeney, T. J. & Witmer, J. M. Who says you're a counselor? *Personnel and Guidance Journal,* 1977, 56, 589–594.

Winborn, B. B. Honest labeling and other procedures for the protection of consumers of counseling. *Personnel and Guidance Journal,* 1977, 56, 206–209.

This article is formally published here for the first time. It originally appeared in *Action Line*, the APGA Licensure Committee's Newsletter. It was written by Mel Witmer in response to a document being put in the hands of state legislators by the Council of State Governments. The document "Occupational Licensing: Questions a Legislator Should Ask" was written by Benjamin Shimberg and Doug Roedener and published in 1978. It raises many good questions that we believe receive equally good answers in this article.

[From: *APGA Licensure Action Line*, No. 3, March 1973]

The Politics of Licensure: Questions Legislators Are Asking

J. Melvin Witmer

In my series of articles on *power, love, money, and politics, I* proposed to write on *money* in the third issue. Everett Dirksen, the late senator from Illinois, once suggested that a good politician reserves the right to change his/her mind when new information is made available. I have changed my mind and chosen to write on *politics* instead of *money*, which will be my topic for my fourth article. The new information I have received is Shimberg and Roederer's *Occupational Licensing: Questions a Legislator Should Ask*. If you haven't read it, I suggest you do so before approaching any legislators on counselor licensure. At a recent meeting of the APGA Licensure Committee we discussed how we might respond to the questions posed in this publication put out by the Council of State Governments. I agreed to treat it in this issue of the *Action Line* and organize my discussion around the questions in the booklet. The responses are based on material from the APGA *Action Packet*, ASCA's *Educational Package*, brochures and newsletters from state licensure committees, APGA Licensure Committee discussions, and my own experience in licensure legislation.

In one way or another I have been asked most of these questions over the last 4 years. Please be aware that answers to them will vary from state to state, depending on the nature and history of counseling and psychological services in that state and the existent political and professional circumstances. Without due regard to these unique state conditions, your use of these answers may be hazardous to your cause for counselor licensure. Now that I have stated this disclaimer I will try to respond to the questions briefly, but in sufficient length to be helpful. In doing so it seems logical for me to arrange the questions in an order which would be most meaningful, but one which is a slight departure from the order found in the booklet.

Question: *What Is the Problem?*
Answers:
1. While counseling as a profession does exist, it has no legal recognition or definition except in the states of Virginia, Arkansas, and Alabama, where counselor licensure laws have recently been passed.

Anyone can use the title "counselor" and hold himself/herself out to the public as providing "counseling services."

2. There is no legal recourse for: (1) establishing standards, (2) enforcing professional ethics, and (3) correcting abuses, negligence, malpractice or incompetence. Little data are available as to who is practicing and how many persons are holding themselves out as counselors. Counselors are employed in many diverse settings and offer a wide range of services. Consequently, it is difficult to document unethical practices and unsatisfactory services. We are trying to anticipate and prevent potential harm to the public. There is documentation of counselors providing misleading or false information, providing services for which they are not qualified, and exhibiting behavior not in the client's best interests.

3. Counselors are being denied employment in the human, health, and social services because they are not appropriately licensed or certified. For example in a recent survey, 70 ACES members reported that in spite of training at the doctoral level in counseling they were denied employment as professional counselors in a clinic or agency because of Medicaid or other insurance coverage requirements for licensed service providers. In addition guidelines in government agencies and Federal grants frequently stipulate that persons providing human and social services have some form of credentialing such as licensure or certification. In making third party payments insurance carriers limit reimbursement to persons appropriately credentialed, often by statutory code.

4. In several states counselors have been ordered by the Board of Psychology to discontinue their practice because they are alleged to be in violation of the state's psychology law, even though these individuals were not calling themselves psychologists. The basis for this action comes from the fact that many state psychology licensure laws incorporate a definition which includes the kinds of activities that most counselors, as well as other helping professionals, do in working with people.

It is estimated that legal grievance procedures involving counseling professionals, either as a plaintiff or as a defendant, have been filed in at least 20 states. In one case which reached the court, a decision was handed down which acted to define counseling and guidance as a profession. Two cases centered on the issue of the applicant's right to take the examination in psychology. Another case alleged that a counselor was practicing psychology without a license. The cost for defense in individual cases has amounted to over $20,000 each.

5. State boards of psychology have increasingly refused to permit individuals trained outside departments of psychology to take the state licensure examination, even though the applicant's educational program has been "primarily psychological in nature." State psychology boards are placing the responsibility for designation of the program as "psychological in nature" with the educational institution. More than one-half of the counselor training programs are not located in psychology departments. With the criteria set forth by psychologists, persons graduating from programs that are equivalent to a psychology program will find it extremely difficult to qualify for taking the psychological examination administered by the state board of psychology. Professional counselors thus need an alternative credential, such as being designated as a licensed professional counselor.

Question: *Why Should the Occupational Group be Regulated?*
Answers:
　1. There is currently no legal definition of counseling services and no responsibilities for regulating the profession except in the three states previously mentioned. If counselors were licensed, the individual practitioner could be held accountable.
　2. Licensure would protect the public's right to be served by qualified counselors and their right to freedom of choice in selecting counseling services. Consumers are entitled to the use of any counseling services which meet their needs.
　3. Licensure would protect the constitutional right of counselors to practice their profession. It would offer employment options for counselors in a variety of work settings, including private practice.
　4. While the largest counselor association in the world has preparation standards for counselors, there is no single or common set of standards accepted by sister associations. Licensure would provide the public with more information criteria and information for evaluating the qualifications of those providing the service.
　5. Professional counseling is an occupation in which there is considerable autonomy and independent judgment required because of the private and confidential nature of the service. It is usually performed in a private one-to-one or small group setting, and continuing on-site supervision is not usually possible or desirable. Persons engaging in independent practice generally have no supervision, other than consultation with another professional, when initiated by the practitioner. The nature of the service requires considerable objectivity in dealing with subjective information. Regulation, therefore, by state legislation is desirable.
　6. The process of counseling is essentially an interpersonal relationship which involves the client's mental health, life style, career planning and placement, and personal development. Persons, not products, are at stake. In most states barbers and beauticians, for instance, are required to complete classroom instruction and, in some states, as many as 1500 clock hours of experience, to qualify for licensure. How does one explain there being no minimum requirements for counselors who help people get their heads together and chart their own destiny?

Question: *Why is Regulation Being Sought?*
Answers:

1. The publication, "Standards for the Providers of Psychological Services," (APA, 1974) calls for supervision by a psychologist of all unlicensed persons in schools, colleges, community or government agencies that provide "psychological services." Counselor licensure would deter such monopolistic intentions.

2. Currently psychologists and psychiatrists qualify for third party payments under federal and state programs as well as private health insurers. Counselors do not. Counselor licensure is necessary to insure the right of the consumer to be reimbursed for the cost of qualified counseling services.

3. Counselor positions in some statewide agencies are being eliminated because of the proviso that only licensed providers, such as psychologists or social workers, may perform psychological counseling and social service functions in the future.

4. The Veterans Administration recently established a policy to require all individuals employed as "psychologists" in VA hospitals to be licensed by State Boards of Psychology. Many individuals with a counseling psychology background would not be eligible to take the examination under current Board practices in many states.

5. At the federal level, the Department of HEW published a report in 1977 calling for national certification of health professionals and the establishment of national standards for professional training. Certain recommendations would limit federal reimbursement to those professionals licensed by State Boards adhering to national standards. If implemented, the counseling profession would be excluded from all federal programs, thus denying counselors jobs and opportunity for employment and also denying the public access to their services in many programs and settings.

6. Qualified counselors are being prevented from rendering services because of a "scope of practice" statement of another profession, namely psychology. State psychology laws and board regulations are exclusionary and restrictive, consequently placing undue restraint upon the practice of counseling, and limiting services available to the public.

7. Efforts have been made at the national level between the American Personnel and Guidance Association (APGA) and the American Psychological Association (APA) to resolve differences regarding the exclusionary nature of psychology licensure and the restrictive effect on the practice of counseling. No progress has been made at either the state or national level.

PART II

Credentialing: Accreditation, Certification/Registry, and Standards

As stated in the introduction, the area of professional credentialing includes accreditation, certification/registry, and professional standards in addition to licensure. It is important for the reader to understand that the four-fold thrust of APGA in the area of credentialing is a concerted effort. None of the individual efforts, including the licensure effort, will stand alone. The licensing of professional counselors would become a sham unless those counselors are being prepared in programs that are of the highest quality. To ensure that quality, we must, as a profession, begin to accredit our own programs. Most counselor education programs are now located in schools of education and are, therefore, accredited under the National Council for the Accreditation of Teacher Education. Although this accreditation is helpful in ensuring quality programs, it is not as effective as it should be.

To accredit programs, a professional association must have developed a realistic and quality list of professional standards. The American Personnel and Guidance Association now has standards related to the preparation of individuals at both the master's and doctoral levels. Counselor education programs and agencies that employ counselors must begin using both sets of professional standards.

Although licensure has the advantage of giving legal status to a profession, in and of itself, it only establishes minimum levels of competency for practice. If a professional association desires to go beyond the establishment of minimum levels of competency, it must investigate and develop procedures for certifying its practitioners. Publication of a list of individuals so certified by professional association is often referred to as a registry. This can be confusing because registries often are simply a list of individuals who have submitted certain credentials to a central organizing body. This organizing body may not really examine the credentials submitted but may simply accept them as evidence of competence. Although this is the weakest form of registry, it is the most prevalent. The registry that the APGA Registry Committee is considering would include a process of certification similar to that developed by the National Academy of Certified Clinical Mental Health Counselors.

In Part II, we will briefly examine each of the areas mentioned above. The material presented is, in our judgment, the best available material related to these topics.

Accreditation/Standards. The Association for Counselor Education and Supervision (ACES), a division of the American Personnel and Guidance Association, was charged by the APGA Board of Directors in July of 1978 to develop guidelines and procedures for the accreditation of counselor education programs based on the APGA standards. A procedural manual has been produced and regional workshops have been held to train a cross section of individuals as potential accreditation team members. Several counselor education programs will be reviewed by ACES in a pilot study basis during the 1979–80 academic year. This will be the first time these programs have been reviewed using professional counseling standards rather than teacher education or general graduate study criteria under the National Council for the Accreditation of Teacher Education. Based on this pilot study, revisions will be made in the accreditation procedures in conjunction with the APGA accreditation committee. It is hoped that a number of programs will seek APGA accreditation in the years ahead.

Professional standards that define both the ethical practice and the nature of preparation programs are the foundation of the credentialing process.

Certification/Registry. Certification for school counselors is the most widespread form of credentialing that affects the counseling profession; however, only 33% of APGA's membership is presently employed in the K–12 school setting.

National certification procedures have been implemented by two other divisions of the American Personnel and Guidance Association. The American Rehabilitation Counseling Association (ARCA) is a charter member of the Commission on Rehabilitation Counselor Certification, a coalition of professional rehabilitation organizations that administers the national certification system for rehabilitation counselors. The American Mental Health Counselors Association (AMHCA), APGA's newest division, was responsible for the development of a national certification process for professional counselors with somewhat broader application. The National Academy for Clinical Mental Health Counselors is now in existence and is designed to provide a certification system for community mental health counselors operating in agencies and in the private sector. A by-product of both certification processes is the publication of a registry of certified individuals. The establishment of these two certification/registry procedures is a giant step forward for our profession. The articles that follow are directly related to these two processes.

APGA adopted its ethical standards in 1961 and revised them in 1974. The Association for Counselor Education and Supervision (ACES) adopted standards for the preparation of counselors and other personnel service specialists in 1973. The ACES standards have been adopted by the American School Counselor Association (ASCA) and have been designated by the APGA Board of Directors as the official statement of professional preparation standards. Preliminary standards for the preparation of counselors at the doctoral level have also recently been accepted by the APGA Board of Directors. Compliance with the APGA standards by counselor education programs has been on a voluntary basis because of the lack of accreditation procedures.

Jerald R. Forster's article provides an excellent introduction to the APGA standards for the preparation of counselors and other personnel services specialists. Following the presentation of this article are the guidelines for doctoral preparation in counselor education that was formally adopted by the ACES membership in July 1977.

[From: *Personnel and Guidance Journal*, Vol. 55, No. 10]

An Introduction to the Standards for the Preparation of Counselors and Other Personnel Services Specialists

Jerald R. Forster

The standards that follow represent the culmination of an extensive amount of effort occurring around the country during the past two decades. These standards incorporate many of the ideas developed during the early sixties when a committee of the Association for Counselor Education and Supervision (ACES) conducted a five-year Planning Cooperative Study of Counselor Education Standards. Stripling (1965) gives an account of this study that tapped the reactions of 150 grass roots committees in all 50 states and resulted in a final report at the 1964 APGA convention in San Francisco. The standards included in that report were used on an experimental basis for a three-year period for institutional self-evaluation and officially adopted in 1967 (Standards 1967). A manual for applying the standards to counselor education programs was also developed in 1967. Concomitant with these efforts were other major studies by the American School Counselor Association (ASCA), which developed a statement of policy and implementation guidelines for secondary school counselors.

Having worked out standards for secondary school counselors, ACES next turned its attention to standards for preparing elementary school counselors and approved these standards in 1968, after a committee had spent three years developing the final product. Yet another set of standards for the preparation of student personnel workers was adopted by ACES in 1969.

The development of separate standards for each specialization led to a diffusion of energy, and members of the profession urged that the various standards be combined into a comprehensive document covering all subspecialties. A Commission on Standards and Accreditation was formed, chaired by Robert Stripling, and in 1971 the Commission was assigned the task of developing a revised and combined set of standards that would serve the whole profession. The activities of that Commission led to the development of the standards that follow. The Commission, which included members from each of the APGA regions, took the position that the development of the standards of preparation should be an educational process that was to involve as many members of the profession as possible. In the letter sent out to the ACES membership in 1973, the Commission said:

During the course of the hearings on the standards at the five ACES regional meetings in the fall of 1972 and at the three 1972–73 APGA regional meetings, the Commission learned much about the many important changes in counselor education that are taking place throughout the country. A conscientious attempt was made to incorporate in the attached final draft of the standards the flexibility needed to accommodate the different models of professional preparation which are emerging. Certainly, the attached standards were meant, in no way, to inhibit creativity in the improvement of counselor education.

The ACES membership overwhelmingly approved the revised, combined standards in October 1973. The standards were subsequently adopted by ASCA and the Board of Directors of APGA.

Despite the fact that the standards have not had widespread distribution, they have received many positive descriptions. Dash (1975) examined them in relationship to competency-based counselor education and found the two to be complementary.

While the standards are designed to be used for counselors of many subspecialties, they were not intended for use in preparing doctoral students or paraprofessionals. An ACES committee was formed in 1976 to develop guidelines for advanced graduate degree programs in counselor education. Robert Stripling, a counselor educator whose name is synonymous with professional standards for counselors, will lead the committee. P&G

References

Dash, E. G. Counselor competency and the revised ACES standards. *Counselor Education and Supervision*, 1975, 24, 221–227.
Standards for the preparation of secondary school counselors, 1967, (George Hill, Chairperson), APGA, Washington, D.C.
Stripling, R. O. Standards for the education of school counselors. In J. Loughary, R. Stripling & P. Fitzgerald, (Eds.), *Counseling, a growing profession*. Washington, D.C.: APGA, 1965.

Standards for the Preparation of Counselors and Other Personnel Services Specialists

(Adopted by ACES Membership October 1973)

Introduction

These Standards are intended as guidelines for the graduate preparation of counselors and other personnel services specialists. They should be beneficial to college and university staff who are involved in initiating programs of preparation or in evaluating existing programs. The Standards can also be helpful to state, regional, and national accrediting agencies. While the Standards are designed to serve as guidelines for minimum preparation, they are flexible enough to allow for creative approaches to counselor education. The Standards do not include guidelines for the preparation of support personnel or professional personnel at the doctoral level.

These Standards recognize that:

> The faculty has developed a written statement of philosophy for the counselor education program and that this statement has been accepted by the institution.
>
> The trend toward the development of competency-based/performance-based counselor education programs is likely to continue. Whether or not a counselor education program is developed upon such a base, however, the Standards reflect the concern that all programs should give to the assessment of demonstrated competencies by students during various stages of their development.

Students take varying rates of time to demonstrate the competencies and professional maturation demanded in the complexities of counseling and personnel services work. While the Standards recommend minimum hours of study in certain areas, these stated minimum hours should be interpreted in the context that some students will demonstrate the desired competency and professional maturation levels in a shorter time than indicated while others may take substantially longer.

The need of counselors and other personnel services specialists for self-renewal and in-service education beyond minimum preparation or certification will increase. Therefore, the counselor education program should provide enriching experiences for those who have already completed the minimum program.

Minimum study in counselor education will increasingly extend beyond the one-year program of graduate preparation. Such programs might include (a) a combination of an undergraduate major in guidance and a year of graduate study in counselor education, (b) two years of graduate study in counselor education, or (c) other models that include a minimum of one year of graduate study.

All counselor education programs are not expected to prepare counselors and other personnel services specialists for all the work settings encompassed by the Standards. Institutions should offer preparation programs only in those areas where sufficient qualified full-time staff and other resources are available.

The Standards reflect current thinking concerning the preparation of counselors and other personnel services specialists and combine the three existing statements on counselor preparation previously adopted by the Association for Counselor Education and Supervision (ACES): "Standards for the Preparation of Secondary School Counselors—1967"; "Standards for the Preparation of Elementary School Counselors," February, 1968; and "Guidelines for Graduate Programs in the Preparation of Student Personnel Workers in Higher Education—1969."

In addition to acknowledging the similarity of preparation among the various specialists, the Standards also provide for different goals that may exist in various work settings. While this single document has been developed for the entire profession, the respective divisions of the American Personnel and Guidance Association and other professional groups are encouraged to develop jointly, with ACES, specific statements concerning the specialized needs of counselors and other personnel services specialists who work in different settings. In this respect, attention is called to Section II.B.2 of the Standards, "Environmental and Specialized Studies."

Leadership for the development of these Standards was assumed by the ACES Commission on Standards and Accreditation,* working under the supervision of the Executive Council of ACES. The Standards were adopted by the membership of ACES in October 1973.

Standards

SECTION I. OBJECTIVES

A. Objectives of the Program to Prepare Counselors and Other Personnel Services Specialists

1. *The faculty has developed program objectives.*

   a. Objectives reflect a knowledge of studies and recommendations of local, state, regional, and national lay and professional groups concerned with counseling and personal services needs of society.

   b. Objectives reflect the needs in society that are represented by different ethnic and cultural groups served by counselors and other personnel services specialists.

   c. Objectives are reviewed and revised continuously through student as well as faculty participation.

   d. Objectives are developed and reviewed with the assistance of personnel in cooperating agencies.

   e. Objectives are written in such a way that evaluation of a student can be based on demonstrated competencies as he progresses through the program.

2. *Objectives are implemented on a planned basis in all areas of the program including selection, retention, and endorsement of students; curriculum; instructional methods; research activities; and administrative policies, procedures, and execution.*

3. *Personnel in cooperating agencies and faculty members with primary assignments in other disciplines are aware of and are encouraged to work toward the objectives of the counselor education program.*

---

* Membership of the Commission is listed at the end of this document.

4. *There is a planned procedure for a continuing evaluation of the outcomes of the program.*

   a. The program is evaluated in terms of demonstrated competencies of each student as he or she progresses through the program.

   b. Evaluation of the effectiveness of preparation is accomplished through evidence obtained from (a) former students, (b) supervisors in agencies employing graduates of the program, and (c) personnel in state and national licensing and accrediting agencies.

SECTION II: CURRICULUM— PROGRAM OF STUDIES AND SUPERVISED EXPERIENCES

A. General Program Characteristics

1. *The institution provides a graduate program in counselor education designed for the preparation of counselors and other personnel services specialists.*

   a. The opportunity for full-time study throughout the academic year is provided and actively encouraged.

   b. Flexibility is provided within the curriculum to allow for individual differences in competencies and understandings developed before entering the program.

   c. Descriptions of the various program options and requirements for graduate studies are published and distributed to prospective students.

   d. Concepts relating to differentiated staffing and preparation in counseling and personnel services are reflected in the program. The faculty is aware of lifetime opportunities for development and advancement in the field of counseling and personnel services. There is also an emphasis on the use of support personnel to free more professionally prepared personnel for the performance of higher level functions.

2. *Continuing and/or in-service education offerings in counselor education meet all of the criteria in faculty qualifications, faculty load, physical facilities, and faculty-student ratios, as described in these Standards.*

3. *There is evidence of high quality instruction in all aspects of the program.*

   a. Syllabi or other evidence of organized and coordinated instructional units of the curriculum are available.

   b. Resource materials are provided.

   c. Responsibilities are assigned to, or assumed by faculty members only

in those areas of the counselor education program for which they have demonstrated professional competency.

   d. Provisions are made for periodic evaluation by students and staff of all aspects of the program; i.e., course content, methods of instruction, and supervised experience, both on and off campus.

4. *Planned sequences of educational experiences are provided.*

   a. Within the minimum counselor education program a sequence of basic and advanced graduate studies and other associated learning experiences is defined and provided.

   b. The program provides for the integration of didactic studies and supervised experiences.

   c. All prerequisite studies and other experiences are identified.

   d. Representatives of departments offering studies in related fields are regularly consulted regarding how related studies can be made more useful to counselor education majors.

   e. The faculty has identified performance indicators to determine whether the professional competencies to be developed by the sequence of educational experiences are achieved.

5. *A close relationship exists between the faculty of the counselor education program and the staff members in work settings.*

   a. The staff in the work settings is consulted in the design and implementation of all aspects of the program, including practicum and internship experiences.

   b. The faculty of the preparation program is consulted in the design and implementation of in-service preparation of staff in work settings.

6. *Within the framework of the total program, there are opportunities for the student to develop understandings and skills beyond the minimum requirements of the program.*

   a. Elective courses and related experiences are available.

   b. Supervised individual study is available.

   c. Enrichment opportunities are provided and faculty encourage students to take part in them.

7. *The spirit of inquiry and the production and utilization of research data are encouraged among both faculty and students.*

   a. The statement of objectives of

Standards

the program reflects an awareness of the role of research in the counseling and personnel services field.

b. Instructional procedures make frequent use of, and reference to, research findings. Areas in which research is needed are identified.

8. *Opportunities for planned periodic self-evaluation and the development of greater self-understanding are provided for both students and faculty.*

a. Self-analysis is encouraged through such activities as laboratory experiences, including audio- and/or videotape recordings.

b. Opportunities for improvement of interpersonal relationships are provided through small-group activities.

c. Counseling services for students are available and are provided by qualified persons other than counselor education faculty.

B. Program of Studies

1. *Common core: The common core is composed of general areas considered to be necessary in the preparation of all counselors and other personnel services specialists.*

a. Human growth and development: Includes studies that provide a broad understanding of the nature and needs of individuals at all developmental levels. Emphasis is placed on psychological, sociological, and physiological approaches. Also included are such areas as human behavior (normal and abnormal), personality theory, and learning theory.

b. Social and cultural foundations: Includes studies of change, ethnic groups, subcultures, changing roles of women, sexism, urban and rural societies, population patterns, cultural mores, use of leisure time, and differing life patterns. Such disciplines as the behavioral sciences, economics, and political science are involved.

c. The helping relationship: Includes (a) philosophic bases of the helping relationship; (b) counseling theory, supervised practice, and application; (c) consultation theory, supervised practice, and application; and (d) an emphasis upon development of counselor and client (or consultee) self-awareness and self-understanding.

d. Groups: Includes theory and types of groups, as well as descriptions of group practices, methods, dynamics, and facilitative skills. It also includes supervised practice.

e. Life-style and career development: Includes such areas as vocational choice theory, relationship between career choice and life-style, sources of occupational and educational information, approaches to career decision-making processes, and career development exploration techniques.

f. Appraisal of the individual: Includes the development of a framework for understanding the individual, including methods of data gathering and interpretation, individual and group testing, case study approaches, and the study of individual differences. Ethnic, cultural, and sex factors are also considered.

g. Research and evaluation: Includes such areas as statistics, research design, development of research and demonstration proposals. It also includes understanding legislation relating to the development of research, program development, and demonstration proposals, as well as the development and evaluation of program objectives.

h. Professional orientation: Includes goals and objectives of professional organizations, codes of ethics, legal considerations, standards of preparation, certification, licensing and role identity of counselors and other personnel services specialists.

2. *Environmental and specialized studies: The counselor education program includes those specialized studies necessary for practice in different work settings. There is evidence that the faculty, in planning and evaluating the counselor education curriculum, has taken into consideration statements made by other professional groups relating to role, function and preparation.*

a. Environmental studies: Includes the study of the environment in which the student is planning to practice. This includes history, philosophy, trends, purposes, ethics, legal aspects, standards, and roles within the institution or work setting where the student will practice.

b. Specialized studies: Includes the specialized knowledge and skills needed to work effectively in the professional setting where the student plans to practice. For example, the student preparing to be an elementary school counselor may need to take, among other specialized courses, work in diagnosis of reading dysfunction; the student preparing to be a personnel services educator in higher education might need, among other specialized work, both course work and supervised experiences in student financial aid; or the student preparing to work in employment counseling may need additional information about employment trends as well as the sociology and psychology of work. The different professional associations jointly concerned with the preparation of counselors and other personnel services specialists are encouraged to develop statements concerning environmental and specialized studies and make these statements available to the ACES Commission on Standards and Accreditation and to the profession in general.

C. Supervised Experiences

1. *Appropriate supervised experiences provide for the integration and application of knowledge and skills gained in didactic study.*

a. Students' supervised experiences are in settings that are compatible with their career goals.

b. Supervised experiences include observation and direct work with individuals and groups within the appropriate work setting.

c. Opportunities are provided for professional relationships with staff members in the work settings.

2. *Supervised experiences include laboratory, practicum, and internship.*

a. Laboratory experiences, providing both observation and participation in specific activities, are offered throughout the preparatory program. This might include role playing, listening to tapes, viewing videotape playbacks, testing, organizing and using personnel records, interviews with field practitioners, preparing and examining case studies, and using career information materials.

b. Supervised counseling practicum experiences provide interaction with individuals and groups actually seeking services from counselors and other personnel services specialists. Some of these individuals and groups should come from the environments in which the counselor education student is preparing to work.

(1) Specific counseling practica have sufficient duration and continuity to assure optimum professional development. The minimum recommended amount of actual contact with individuals and groups is 60 clock hours extending over a minimum nine-month period.

(2) Supervision in consultation is also provided.

(3) The supervisor's role is clearly identified and sufficient time for supervision is allocated. The recommended

weekly minimum of supervision is one hour of individual supervision and one hour of supervision in a group for the duration of the practicum experiences. Supervisory responsibilities include critiquing of counseling, either observed or recorded on audio- or videotape.

c. Internship is a postpracticum experience that provides an actual on-the-job experience and should be given central importance for each student.

(1) The internship placement is selected on the basis of the student's career goals.

(2) The internship includes all activities that a regularly employed staff member would be expected to perform. In the setting the intern is expected to behave as a professional and should be treated as one.

(3) For those students who have no prior work experience in their particular setting, an intensified or expanded internship is provided.

(4) The intern spends a minimum of 300 clock hours on the job. It is desirable that the internship be a paid experience.

(5) Supervision is performed by qualified staff in the field placement setting who have released time from other regular duties.

(6) The counselor education faculty provides these field supervisors opportunities for in-service education in counseling and personnel services supervision.

(7) There should be close cooperative working relationships between staff in field placement settings and the counselor education faculty.

3. *A qualified faculty and staff with adequate time allocated to supervision is provided for laboratory, practicum, and internship experiences.*

a. Members of the on-campus faculty responsible for supervision includes those who:

(1) have earned doctoral degrees, preferably in counselor education, from accredited institutions.

(2) have had experience and demonstrate competencies in counseling and other personnel services at the level appropriate for the students supervised.

b. Doctoral students serving as supervisors of practicum experiences are themselves supervised by qualified faculty.

c. The practicum and internship experiences are tutorial forms of instruction; therefore, the supervision of five students is considered equivalent to the teaching of one three-semester-hour course. Such a ratio is considered maximum.

4. *Facilities, equipment, and materials are provided for supervised experiences in both on- and off-campus settings. (See also Section IV.)*

D. Program Development Outreach

1. *The counselor education faculty assists individual counselors and other personnel services specialists in off-campus agencies providing supervised experiences in the program of preparation.*

a. The institution encourages agency personnel to seek the counselor education faculty's assistance in planning and conducting in-service education and in developing program improvement models.

b. The counselor education faculty is provided a teaching-work load recognition for their part in in-service and program development activities in cooperating agencies.

c. The counselor education faculty involves advanced graduate students in programs of in-service education and in program development planning and implementation at the agency level.

2. *The counselor education faculty provides on-campus assistance to agency personnel in resolving unique problems or difficulties.*

a. The faculty encourages agency personnel to seek assistance through the use of such techniques as personal appointments, telephone access programs, information storage and retrieval, position papers, and various audio and/or visual media.

3. *The counselor education faculty integrates the experiences of the outreach activity into its counselor education program by adapting or modifying the counselor education program as may be appropriate. Outreach activities are viewed as a significant function in the preparation program.*

SECTION III: RESPONSIBILITIES CONCERNING STUDENTS IN THE PROGRAM

A. Information

1. *Information concerning major aspects of the counselor education program and the faculty is available in a variety of media for prospective students.*

a. The academic areas in which the program offers preparation and the degrees offered are clearly stated.

b. Counselor education faculty are available to discuss the program of preparation.

c. Personnel in various counseling and related job settings have been designated as referral sources for discussion of their areas of interest with prospective students.

B. Selection

1. *Applicants accepted meet the institution's standards for admission to graduate study.*

a. There is evidence that staff in cooperating agencies have been consulted relative to admission policies and procedures.

b. Students in the program reflect an effort, on the part of the faculty, to select individuals who represent a variety of subcultures and subgroups within our society.

c. A committee of faculty members makes the decisions concerning admission of applicants to the program based upon established criteria such as:

(1) Potential effectiveness in close interpersonal relationships.

(2) Aptitude for counseling and related human development responsibilities.

(3) Commitment to a career in counseling and personnel work.

(4) Potential for establishing facilitative relationships with people at various levels of development.

(5) Openness to self-examination and commitment to self-growth.

C. Retention

1. *A continuing evaluation through systematic review is made of students as they progress through the program.*

2. *In situations where evaluations of a student indicate an inappropriateness for the counseling field, faculty members assist in facilitating change to an area more appropriate for the student.*

D. Endorsement

1. *A statement of policy relating to the institution's procedure for formal endorsement has been adopted and approved by the faculty and administrative authorities.*

a. Each candidate is informed of procedures of endorsement for certification, licensing, and employment.

b. Insofar as possible, all faculty members acquainted with the student, including supervisors of practicum and

Standards

internship experiences should participate in the endorsement process.

    2. *Endorsement is given by the counselor education faculty only for the particular job setting for which the student has been prepared.*

    3. *Endorsement is given only on the basis of evidence of demonstrated proficiency. The candidate should have completed a substantial part of his graduate work in counselor education, including supervised counseling experience, at the endorsing institution.*

E. Placement

    1. *The institution has a placement service with policies and procedures consistent with recognized placement practices.*

      a. The faculty assist the student with the preparation of placement papers and the selection and securing of a suitable position.

      b. Placement services are available to graduates of the program throughout their professional careers.

      c. Opportunities are provided for students to participate in local, state, and federal examinations for employment opportunities.

F. Research and Evaluation

    1. *Policies and procedures relating to recruitment, selection, retention, and placement are continually studied through various research and evaluative methods.*

      a. Regular follow-up studies are made of former students, including dropouts, students removed from the program, and graduates.

      b. Evaluation is followed by appropriate revisions and improvements in the preparation program.

SECTION IV: SUPPORT FOR THE COUNSELOR EDUCATION PROGRAM, ADMINISTRATIVE RELATIONS, AND INSTITUTIONAL RESOURCES

    1. *Administrative organization and procedures provide recognition and designated responsibilities for a counselor education program.*

      a. The program is a clearly identified part of the institution's graduate program.

        (1) There is preferably only one unit directly responsible for the preparation of counselors and other personnel services specialists.

        (2) If more than one unit in the institution is directly involved in the preparation of counselors and other personnel services specialists, there is evidence of close cooperation and coordination.

      b. Cooperative relationships exist between the counselor education program and other units of the institution related to the program.

        (1) Contributions of other units to the program are defined.

        (2) Channels of communication with faculty members in other units are identified and maintained.

      c. Use is made of a wide range of professional and community resources. Evidence of positive working relationships exists with agencies off the campus that have the potential for contributing to the preparation of counselors and other personnel services specialists. They may be potential employers of graduates of the program.

    2. *The institution provides for the professional development of the counselor education faculty as well as students in the counselor education program.*

      a. Faculty are involved in professional activities on local, state, regional, and national levels.

      b. Faculty participate in voluntary professional service capacities.

      c. The institution provides encouragement and financial support for the faculty to participate in professional activities.

      d. Faculty engage in programs of research and contribute to literature of the field.

      e. Students participate in the activities of professional organizations.

    3. *The institution provides adequate faculty and supporting staff for all aspects of the counselor education program.*

      a. An individual is designated as the professional leader of the counselor education program.

        (1) This individual is an experienced counselor and possesses an earned doctorate in counselor education from an accredited institution.

        (2) This individual has full-time assignment to the counselor education program.

        (3) This individual is recognized for his or her leadership in the counseling profession.

        (4) This individual is qualified by preparation and experience to conduct and to supervise research activities.

    4. *In addition to the designated leader there are at least two full-time faculty members with comparable qualifications.*

      a. Additional faculty are provided at the ratio of one full-time staff member for every 10 full-time graduate students or their equivalent in part-time graduate students. This ratio should be reduced in institutions where a large percentage of the counselor education students are enrolled on a part-time basis and/or when program changes create the need for the faculty to spend more time in the evaluation of each student.

    5. *The full-time teaching load of faculty members is consistent with that of other graduate units in the institution that require intensive supervision as an integral part of professional preparation.*

      a. The faculty load is modified in proportion to assigned responsibilities for graduate advisement and research supervision on a formula that is consistent with established graduate school policy in the institution.

      b. Time is provided within the total faculty work load for cooperative interdisciplinary activities with teaching faculty in related fields.

      c. The total work load of faculty members includes a recognition of time needed for professional research.

    6. *Faculty in closely related disciplines are qualified in their respective areas and also are informed about the objectives of the counselor education program.*

    7. *Off-campus agency personnel who supervise students are qualified through academic preparation and professional experience.*

      a Such staff members have two or more years of appropriate professional experience.

      b. These staff members have at least two years of graduate work in counselor education or can demonstrate equivalent preparation.

    8. *Graduate assistantships are provided to assist the faculty and to provide additional experiences for students in the program.*

      a Regular procedures are established for the identification and assignment of qualified students to assistantships.

      b. A minimum of one half-time graduate student is assigned to the counselor education program for each 30 full-time equivalent students.

c. Assignments are made in such a way as to enrich the professional learning experiences of the graduate assistants.

9. *Secretarial, clerical, and other supportive staff are provided in the counselor education program.*

a. A minimum of one full-time secretary or equivalent is provided for the clerical work of the counselor education program.

b. Additional clerical service is provided at the ratio of one full-time clerical assistant for the equivalent of every three faculty members.

c. Responsibilities of secretarial, clerical, and other supportive staff are defined and adequate supervision is provided.

10. *The institution provides facilities and a budget that insures continuous operation of all aspects of the counselor education program.*

a. The institution provides a designated headquarters for the counselor education program.

(1) The headquarters is located near the classroom and laboratory facilities used in the counselor education program.

(2) The headquarters area includes a private office for each faculty member.

(3) The headquarters area includes office space for secretarial, clerical, and other supportive staff.

(4) The headquarters provides appropriate work space, equipment, and supplies for graduate assistants.

b. Facilities for supervised experiences are provided in a coordinated laboratory setting on campus. Consideration is given to:

(1) Facilities for individual counseling in rooms with assured privacy and adequate space for related equipment.

(2) Facilities for small-group work. The area provides for small-group counseling, testing, staffing, meetings, and so forth.

(3) Classroom and seminar meeting rooms.

(4) Facilities appropriately equipped with the following:

(a) recording and listening devices, both portable and permanent;

(b) one-way vision glass;

(c) videotape recording and playing devices, both portable and permanent.

(5) Technical assistance for both operational and maintenance services.

(6) Acoustical treatment throughout the facility.

(7) Facilities that are conductive to modeling and demonstrating exemplary environments and practices in counseling and personnel services. The facilities should include a "model" counseling laboratory with related resource materials and audiovisual equipment. Included as resources in the "model" laboratory are:

(a) career, occupational, and educational information materials;

(b) standardized tests and interpretation data;

(c) a variety of media, equipment, and materials;

(d) space for teaching and laboratory experiences.

(8) Data processing assistance and equipment that are available for both teaching and research.

(9) Facilities that are located in close approximation to the counselor education faculty offices and away from centers of extreme noise and confusion.

c. Library facilities provide an appropriate supply of resource materials for study and research in counselor education.

(1) The facilities include basic resources, both books and periodicals, in areas in which the counselor education program provides preparation. Resources in related areas such as psychology, sociology, and economics are also available.

(2) Both current and historical materials are available.

(3) Library resources are available during evening and weekend hours.

(4) Interlibrary loans, ERIC services, microfilm, and photocopy services are available.

(5) Multiple copies of frequently used publications are available.

11. *Research facilities are available to faculty and students in counselor education.*

a. Facilities include offices and laboratories equipped to provide opportunities for the collection, analysis, and synthesis of data.

b. Consultant services are available from research specialists on the institution's faculty.

c. Campus computer centers and other data-processing facilities are available.

d. Appropriate settings for research, both off and on campus, are provided.

12. *The institution recognizes the individual needs of graduate students and provides services for personal as well as professional development.*

a. Since full-time academic-year attendance is possible for most graduate students only if some form of financial assistance is available, efforts are made to develop financial assistance for students in the counselor education program.

(1) The counselor education program is assigned a proportionate share of the institution's funds for student assistance.

(2) Part-time work opportunities appropriate for students in the program are identified, and efforts are made to secure assignments for those desiring such opportunities.

(3) Loan resources are available to students in counselor education.

(4) Prospective students are provided information about possible sources of financial assistance.

b. Personal counseling services are available to all counselor education students.

(1) A counseling service is available from professionals other than the members of the counselor education faculty.

(2) Procedures for referral are known by all faculty members.

Commission on Standards and Accreditation
Association for Counselor Education and Supervision
(At the time of adoption)

ACES Region		Term Expires June 30
Chairperson	Dr. Robert O. Stripling	1974
North Atlantic	Mrs. Cynthia Atlas	1976
North Central	Mr. William J. Erpenbach	1974
Rocky Mountain	Mr. Emery A. Morelli	1975
Western	Dr. Jerald R. Forster	1975
Southern	Dr. Doris S. Cantey	1976

Former members of the Commission who participated actively in the development of the Standards: Dr. James Winfrey; Dr. Phelon Malouf; Dr. Laurabeth H. Hicks; and Mrs. Elizabeth (Betty) Bernos. Dr. E. Gordon Poling, chairperson of the APGA Professional Preparation and Standards Committee from 1971–73, worked closely with the Commission during the development of these Standards.

Guidelines For Doctoral Preparation in Counselor Education

Association for Counselor Education and Supervision

In 1973, the Association for Counselor Education and Supervision (ACES) adopted *Standards for Preparation of Counselors and Other Personnel Services Specialists* (Standards). These Standards which relate to entry preparation for counselors and other guidance and personnel services specialists working in any setting in our society suggest several models of preparation, including two years of graduate work which could lead to the specialist in education degree or a similar intermediate graduate degree. A copy of the Standards may be obtained from the American Personnel and Guidance Association (APGA). Also, they were published in the September, 1974, issue of the *Journal of Employment Counseling* and the June, 1977, issue of the *Personnel and Guidance Journal*.

The Guidelines given below for doctoral programs are intended for use in evaluating existing doctoral programs or in establishing new programs. Also, they may be used by state, regional, and national accrediting associations. However, the application of these Guidelines to a doctoral program is predicated upon two assumptions: (1) those using the Guidelines are thoroughly familiar with the Standards mentioned above, and (2) the entry program in counselor education substantially meets these Standards. These Guidelines were adopted by the Membership of ACES in July, 1977.

Section I: Objectives of Doctoral Program in Counselor Education

The primary objective of the doctoral program in counselor education is to prepare leaders for all areas of counseling, guidance, and student services as well as counselor educators. Graduates of the program should have a strong background in the behavioral sciences. Through both didactic work and supervised experiences they should possess strong competencies in the core areas of preparation: counseling (both individual and group), consulting, and research. Other core areas for the development of a high degree of competency might be supervision, management/administration, and facilitative or clinical teaching.

In addition to the core areas of preparation the doctoral program should provide students with an opportunity to gain a depth of knowledge and skills in one or more areas such as learning theory, career guidance, research, testing, and evaluation.

Section II: Curriculum—Program of Studies and Supervised Experience

The doctoral program consists of a minimum of four academic years of graduate preparation, including the entry program and a year of internship. A minimum of one academic year of full-time graduate study beyond the entry program is required. The doctoral student should be given an opportunity to participate in course work and seminars which extend knowledge, understanding, and skills beyond those obtained in the core program outlined in the Standards. In addition, doctoral students should be encouraged to participate in conferences, workshops, special training programs, and other professional activities which will assist in bridging the gap between the campus and the broader professional world.

Supervised experiences should include opportunities to gain insights and skills beyond those provided in the entry program.* These supervised experiences are intended to provide both depth and breadth of preparation. Also, such experiences should be related to the doctoral student's professional objectives. Both on campus and off campus supervised experiences should be under the supervision of doctoral level personnel whose area(s) of specialization is compatible with the professional objectives of the doctoral student.

Supervised experiences should include the completion of at least one academic year (36 weeks) of full-time internship, including the one term of internship provided in the entry program.

All doctoral students should acquire competencies in statistics, research design, and other research methodology. Faculty should be involved in research which can be observed by students; and, when appropriate, students should become involved as active participants. In addition students should have opportunities to collaborate with faculty in the development of scholarly reports and papers.

Doctoral research seminars serve as a form of instruction for students as well as an opportunity for inservice education of the faculty.

A sequence of courses relating to the environmental area (or work setting) in which the doctoral student plans to work should be available.

---

*The standards for the entry program provide for practicum experiences in counseling totalling a minimum of 60 clock hours of "actual contact with individuals and groups' over one academic year plus a minimum of one term of a full-time postpracticum internship. This internship in a semester program would provide an additional 720 clock hours (40 hours per week times 18 weeks) of supervision or a total of 780 clock hours for the entry program. It is expected that similar supervised experiences will continue throughout the remainder of the doctoral program.

Section III: Responsibilities Concerning Students in the Program

Areas of specialization in which the counselor education program offers doctoral work should be clearly defined. The counselor education faculty should have the sole responsibility for selecting doctoral candidates, including the option of establishing criteria for admission which exceed those of the graduate division of the institution. These criteria should include evidence that the applicant for the doctoral program is committed to the profession of counseling and guidance through successful entry level preparation and experience.

Students in the doctoral program should reflect an effort on the part of the faculty to select individuals who represent a variety of subcultures and subgroups within our society. In order to accomplish this objective there should be evidence of a continuing search on the part of the counselor education faculty for ways of identifying students who possess the potentiality for doctoral work but who do not meet some of the more traditional criteria for entry into doctoral programs.

The acceptance of a doctoral candidate into a counselor education program represents a serious commitment on the part of the counselor education faculty to support the student. Consequently, there should be evidence that the counselor education faculty continuously is studying ways to improve and enhance student selection, retention, and endorsement, as well as placement and follow-up upon completion of the program.

Section IV: Support for the Counselor Education Program, Administrative Relationships, and Institutional Resources

The doctoral program in counselor education should be a clearly identified part of the institution's graduate program. There should be evidence that the counselor education faculty is utilizing fully all appropriate resources (both human and physical) of the institution to provide the best preparation possible for doctoral students. The institution should provide adequate support for a sound program of research in the various aspects of counseling, guidance, and student service. Furthermore, there should be evidence that the institution is supporting the counselor education faculty in efforts to provide cooperative relationships with agencies and individuals off the campus who can contribute to the enhancement of the quality of preparation in counselor education.

The institution provides the inducements necessary to attract and retain an outstanding faculty in counselor education. Faculty members should possess earned doctoral degrees in areas appropriate for their responsibilities in the doctoral program. They should be individuals who are recognized for their professional competencies and commitment to quality preparation of doctoral students.

The institution should support the counselor education faculty in its efforts to contribute to the improvement of counseling, guidance, and student services through participation in the activities of learned societies and professional associations at the local, state, regional, national, and international levels.

Faculty loads should be adjusted to reflect the institution's recognition of the intimate professional relationship between the doctoral student and the faculty, especially those faculty who provide practicum and internship supervision, and the doctoral research committee chairperson. Doctoral committee chairpersons should be recognized leaders in one or more aspects of counseling, guidance, and student services. They should have recognized competencies in both research and writing.

Computer facilities and library resources available to doctoral students reflect the institution's strong commitment to provide an outstanding environment which encourages both research and writing on the part of both faculty and doctoral candidates.

The institution supports the counselor education faculty in making funds available through tuition grants, scholarships, special grants, assistantships, and other ways to provide financial assistance for doctoral students.

Specialization in the doctoral programs is offered only in an area where there are at least two full-time counselor education faculty members with specialization in that area. This full-time faculty should be supplemented by either doctoral level full-time staff or doctoral level part-time staff on/off campus.

Members of the ACES Committee to Develop Guidelines
for Doctoral Preparation in Counselor Education

Lawrence K. Jones, North Carolina State University
Jack A. Duncan, Virginia Commonwealth University
K. Richard Pyle, Georgia College (Milledgeville)
Richard Schumacher, committee co-chairperson, North Carolina State Department of Education
Robert O. Stripling, committee chairperson, University of Florida
William H. Van Hoose, University of Virginia
Thomas J. Sweeney, ex-officio member, Ohio University

Robert Stripling, who has a long and distinguished career of service to the profession of counseling and who is currently chairperson of the ACES committee that proposed the 1977 guidelines for doctoral programs in counselor education, has developed a comprehensive proposal in his article on "Standards and Accreditation in Counselor Education." The article gives an excellent historical background on the development of the standards and an overview of APGA's involvement in the accreditation process. The article is must reading for individuals interested in understanding the relation between standards and accreditation.

[From: *Personnel and Guidance Journal,* Vol. 56, No. 10]

Standards and Accreditation in Counselor Education: A Proposal

At the heart of professional development are standards of preparation. There must also be some way to evaluate the quality of preparation when issues of licensure and certification are being considered. Historically in American higher education, program quality has been measured through the process of accreditation. This article gives a brief history of the development of standards by APGA and the nature of APGA involvement in the accreditation process. Suggestions are made as to how APGA might at present strengthen the process of accreditation as it relates to counselor education.

Before approval by ACES and APGA in 1964 of the "Standards for Counselor Education in the Preparation of Secondary School Counselors" (1964) the profession had relied on the U.S. Office of Education to provide guidelines for counselor preparation. The 1964 standards were the result of a five-year grass-roots study of preparation needs in counselor education, which involved over 700 counselor educators, supervisors, and practicing counselors in 50 states working on 150 local committees (Stripling 1965; Stripling & Dugan 1961).

Paralleling the ACES study were two other national projects relating to professional development. ASCA assumed leadership in developing a statement of policy for secondary school counselors as well as guidelines that could be used in implementing the policy. The other was a study by the APGA Committee on Professional Preparation and Standards (1964). The committee's report stated that there should be a "year-round program of counselor education that makes possible full-time graduate study" and that the entry program in counselor education should "consist of a minimum of two years of graduate study, a substantial portion of which should be in full-time graduate study."

Based on their use in more than 100 institutions and on reactions from more than 1,000 members of the Association, minor revisions were made in the 1964 Standards and were approved in 1967 by ACES and APGA ("Standards for the Preparation of Secondary School Counselors" 1967). At the same time a manual was developed that could be used as a guide in applying the Standards to a counselor education program (*Manual for Self-Study* 1967). In 1968 APGA approved the "Standards for Preparation of Elementary School Counselors."

In 1969 a joint committee composed of representatives from APGA, ACPA, SPATE, ACES, and the Council of Student Personnel Associations in Higher Education (COSPA) completed the development of "Guidelines for Graduate Programs in the Preparation of Student Personnel Workers in Higher Education" (1969). These guidelines, subsequently approved by constituent groups of the joint committee, were based, in part,

Robert O. Stripling *is a Distinguished Service Professor at the University of Florida where he teaches in the Department of Counselor Education. A past president of ACES, he cochaired with Willis Dugan and later chaired the five-year study, the results of which evolved into the original set of counselor education standards developed in 1964. Later he chaired the committee that developed the 1973 combined* Standards for the Preparation of Counselors and Other Personnel Services Specialists. *He also chaired the ACES committee that prepared the 1977* Guidelines for Doctoral Programs in Counselor Education.

on a 1964 proposal developed by COSPA (Commission on Professional Development 1964). In 1972 COSPA adopted *Student Development Services in Higher Education*, which elaborated on the developmental aspects of student personnel services and outlined a program of professional preparation in broad terms.

In the early seventies it became apparent that there was too much overlapping in the several sets of standards and an ACES committee was appointed to combine these standards into one document that could be used in initiating programs of preparation or in evaluating existing counselor education programs. It was felt that such a document could also be helpful to state, regional, and national accrediting agencies. In 1972 the committee presented its report, "Standards for the Preparation of Counselors and Other Personnel Services Specialists" (1973), which was adopted overwhelmingly by the ACES membership. The standards were subsequently approved by the Board of Directors of APGA and ASCA. These standards, which relate only to entry programs of preparation, state:

> Minimum study in counselor education will increasingly extend beyond the one-year program of graduate preparation. Such programs might include: (1) a combination of an undergraduate major in guidance and a year of graduate studies in counselor education, (2) two years of graduate study in counselor education, or (3) other models which include a minimum of one year of graduate study.
>
> All counselor education programs are not expected to prepare counselors and other personnel services specialists for all the work settings encompassed by the standards. Institutions should offer preparation programs only in those areas where sufficient qualified full-time staff and other resources are available.

Standards of Preparation for Doctoral Programs

In 1977 the ACES membership approved "Guidelines for Doctoral Preparation in Counselor Education" (1978). The use of these guidelines is predicated on two basic assumptions: The counselor education faculty is thoroughly familiar with the 1973 standards for entry preparation and the entry program in counselor education substantially meets these standards.

The Guidelines state that the "primary objective of the doctoral program in counselor education is to prepare leaders for all areas of counseling, guidance, and student services as well as counselor educators" (p. 163). Through didactic work and supervised experiences at advanced graduate levels doctoral students should develop strong competencies in "core areas of preparation: counseling (both individual and group), consulting, and research." Other areas in which students may elect to develop high degrees of competency might be "supervision, management/administration, and facilitative or clinical teaching." Although the Guidelines, to some degree, are prescriptive in nature they are not intended to stifle creative approaches to advanced preparation.

Relating to practicum and internship experiences, the guidelines state:

> The standards for the entry program provide for practicum experiences in counseling totaling a minimum of 60 clock hours of actual contact with individuals and groups for 1 academic year plus a minimum of one term of a full-time postpracticum internship. This internship in a semester program would provide an additional 720 clock hours (40 hours per week times 18 weeks) of supervision or a total of 780 clock hours for the entry program. It is expected that similar supervised experiences will continue throughout the remainder of the doctoral program. (p. 164)

Thus, it is possible for the counselor education faculty to provide supervised experiences that will meet the requirements of the different professional areas to which doctoral graduates wish to relate, for example, marriage and family counseling, community mental health counseling, or higher education administration of student development services.

Accreditation in the U.S.

The accreditation process for education at all levels in our country is unique since it is both nongovernmental and voluntary. Accreditation grew out of attempts in the late 1800s by certain colleges and universities to achieve more meaningful articulation between themselves and secondary schools. Since that time there has been a proliferation of accrediting groups at all levels of education and many struggles have occurred in an attempt to develop rational approaches that would protect all concerned. Currently, we still face many unresolved issues in the accreditation of higher education (Seldon 1960; Young 1976). Some of these issues, which relate more directly to the membership of APGA, are mentioned briefly in this article.

Who Accredits Counselor Education? Over 95 percent of the counselor education programs in the United States are under the control of colleges, schools, or departments of education. Consequently, the accrediting agency for counselor education is the National Council for Accreditation of Teacher Education (NCATE). Although professional organizations such as the American Library Association, the National Council of Teachers of Mathematics, and APGA may have an interest in the accreditation process in teacher education, these groups have only peripheral authority. The role of professional organizations such as APGA in accreditation was rather ill defined until some four years ago when NCATE recognized the need for better channels of communication with other professional associations interested in teacher education and established Standard G-1.5 for graduate programs: "In planning and developing curricula for its advanced programs, the institution gives due consideration to guidelines developed by national societies and professional associations for the preparation of teachers and other professional personnel" (NCATE 1970, 1975).

The establishment of the standard marked a milestone in the relationship between APGA and NCATE. This standard made it possible to relate the APGA standards directly to the accreditation process of NCATE. This did not, of course, constitute an endorsement by NCATE of the APGA standards or similar standards by other professional groups but it did provide the way for the involvement of the APGA standards, if visiting NCATE teams wish to use them.

During the last several years NCATE has periodically invited the membership of APGA to submit a list of counselor educators, supervisors, and practicing counselors who would be available to serve on NCATE visiting teams in institutions where counselor education programs are being considered for accreditation. This has resulted in most, if not all, such teams including at least one APGA member.

Who Controls Accreditation in the U.S.? The Council on Post-Secondary Accreditation (COPA) was organized in 1975 through the merger of two accrediting groups, the National Council

Accreditation Proposal

on Accreditation and the Federation of Regional Accrediting Commissions of Higher Education (Council on Postsecondary Education 1977). COPA is now the umbrella organization of all accrediting groups in higher education and is therefore the parent organization of NCATE. With its 36-member governance board, composed of both lay and professional personnel, COPA has been described as a unique "balance wheel" in relationship to the 4,000 institutions of postsecondary education in the United States and the approximately 50 regional and national accrediting bodies such as NCATE (COPA 1976).

Since NCATE accredits only programs preparing personnel for elementary and secondary schools there is an increasing amount of confusion with respect to the role of accreditation in counselor education. This is caused primarily by the fact that many counselor education programs are preparing a large percentage of their students for positions outside elementary and secondary schools. Thus, the answer to the question of what agency should accredit counselor education becomes increasingly confusing. This problem has been called to the attention of leaders in both NCATE and COPA (Stripling 1968). At present, however, the reality that NCATE and COPA control accreditation in counselor education must be accepted. Presently, approximately 275 counselor education programs in the country have NCATE accreditation at one or more of the three levels of accreditation recognized by NCATE: master's, specialists, and doctoral (NCATE 1977).

Two professional groups closely allied to counselor education, counseling psychology and rehabilitation counseling, have established accrediting bodies that relate directly to COPA. Of the 22 accredited counseling psychology programs in institutions of higher education, approximately half are solely in colleges of education or are joint programs between departments of psychology and counselor education (APA 1976). Recently, leaders in the accreditation movement of APA have expressed concern over the possibility that accreditation in counseling psychology will become accreditation for an entire counselor education program. The accreditation committee of APA is setting up safeguards in an effort to avoid this possibility.

The Council of Rehabilitation Education (CORE) was recognized in 1975 by COPA as the accrediting group for rehabilitation counselor education. At present, 38 rehabilitation counselor education programs have been accredited by CORE and it is expected that this number will eventually total between 50 and 55. A number of these programs are in counselor education departments or in other units of colleges of education. At this time CORE accredits only master's degree programs; however, plans are being made to develop accrediting standards for undergraduate programs in rehabilitation education. CORE now has no plans to accredit advanced graduate programs.

The justification for independent accrediting groups in counseling psychology and in rehabilitation counseling has been that the primary purposes of these programs are to prepare professional personnel for nonschool settings. This position becomes questionable when it is recognized that APA also accredits school psychology programs (APA 1976).

Challenges Facing Accreditation.
The controversy over the purposes of accreditation is escalating. The National Education Association (NEA), a major financial supporter of NCATE, has advocated the position that accreditation groups should take a more rigorous stand against weak programs. Different state branches of NEA are insisting on more drastic steps in the direction of eliminating weak programs at both the undergraduate and graduate levels. In 1972, NEA withdrew its financial support of NCATE for a year, thus precipitating a crisis for NCATE. NEA now has increased representation on the NCATE Council and is working more closely with NCATE in the accreditation process.

Another point of view concerning the purposes of accreditation is held by the American Association for the Colleges of Teacher Education (AACTE), another major financial supporter of NCATE. AACTE, in general, has supported the position that the primary responsibility of an accrediting association is to encourage the strengthening of weak programs and that withholding accreditation should be a last resort measure.

During the past two years, while NCATE was revising its standards, AACTE raised serious questions about the procedures used for considering possible revisions for accrediting standards, the shortness of the time provided for constituent groups to respond to proposed revisions, the revision of standards without considering how they are to be applied, and some of the revisions themselves (Council on Postsecondary Education 1976). It remains to be determined if AACTE will be satisfied with the newly revised NCATE Standards adopted by NCATE in May 1977 to become effective January 1, 1979. A movement is already under way in NCATE to adopt some quantitative measure that can be incorporated into the 1977 revised standards. This would bring NCATE standards more in line with APGA standards at both the entry and doctoral levels.

The Executive Committee of the Association of Colleges and Schools of Education in State Universities and Land Grant Colleges, composed primarily of deans of education in land grant institutions and affiliated private universities, has stated, in a 1976 letter to Rolf Larson, Executive Director of NCATE, that the NCATE accreditation procedure "fails to provide assurance of quality for recognized professional education programs to interested publics." The position this group will take concerning use of the 1977 NCATE Standards is not clear at this time.

As indicated, NCATE has been most receptive to the idea that a member of APGA be on each NCATE visiting team where counselor education programs have requested accreditation. No position has been taken with respect to the role of the APGA member on a visiting team. In the past, this role has been determined by the member's own philosophical orientation with respect to the purposes of accreditation.

Should APGA Establish Its Own Accreditation Body?

There are two primary reasons why, at this time, such a step would be most difficult. First, NCATE, as well as deans of education and university presidents, would oppose this action. It is also reasonable to expect that COPA would oppose a further proliferation of accrediting groups. Second, a cost factor is involved. For example, a committee of rehabilitation counselor educators received approximately $150,000 over a three-year period from the Rehabilitation Services Administration to develop standards in rehabilitation education and to organize its accrediting agency, CORE. At present, it costs CORE an average of $1,000 per institution to operate its accrediting procedure; the fee received from each institution is $500. In a time of declining university financial resources, it is unreasonable to expect constituent institutions to pay substantially higher accrediting fees to CORE or any other accrediting group. With no outside support for its program of accreditation, CORE is facing a financial crisis.

Another problem with respect to APGA financing of an accreditation agency under the COPA umbrella is that of numbers. When one considers the relatively few programs accredited to date by APA and CORE in contrast to the approximately 275 counselor education programs now accredited by NCATE and that the cost factor seems to escalate for an accreditation agency as more programs are approved, it would make it impossible for APGA to establish an accrediting agency without substantial financial support from the membership or from some outside source.

The ultimate goal of APGA might be to establish, at some time in the future, an independent accreditation body that would relate directly to COPA. In the meantime, it might be important to undertake the following actions:

1. Press both NCATE and COPA for an accreditation procedure that will include programs of preparation in counselor education for nonschool settings.

2. Develop within APGA a clarification of the role of the APGA member on NCATE visiting teams. This, of course, would need to be accomplished with NCATE cooperation.

3. Become more aggressive in providing leadership in the application of both APGA standards and the revised NCATE Standards. This seems feasible since the 1977 NCATE Standards seem to encourage a more active role on the part of professional groups such as APGA.

4. Provide financial support to NCATE and thus gain a stronger voice in the accreditation procedure.

Because of issues of accountability, licensure, and state certification, it is important that the membership of APGA become more involved in both standards of preparation and accreditation. Through such efforts we can gain more visibility for the counseling profession and can play a more responsible role in providing quality counseling and guidance services to the citizens of our country.

P&G

References

American Psychological Association. *APA Approved Doctoral Programs in clinical, counseling and school psychology.* Washington, D.C.: Author, 1976.

Commission on Professional Development, Council of Student Personnel Associations in Higher Education. *A proposal for professional preparation in college student personnel work.* Washington, D.C.: APGA, 1964.

Commission of Professional Development, COSPA. *Student development services in higher education.* Washington, D.C.: APGA, 1972.

Committee on Professional Preparation and Standards, APGA Report. *Personnel and Guidance Journal,* 1964, *42,* 536–541.

Council on Postsecondary Accreditation. *The balance wheel for accreditation.* Washington, D.C.: Author, 1976.

Council on Postsecondary Accreditation. *Accredited institutions of postsecondary education and programs, 1976–77.* Washington, D.C.: Author, 1977.

Guidelines for doctoral preparation in counselor education, 1977. *Counselor Education and Supervision,* 1978, *17,* 163–168.

Guidelines for graduate programs in the preparation of student personnel workers in higher education. Washington, D.C.: APGA, 1969.

Manual for self-study by a counselor education staff. Washington, D.C.: APGA, 1967.

National Council for Accreditation of Teacher Education. *Standards for the accreditation of teacher education.* Washington, D.C.: Author, 1970, 1975.

National Council for the Accreditation of Teacher Education. *Standards for the accreditation of teacher education, 1977.* Washington, D.C.: Author, 1977.

Seldon, W. K. *Accreditation: A struggle over standards in higher education.* New York: Harper & Bros., 1960.

Standards for counselor education in the preparation of secondary school counselors. *Personnel and Guidance Journal,* 1964, *42,* 1,061–1,073.

Standards for the preparation of secondary school counselors. Washington, D.C.: APGA, 1967.

Standards for preparation of elementary school counselors. Washington, D.C.: APGA, 1968.

Standards for the preparation of counselors and other personnel services specialists. *Personnel and Guidance Journal,* 1977, *55,* 596–601.

Stripling, R. O. Standards for the education of school counselors. In J. Loughary (Ed.), *Counseling, A growing profession.* Washington, D.C.: APGA, 1965.

Stripling, R. O. Current and future status of accrediting. *Counselor Education and Supervision,* 1968, *7,* 200–209.

Stripling, R. O., & Dugan, W. E. The cooperative study of counselor education standards. *Counselor Education and Supervision,* 1961, *1,* 34–35.

Young, K. E. *Major issues in accrediting, 1975–1976.* Washington, D.C.: Council on Postsecondary Accreditation, 1976.

In the first section of the following article, Daniel C. McAlees, former chairperson of the Commission on Rehabilitation Counselor Certification, presents a comprehensive overview on the definition, origin, and specific features of certification in rehabilitation counseling. As an individual who is actively involved in the development of the first certification process for counselors, McAlees' comments are of extreme importance.

In section two, Brockman Schumacher, past president of Council on Rehabilitation Education (CORE), discusses accreditation in a style similar to McAlees's. Emphasis is given to how accreditation is developed within rehabilitation counseling. The dialectic style used by both authors in this section provides greater insight into the issues of certification/accreditation as they relate not only to rehabilitation but to the profession of counseling.

[From: *Rehabilitation Counseling Bulletin,* Vol. 18, No. 3]

special feature

Toward a New Professionalism: Certification and Accreditation

CERTIFICATION

Daniel C. McAlees, *Chairman*
Commission on Rehabilitation Counselor Certification

What Is Certification in Rehabilitation Counseling?

The primary purpose of certification is to establish professional standards whereby disabled individuals, related professionals, agency administrators, and the general public can evaluate the qualifications of persons practicing rehabilitation counseling. Certification has as its primary impetus the provision of assurances that professionals engaged in rehabilitation counseling will meet acceptable standards of quality in practice. Such standards are considered to be in the clients' best interests.

How Did Certification Develop, and How Is It Organized in Rehabilitation?

The certification program is a direct outgrowth of the concern of the two professional associations—American Rehabilitation Counseling Association (ARCA) and National Rehabilitation Counseling Association (NRCA)—to establish standards and consequently stabilize the field of rehabilitation counseling and to provide a baseline for future professional growth. These two associations appointed a joint committee on certification which became an independent incorporated Commission on Rehabilitation Counselor Certification. The Commission consists of five appointees from ARCA, five appointees from NRCA, and one each from the Council of Rehabilitation Education, Council of State Administrators of Vocational Rehabilitation, International Association of Rehabilitation Facilities, National Association of Non-White Rehabilitation Workers, Council of Rehabilitation Counselor Educators, and a representative from a national consumer organization.

Who Is Eligible for Certification?

Professional rehabilitation counselor certification may be established by:

- graduation with a master's degree from an accredited rehabilitation counseling training program, which includes a supervised internship and one year of acceptable experience in rehabilitation counseling;

- attainment of a master's degree in rehabilitation counseling, not including a supervised internship, or a master's degree in a related area (as defined by the Commission) along with two years experience in rehabilitation counseling;

- attainment of a master's degree equivalency level by (a) graduation with a bachelor's degree in rehabilitation, along with four years of acceptable experience in rehabilitation counseling or (b) graduation with a bachelor's degree, along with five years of acceptable experience in rehabilitation counseling.

"Grandfathering" those members who meet the above criteria will be carried out until July 1975. Membership in ARCA, NRCA, and/or an allied professional association will be a prerequisite for "grandfathering." After July 1975, all persons who qualify for certification will be required to demonstrate competence in the following content areas on a certification examination: (a) rehabilitation philosophy, history, and structure; (b) medical aspects of disability; (c) psychosocial aspects of disability; (d) occupational information and the world of work; (e) counseling theory and techniques; (f) community organization and resources; (g) placement processes and job development; (h) the psychology of personal and vocational adjustment; (i) evaluation and assessment; (j) the ability to use research findings and professional publications.

What Are Specific Features of the Certification Program?

The main features include (a) a commission broadly representative of the entire field of rehabilitation; (b) participation in the development of a certification examination by all present members of the profession who apply for grandfathering; (c) the use of supervisor and peer evaluations to supplement examination data; and, most importantly, (d) the establishment of minimum standards for practice as rehabilitation counselor.

What Is Grandfathering?

Those persons currently working in the profession who meet the minimum educational, experiential, and professional affiliation standards outlined above will not be required to demonstrate competence on a certification examination. They will be required, however, to take the examination for field review purposes.

How Do I Apply for Certification?

All inquiries regarding certification and requests for application forms should be directed to the Commission on Rehabilitation Counselor Certification, 520 North Michigan Avenue, Suite 1504, Chicago, Illinois 60611; telephone—(312) 644-4329

Please Discuss the Examination— What Is It? How Do I Prepare for It? And Where Do I Take It?

The examination is a practice-based examination; therefore, it is not necessary for an individual to do a great deal of studying prior to the examination. In fact, intensive study may not help a person pass this kind of examination. Items included in the examination put a higher premium on the application of knowledge in managing clients rather than on isolated bits of factual information.

The first field review was held on 19 July 1974 at 40 sites, and the second on 15 October 1974 at 21 sites. The third field review will be held 22 March 1975. The primary site for this field review will be New York City in conjunction with the annual ARCA-APGA meeting.

Two additional field reviews have been scheduled: one on 18 July 1975 (deadline for applications, 1 April 1975) and one on 12 October 1975 (deadline for applications, 1 July 1975). Sites for these field reviews will be selected based on the location of the applicants. Any geographical or organizational entity of rehabilitation counselors may determine the most appropriate site for administering the field review within their area. When twenty or more counselors can be brought together under the conditions set by the Commission for the field review, the Commission will administer the examination at the site requested. A checklist detailing criteria for site selection is available on request. If you would like to arrange for a site in your area, please contact the Commission office.

The field review will be available in a Spanish translation, and the Commission will provide equal access and opportunity to participate to all disabled counselors who apply.

What Will Certification Cost Me?

The total fee for certification during the grandfather period is $45. Fifteen dollars of this total fee should be sent with the completed application. When approved, you will be assigned to a field review site and requested to send the remaining $30 of this fee. These fees reflect the total cost for certification and no additional fees will be assessed for annual renewal of the certification certificate.

What Will Be the Effects of Certification on Rehabilitation Counseling as a Profession?

The intent is not to certify that any individual is suitable for employment or attempt to impose personnel requirements upon any agency; the intent is to establish a national professional scale which any interested group, agency, or individual may use as a measure. It would be hoped that voluntary cooperation by a majority of rehabilitation counselors would, over time, exercise an increasing influence on the field and ultimately guide legislation, personnel practices, and training programs. Aside from establishing a good measure of professional qualifications for the counselor, certification will further the public interest and the confidence of other professions and clients.

To date, more than 5,000 rehabilitation counseling professionals have made application to participate in the certification program, an overwhelming and revealing response. It is evident that rehabilitation counselors are encouraging, through certification, a higher level of performance and qualifications that will benefit both the public and the profession.

ACCREDITATION?

Brockman Schumacher, *President Council on Rehabilitation Education (CORE)*

What Is Accreditation?

Since the United States has no federal ministry of education, the responsibility to ensure quality training programs for practicing professionals rests with individual states, educational institutions, and professional organizations. Thus, accreditation is concerned with the quality of educational programs in certain institutions and professions. This process entails nongovernmental self-evaluation of training within a professional discipline. It serves to identify acceptable levels of training so as to maintain high standards and to establish goals for self-improvement in professional education.

Is There Any Relationship Between Accreditation and Certification?

Although both accreditation and certification are assessment processes, there is no formal or procedural relationship between the two. However, both these processes are concerned with evaluation and improvement of professional practice and, therefore, they are parallel in nature. Constant dialogue concerning issues, criteria, objectives, and goals is necessary to deal with ongoing, crucial matters associated with a profession.

How Did Accreditation Develop in Rehabilitation Counseling?

In 1970, leadership from the American Rehabilitation Counseling Association (ARCA), the National Rehabilitation Counseling Association (NRCA), the Council of Rehabilitation Counselor Educators, the Council of State Administrators of Vocational Rehabilitation, and the International Association of Rehabilitation Facilities recommended establishing a planning committee to address itself to the issues of accreditation. This planning committee became incorporated and developed strategies for the accreditation process. These strategies included procedures, instruments, and standards, which received approval of the National Commission on Accrediting.

Presently the Council on Rehabilitation Education (CORE) is composed of two representatives from each of the participating professional rehabilitation organizations. CORE's major responsibility now is the implementation of the accreditation process, program assistance, and development.

What Are the Features of the CORE Approach to Accreditation?

The major emphasis of CORE's approach to accreditation is on program development and improvement, rather than mere formal approval. During the pilot phase of developing the accreditation process, site visits were used as a basis for evaluation. These have now been replaced by a systematic, research-based collection of data on a particular training program, although site visits may be used as supplemental sources of data when needed. The data include both a review of the training program itself and employer evaluation of the program's graduates. The accreditation process also stresses continued reevaluation of its methods, criteria, and standards.

How Does a Training Program Become Accredited?

A training program must meet initial eligibility criteria and be evaluated and approved by CORE's Commission on Standards and Accreditation.

What Is Expected from a Program Undergoing the Accreditation Process?

The faculty is expected to carefully complete a Program Evaluation Self-Report Schedule, which reviews curriculum, faculty, and students. Cooperation in supplying further information or collecting more data for the Commission is essential. Successful implementation of specific recommendations for improving a program's standards is also expected.

What Advantages Are There to a Program's Being Accredited?

The major advantages in accreditation are to ensure self-evaluation and to assist in the improvement of preparation programs for rehabilitation counselors. The achievement and maintenance of quality in preparation programs accrue special advantages to consumers—applicants, students, graduates, employers, and the general public. Publication of a program's mission and status among other programs in the country lead to the knowledge of its standing in relation to accepted professional criteria of preparation in rehabilitation counseling.

What Does It Cost?

A fee of five hundred dollars is charged for the accreditation year or initial participation in the process. In order to sustain accreditation, the program must continue contact with the Commission yearly. A fee of two hundred dollars is charged for this continued support.

The individual program must bear the cost of accreditation and any additional expenses, if a site visit is necessary. In the case of providing assistance in program development, CORE has a separate fee schedule.

How Often Does a Program Need to Be Reevaluated?

Reevaluation for continued accreditation must occur every five years. In some instances, special conditions will be set which might make accreditation more frequent.

What Is the Value of Accreditation to the Profession of Rehabilitation Counseling?

The basic purpose of accreditation is to assure quality education of rehabilitation counselors, thereby promoting the effective delivery of vocational rehabilitation services to persons with handicaps. The accreditation procedure will promote program self-improvement as a regular system. Accreditation will assist in placing rehabilitation counseling on a par with other professional disciplines. Finally, and most importantly, such procedures ensure a level of excellence in professional training with the ultimate goal of improving service delivery to rehabilitation clients.

This important article, which appeared in the *Journal of Applied Rehabilitation Counseling,* details the important history of the development of the certification process for rehabilitation workers. This effort was the first development of its kind by the American Rehabilitation Counseling Association (ARCA), which worked in cooperation with the National Rehabilitation Association. ARCA is an APGA division.

[From: *Journal of Applied Rehabilitation Counseling,* Vol. 10, No. 3]

The History of Rehabilitation Counselor Certification

Roger Livingston

The history of the rehabilitation counselor certification movement began in late 1962 during an informal conversation between four individuals returning from a National Easter Seal Society meeting in Denver, Colorado (Natress, 1977). Prior to examining this movement, however, one should consider the origins of certification.

First, one should consider what is meant by *certification*. Certification is a process "by which a nongovernmental agency or association grants recognition to an individual who has met certain predetermined qualifications specified by that agency or association" (Certification in Allied Professions, 1971). Licensure, on the other hand, is the granting of permission by an agency of the state or federal government that allows a person to engage in a particular profession or occupation (Weber, 1977). Licensure has been considered a mandatory screening-out process whereas certification is seen as a voluntary screening-in process (Hecht, 1974). One of the earliest certifying bodies was the American Board for Certification in Orthotics and Prosthetics in 1948. In the 1950's there were a number of certifying boards established, which included: Speech and Hearing, Corrective Therapist Association, Dental Laboratory Technology, Occupational Therapists, and Medical Assistants. The 1960's saw the certification of inhalation therapists.

All of the groups mentioned require, at minimum, a written examination and some require oral and practical examinations, and certified dental assistants, for example, must be graduates of an American Dental Association accredited program and pass a written and practical examination. To maintain certification they are required to pay a fee and provide evidence of continuing education.

The earliest official discussion of rehabilitation counselor certification occurred in February 1963 when Mr. Harley Reger, who was chairperson of the Professional Standards Committee of National Rehabilitation Counseling Association (NRCA), presented a report to the Executive Committee proposing the development of a certifying board. The subsequent Certification Board had the task of membership credentialing (in other words, determining if an individual met the membership criteria for NRCA) and did not actually become a part of NRCA until 1967 after an amendment to the NRCA Constitution established this Board's structure and function.

In 1968, the chairperson of the Certification Committee of NRCA, Leroy Natress, outlined in a report to the Executive Committee of NRCA the stages necessary to achieve viable goals in certification. He indicated that in stage one, time would be devoted to identify components of professional competence in rehabilitation counseling. Stage two would involve a critical review of the current procedures to evaluate counselor competencies, and in stage three the Certification Board would devise new instruments and improve upon existing ones. In the fourth and final stage, the Certification Board hoped to assess behaviors identified in stage one. In this same year, a similar report was presented to the NRCA Board of Directors but with additional suggestions that the American Rehabilitation Foundation be contacted and that the American Rehabilitation Counseling Association (ARCA) be contacted to appoint members to serve in a liaison role to the Certification Committee of NRCA.

In early 1969 a joint meeting of the ARCA Professional Relations Committee and the NRCA External Relations Committee was held. A proposal was developed that suggested that a joint ARCA-NRCA Committee be developed with the charge of preparing a statement concerned with the role and functions of counselor-counselor support personnel. Recommendations were also made in that year to examine closely the Muthard and Salamone (1969) study on the "Counselor Role and Function" to determine if it would aid in accomplishing certification goals.

In late 1969 and early 1970, the Minnesota branches of NRCA and ARCA developed and administered a trial questionnaire related to certification. The results suggested that "a nation-wide survey was both desired and necessary at this time" (Brumberg letter, January 23, 1970) because of the strong interest in certification expressed by the group surveyed. A national survey was conducted in the fall of 1971 through a questionnaire that appeared in the *Journal of Applied Rehabilitation Counseling*.

On April 4, 1971, a joint meeting of the NRCA-ARCA Accreditation Committee and Professional Standards Committee was held. The outcome of this meeting was a proposal for a single level of rehabilitation counselor certification. This committee also created a philosophy for the certification of rehabilitation that spelled out problems as well as how certification could be established (Carnes, 1972). To this group of twelve individuals also fell the responsibility of establishing professional standards for eligibility for certification as a rehabilitation counselor. Within these standards, an educational level was specified along with specific content area in which an individual should have work experience.

Concurrent with efforts in the field of rehabilitation, considerable efforts were taking place nationally to determine the implication of Public Law 91–519, the Health Training Improvement Act of 1970. In June 1971, the Health, Education, and Welfare Secretary, Richardson, submitted a "Report on Licensure of Related Health Credentialing" as required by PL 91–519. Contained within this report was a recommendation that all states observe a two year moratorium on the enactment of legislation establishing categories of health personnel whose functions might be statutorily defined. Of prime concern at that time was a hope that rigidly defined training and education programs, as well as job functions, be avoided since national efforts were being made to revise and broaden occupational roles.

In the latter part of 1971, the academic community of rehabilitation began asking for a certification process. Mike Oliverio, the then President of the National Rehabilitation Counseling Association, requested from the chairperson of the joint ARCA-NRCA certification committee that the process for rehabilitation counselor certification be put together during the next twelve months. Dr. Daniel C. McAlees was the chairperson of this joint ARCA-NRCA Certification Committee. At the National Rehabilitation Association (NRA) National Convention in Puerto Rico in September, 1972, in a report of this committee to the NRCA delegate assembly, Dr. McAlees outlined the purpose of the certification process as follows:

1. To promote the effective delivery of vocational rehabilitation services to handicapped persons by stimulating and fostering continuing review and improvement of professional practice in rehabilitation counseling in order to serve the public interest through the professional association.

2. To ascribe to an individual counselor a visible sign that his peers acknowledge his competency to practice and to provide an orderly and systematic procedure by which this competency is measured. (Report of Joint Certification Committee meeting, July, 1972).

During the same period, this committee also indicated that *re-certification* would probably be recommended. The certification philosophy and the concept of re-certification was approved by the delegate assembly at this time. A rather extensive timetable was also prepared that included a recommendation to create a Commission on Rehabilitation Counselor Certification (CRCC) with 15 members.

The first meeting of the Commission of Rehabilitation Counselor Certification was held in Chicago on April 2, 1973. The focus of this meeting was upon the appointment of a subcommittee on "Evaluation and Selection" that was to establish guidelines to be completed by firms interested in bidding on contracts, to develop procedures for the rehabilitation counseling certification process and the evaluation instruments to be utilized in this process. On August 16th of the same year, the Commission reviewed final recommended standards and NatResources, Chicago, Illinois, was selected as the administrative agent of the Commission.

The first task to be accomplished by the Commission after the determination of an administrative agent was the development of the field review examination. The Commission defined 10 areas that it had determined to be the most relevant to the field of rehabilitation counseling. This decision was not an arbitrary one but one based on the training and experience of Commission members. They determined that to be certified as a rehabilitation counselor, each individual had to demonstrate competence in the following areas on a written examination: (a) rehabilitation philosophy, history and structure; (b) medical aspects of disability; (c) psychosocial aspects of disability; (d) occupational information and the world of work; (e) counseling theory and techniques; (f) community organization and resources; (g) placement processes and job development; (h) the psychology of personal and vocational adjustment; (i) evaluation and assessment; and, (j) the ability to use research findings and professional publication.

To accomplish the task of writing the examination questions to assess the ten competency areas the Commission appointed a task force composed of twelve members. This task force included Drs. Engelkes, English, Hansen, McAlees, and Taylor, who were directly involved in rehabilitation counselor training programs in major universities throughout the United States; Florence Curnutt, counselor of handicapped students, San Jose City College; William Joslin, Director, Council Workshop for Senior Citizens in New York City; Barbara Korn, Director, Rehabilitation Services, North Shore University Hospital, New York, New York; George McCrowey, a counselor with the division of Vocational Rehabilitation (DVR), Chicago, Illinois; Ed Navis, a DVR counselor in Richmond, Virginia; Harold Rubin, a counselor in New York City; and Jim Stephens, Staff Development, DVR, Raleigh, North Carolina.

The members of this task force were to formulate 60 multiple choice questions in their own specialty areas as related to the 10 areas defined by the Commission. The writers then exchanged their questions with other members of the task force so that ambiguities in content and form could be clarified. The original writers then received their own questions in return to examine changes and make any necessary corrections. The questions were then forwarded to NatResources Incorporated to be placed in an item pool from which the "field review" was to be constructed. To insure some consistency in the preparation of test items, a workshop in examination item development, and test construction was held in June 1973.

The significant efforts of all individuals working within the rehabilitation counseling certification movement were reported by Dr. McAlees in 1973, and led the way to further discussions and clarifications during the NRA annual meeting in 1974. During this convention in Las Vegas, Nevada, the Education Committee of NRCA presented a report to the delegate assembly on a number of topics, including certification and *re-certification.* After considerable discussion, the concepts of certification and recertification were affirmed by this assembly.

Field Review Examination

The field review examination previously mentioned typically consisted of multiple choice questions. The one notable exception was in March 1975 when two branching simulation exercises were added to one form of the field review. The branching simulation exercises simulated a real-life counseling situation in which the CRCC applicant had to make decisions on the management of a case. Dependent on the decision, certain paths and consequences were available. A sequence of decisions led to the unsuccessful or successful closure of the case. The scoring of this type of questions was found to be problematic; thus, it was eliminated from future forms of the examination.

The prime task related to the examination during the "grandfathering" period was the development of an item pool that contained reliable and valid questions. To facilitate this task, a number of different forms were utilized during each administration of the examination in an attempt to isolate the optimum length and content as well as establishing the difficulty index and discrimination index of the written examination. Also during the early phases of the "grandfathering" period, individuals taking the examination were provided a second scoring sheet and requested to rate each question for its relevance to the practice of rehabilitation counseling. This time-consuming process was completed to insure that a strong emphasis on a field-oriented examination was completed.

The content of the examination during the grandfathering period was consistent in the use of case histories, veracity items and practice-based multiple choice items. An analysis was made of each form of the examination, after each administration and split-half reliabilities were calculated. Individuals who failed to score greater than 75% on the veracity items were not included in the analysis because they apparently were not taking the examination seriously (Lunz, 1976). Internal reliability as measured by split-half reliability (KR-20) was in the range of .66-.76 over five different forms in July and October 1974. In March 1975, the split-half reliability was .69-.72 on four separate forms and improved to approximately .82 during both July and October 1975.

As for the interpretation of these coefficients, Mehrens and Lehman (1973) pointed out "although there is no universal agreement, it is generally accepted that standardized tests used to assist in making decisions about individuals should have coefficients of at least .85" (p. 122). The field review was such an instrument in that it was to be used for certification of rehabilitation counselors. Guilford (1956) pointed out that "all internal consistency formulas that depend upon a single administration of a test probably underestimate the reliability of a test" (p. 455). With this thought in mind, it appears that a statement can be safely made that the field review was a reliable measurement instrument.

As was previously mentioned, the question of the validity of the field review and the certification examination was also of prime concern. On the March 1975 field review, Lunz (1976) reported that

> the items field tested in the March field review measure similarly across educational groups, geographic groups, and work setting experience. While refinement and improvement is still essential, the progress of the quality of the examination indicates movement towards content validity where the criterion is practice-based performance and internal consistency or test reliability across groups. (p. 71)

In early 1975, developmental work began at Michigan State University on a questionnaire that was intended to identify clusters of demographic characteristics that might be utilized to predict examination patterns after the "grandfathering" period. These efforts, utilizing rather sophisticated statistical techniques such as factor analysis and discriminant analysis, did identify a number of common variables (Engelkes & Livingston, 1976).

Livingston (1976) conducted a rather extensive study of the concurrent validity of the field review utilized in July and October 1975 that was taken by 3,982 individuals. The specific focus was upon field review scores and the variables that made up the demographic questionnaire. Generally speaking, in concurrent validity, no significant time intervals elapse between administration of the test being validated and the criterion measure. This is a procedural distinction as compared to predictive validity when the criterion data is collected at a later date. Such validity might be evidence by the correlation between scores on a test and criterion measures that are valid but are less objective. Statements regarding concurrent validity generally indicate the extent to which one measure may be used to estimate an individual's present standing on the criterion.

The demographic questionnaire, which was designed under the supervision of Dr. James Engelkes, chairperson of the CRCC research committee, was closely examined, as was the field review. Support was found to reinforce the notion that the field review fulfilled the required characteristics as proposed by Mehrens and Lehman (1973) for the criterion measure to be considered adequate. Probably the most frequent procedure used in reporting validity is the Pearson product moment correlation coefficient. In July 1975, of the 67 possible predictor variables, these were 37 that were significant at the .05 level and in October, there were 45 variables at this statistical level. Closer examination of all variables revealed that there were 12 common variables in July and October where the correlation coefficients were considerably larger than their standard errors. These data suggested that from a statistical perspective, there were in fact 12 significant variables on which validity could be based. Obviously this is not near the potential number that might have been possible, but then again, one, two, or 12 are more significant than finding no basis for criterion validity.

Weber (1977) conducted an item analysis of performance on the field review utilizing various subgroups of an undergraduate population as compared to rehabilitation counselors taking the same examination. Since CRCC has stated that its purpose is to "establish a national professional scale designed to measure the competencies and judgment abilities of rehabilitation counselors", one could construe this to mean that the field review is designed to measure the construct of "competencies and judgment abilities" of rehabilitation counselors. Validity may be established for a measurement instrument by determining the construct validity of this instrument. In other words, does the instrument measure the construct that it purports to measure? Weber found that on Form I of the July 1975 field review, rehabilitation counselors performed significantly higher on 70% of the field review items as compared to all of the subgroups combined. However, 45 science majors who volunteered as one of the subgroups to participate in the study did score as well as the rehabilitation counselors on 50% of the items. Given that the field review was still in its developmental stage at that point, it appeared that construct validity had been established for at least a portion of the items in the item pool for the certification examination.

A final factor that received considerable attention during the "grandfathering" period was the establishment of a content outline for the certification examination so that meaningful subtest designation could be made in order to provide a useful profile of his/her performance to those individuals who took the examination. The outline also aided in preparing new examination items in deficient areas and in maintaining a content balance. The following areas now compose the subtests of the certification examination: (a) child, (b) adult, (c) aged, (d) physical disability, (e) social deviants, (f) emotional disability, (g) mental retardation, (h) deaf, (i) blind, (j) medical and psychosocial aspects of disability, (k) occupational information, (l) counseling theory, (m) counseling methods, (n) community organization and resources, (o) personal vocational adjustment, (p) evaluation and assessment, (q) research utilization, (r) rehabilitation planning, (s) case management, (t) information dissemination, (u) vocational counseling, (v) personality and adjustment counseling, (w) group counseling, (x) job development and placement, (y) vocational and psychological assessment. The specific number of items per subtest does vary from form to form and from examination to examination.

The activities of the certification movement were discussed by a number of individuals during this period (Miller, 1971; Parker, 1972; Thoreson, 1971), and an article by McAlees (1975) made considerable strides in explaining the movement toward a new professionalism in rehabilitation counseling.

The Present: Certification by Examination

The first Certification Examination of CRCC was administered in April 1976. This group was composed of 110 candidates. Since this was the transition from Field Review to Certification Examination, 295 additional participants who qualified under the "grandfathering" clause were allowed to sit for the examination and to be certified.

The examination consisted of two forms, each containing 150 items which were administered in the morning and afternoon on the date of the examination. Of these 300 items, 229 were included in the final scoring. Sixty items were field test items and the other 11 were found unacceptable after statistical analysis. The instrument was found to be highly reliable, $KR-20 = .93$. Of 110 candidates, 98 passed (89.1%) and 12 failed (10.9%) the examination. Since April 1976, the Certification Examination, following a similar format, has been given six times. These dates included September 1976, April 1977, October 1977, April 1978, October 1978 and April 1979, with 223, 270, 264, 272, 421 and 303 candidates taking part, respectively. From this total of 1,863 candidates, a total of 1,626 or 87%, have passed the examination with 237, or 13% having failed. The reliability of the examination has continued to be quite high, ranging from a $KR-20$ of .80 to .85.

Certification by examination will, of course, be an on-going process within the field of rehabilitation. To date, 8,327 have "grandfathered", an additional 1,626 have been certified by examination, and approximately 400 are scheduled for the certification examination in October 1979. These examinations have been and will continue to be under close scrutiny by the Examinations Committee of CRCC.

The Commission on Rehabilitation Counselor Certification (CRCC) was officially incorporated in January 1974 (Livingston & Engelkes, 1977). This Commission, utilizing considerable foresight, was incorporated as an independent commission. The wisdom of this action was exemplified when on December 2, 1977, the National Commission of Health Certifying Agencies was formally organized after 30 months of planning and a structure for a certifying agency was articulated. This statement read:

In order to be "approved" for membership in the Commission, a certifying agency shall meet the following criteria:

2. Structure of a Certifying Agency
   a) shall be non-governmental
   b) shall conduct certification activities which are national in scope
   c) shall be administratively independent in matters pertaining to certification, except appointment of members of the governing body of the certifying agency. A certifying agency which is not a legal entity in and of itself shall provide proof that the agency's governing body is administratively independent in certification matters from the organization of which it is a part; . . .

The composition of the Commission has been expanded somewhat since the original incorporation and now consists of five appointees from NRCA, five appointees from ARCA, these appointees from the American Coalition of Citizens with Disabilities, Inc., (ACCD) and one from the Council on Rehabilitation Education (CORE), Council of State Administrators of Vocational Rehabilitation (CSAVR), Association of Rehabilitation Facilities (ARF), National Association of Non-White Rehabilitation Workers (NANWR), and National Council on Rehabilitation Education (NCRE) for a total of 18 members, 50% of whom must be practicing rehabilitation counselors and all should be CRC's themselves.

The educational criteria for certification has remained basically the same; however, as of January 1977, the experience portion of the criteria must be completed under the supervision of a CRC.

The question, of course, is what will the effect be of certification on rehabilitation counseling as a profession? It is not the Commission's interest to certify that any individual is suitable for employment or to impose personnel requirements upon any agency. The certification process is intended to provide verification that an individual has met certain minimum standards that have been established by the profession. These standards include educational experience, supervised experience as provided by evaluations of supervisors, an acceptance of a code of ethics, and the demonstration of a knowledge base related to rehabilitation through the certification examination. The intent is to establish a national professional scale, which any interested group, agency, or individual may use as a measure. It is hoped that participation by rehabilitation counselors would exercise an increasing influence on the field and ultimately guide legislation, personnel practices, and training programs. Aside from establishing a good measure of professional qualifications for the counselor, certification will further the public interest and the confidence of other professionals and clients. It is evident to date that rehabilitation counselors are encouraging, through their participation in their certification programs, a higher level of performance and qualifications that will benefit both the public and the profession.

The Future

Effective January 1, 1978, graduates with a Master's degree in rehabilitation counseling from a Council on Rehabilitation Education (CORE) accredited rehabilitation counseling program will not be required to meet a minimum experience requirement of one year; however, this degree program must include 600 hours of clinical experience under the supervision of a CRC. Graduates with Master's degrees in rehabilitation counseling from non-CORE accredited programs will be required to have two years of acceptable experience in rehabilitation counseling, at least one year which must have been under the supervision of the CRC.

On September 11, 1977, CRCC adopted a plan for Certification Maintenance. This plan was adopted in the belief that rehabilitation counselors should continue to demonstrate their competencies to deliver quality rehabilitation counseling services to the public. Certification Maintenance is meant to maintain and enhance the ability of the Certified Rehabilitation Counselor to serve clients. The report by the Commission sets forth the principles of the plan of Certification Maintenance based on continuing education, but includes options for those who find it impossible to particpate in continuing education activities to the extent recommended.

Objectives of the Certification Maintenance plan for Certified Rehabilitation Counselors include:

1. Obtaining Current Information,
2. Exploring New Knowledge in a Specific Content Area,
3. Mastering New Skills and Techniques,
4. Expanding the Approaches Toward the Management of Clients, and
5. Developing Critical Inquiry and Balanced Professional Judgement. (Commission on Rehabilitation Counselor Certification, 1977).

The effective date for beginning Certification Maintenance is January 1, 1978. Should the CRC choose continuing education as the method of Certification Maintenance, 150 contact hours would be required in a period of five years. If the CRC is unable to meet the Certification Maintenance requirements through continuing education or an alternative plan developed by a member organization and approved by the Commission, he/she may sit for the certification examination when it is offered during the year prior to his/her deadline for Certification Maintenance.

A critical question at this point is why should there by any maintenance of certification. First, and most obvious, is that there is precedence for Certification Maintenance, e.g., dental assistants. Second, and of critical importance historically, as was previously mentioned, is the Health Training improvement Act (PL 91–519) passed in 1970, which required the Department of Health, Education and Welfare to submit to Congress a report identifying the issues and setting forth recommendations with respect to the major problems associated with an allied health personnel licensure and certification. The culmination of seven years of efforts by HEW, as noted, was the formation of the National Commission for Health Certifying Agencies in 1977, which was created to establish a monitor national standard for certification of health and allied health professionals.

Included in the National Commission for Health Certifying Agencies are 65 certifying agencies, one of which has been the Commission on Rehabilitation Counselor Certification (CRCC) in affiliation with the National Counseling Association (NRCA). There is a categorical distinction, however, in that NRCA is a member organization and not a certifying group and CRCC is in the process of applying for membership as the certifying body. Other members of this commission include the American Medical Association (AMA), American Dental Association (ADA), American Hospital Association (AHA), along with allied professionals such as occupational therapists and physical therapists. The National Commission for Health Certifying Agencies has established many standards. The Commission on Rehabilitation Counselor Certification has attempted to meet these standards; however, only when the application is approved can full compliance be determined. One of the critical standards is:

The position of HEW is that periodic reassessment or reexamination of all health professionals is needed to protect the public. One condition of membership in the National Commission is that a profession move toward some kind of reassessment.

These previous statements make clear the reasons for CRCC's adoption of a certification maintenance program and bode well for the emerging profession of rehabilitation counseling.

The critical nature of a Certification Maintenance process and the fact that such a process must be meaningful to certified individuals, led the Commission on Rehabilitation Counselor Certification to develop a grant proposal in 1978 to investigate and conduct training on the continuing education needs of the practicing, experienced rehabilitation counselor. The project was funded by the Rehabilitation Services Administration of the Department of Health, Education, and Welfare for a three year period beginning January 1, 1979.

One of the first activities of the continuing education project was the formation of an advisory council to facilitate the objectives of the project. A request was made of organizations directly related to training (deliverers and recipients) to appoint elected officers to represent their organizations. Due to the direct interrelatedness of the project with CRCC, five members of CRCC were appointed. These individuals include the Chairperson of CRCC and the Secretary/Treasurer, along with the Chairpersons of the Certification Maintenance Committee, Examinations Committee and Credentials and Standards Committee. Representatives from American Rehabilitation Counseling Association (ARCA) American Coalition of Citizens with Disabilities (ACCD), Council on Rehabilitation Education (CORE), Council of State Administrators of Vocational Rehabilitation (CSAVR), National Council on Rehabilitation Education (NCRE), National Rehabilitation Counseling Association (NRCA), and Regional Continuing Education Programs (RCEP) were also appointed by their respective organization. These individuals plus a representative of RSA and the project coordinator and director comprise the advisory council.

The first face-to-face meeting of this group occurred in Nashville, Tennessee on April 21–22, 1979. The outcome of this meeting was particularly positive since there was accord on a number of critical factors. *First,* the concepts of certification and its relationship to competency in providing services to the handicapped was affirmed. In relation to this, the point was made that consumers should demand such competency. *Second,* the concept that professionals providing services to clients can maintain their skill level, despite exploding technology in the field of rehabilitation, through continuing education. *Third,* agreement was attained that practicing experienced rehabilitation counselors (CRC's) should be surveyed in the near future on the continuing education they have taken and their future needs in this area. A limited number of demographic characteristics will also be solicited to identify and hopefully facilitate future trends in continuing education. *Fourth,* the established rehabilitation education systems were identified and include: (a) regional rehabilitation continuing education programs; (b) state agency inservices programs; (c) Research and Training Centers; (d) National and Regional Short Term Training; and, (e) private sector agencies and organizations that have an established on-going rehabilitation training program. In relation to the established systems discussion also took place related to alternate mechanisms for the practicing experienced rehabilitation counselor to maintain competency. *Fifth,* agreement was reached that a conference related to continuing education in rehabilitation counseling is needed in 1980, and that the emphasis should be upon strategies for coordination, cooperation, and communication of training and training needs for the practicing, experienced rehabilitation counselor. Mention was also made for the needs for standards of competency and that ACCD's constituency group might best facilitate the development of such competencies. Finally, accord was reached, related to the 1980 conference, that the affirmation of training accomplishments by the established deliverers of training to rehabilitation counselors and the cooperative efforts of these groups should be highlighted along with the fact that these collaborative efforts have moved the profession in a positive direction and will continue to do so.

Plans for a meeting later in 1979 were also tentatively established so that future planning for the aforementioned 1980 conference could be further articulated.

These activities clearly exemplify the existence of a profession called "rehabilitation counseling" and that the need to continually justify its existence is *pass se.*

Summary

The certification movement for rehabilitation counselors has spanned 16 years, and considerable time, effort and cost have gone into a viable means to assess counselor competency and to insure quality services to the clients of the national vocational rehabilitation system. The collective voices of nearly 10,000 certified rehabilitation counselors have had a significant impact on the rehabilitation profession and their united efforts provide a direct impact on this profession. The Commission on Rehabilitation Counselor Certification (CRCC) used considerable foresight and wisdom in establishing criteria that would eventually be a part of the requirements for membership in the National Commission for Health Certifying Agencies.

The certification examination is highly reliable, and there are strong indicators that the instrument is a valid one. The research efforts have allowed for modifications in the examinations as well as to rehabilitation counseling cirriculum and RCEP and inservice training. An extensive plan to enhance and maintain the ability of the CRC to serve clients has been adopted by the Commission. These efforts by the professional organization and the fact that nearly 10,000 professionals have become certified in the field of rehabilitation counseling provide support for the viability of both the professional rehabilitation counselor and the profession of rehabilitation counseling.

REFERENCES

Carnes, C. D. Certification Philosophy and Conclusions. *Journal of Applied Rehabilitation Counseling*, 1972, *3*(1), 19–26.

Commission of Rehabilitation Counselor Certification. *Certification Maintenance Plan*. Chicago: Nat Resources, Inc., 1977.

Engelkes, J. R. & Livingston, R. H., "Implications of the Commission on Rehabilitation Counselor Certification Demographic Data for Rehabilitation Research Curriculum." Paper presented in a program entitled "Teaching Research in Rehabilitation Counseling: Issues, Problems and Alternative." Paper presented at the APGA National Convention, Chicago, Illinois, April, 1976.

Guilford, J. P. *Fundamental Statistics in Psychology and Education* (3rd Edition). New York: McGraw-Hill, Inc., 1956.

Hecht, Kathryn. Paper presented at the Annual Meeting of the National Council on Measurement in Education, Chicago, Illinois, April 16–18, 1974.

Livingston, R. H. A Concurrent Validity Study of Counselor Performance on the C. R. C. C. Field Review Utilizing Demographic Information. Unpublished doctoral dissertation, Michigan State University, 1976.

Livingston, R. H. & Engelkes, J. R. Certified Rehabilitation Counselors: A New Era. *Journal of Applied Rehabilitation Counseling*, 1977, *8*(4), 228–232.

Lunz, M. E. Commission on Rehabilitation Counselor Certification. March, 1975, Field Review Report. *Journal of Applied Rehabilitatoin Counseling*, 1976, *6*(2), 67–72.

McAlees, D. C., Report on Certification Commission. *Journal of Applied Rehabilitation Counseling*. 1973, *4*(3).

McAlees, D. C. & Shumacher, B. Toward a New Professionalism: Certification and Accreditation. *Rehabilitation Counseling Bulletin*. 1975, *18*(3), 160–165.

Mehrens, W. A. & Lehman, I. J. *Measurement and Evaluation in Education and Psychology.* New York: Holt, Rinehart and Winston, Inc., 1973.

Miller, L. A., A Reaction to the Certification of Rehabilitation Counselors. *Rehabilitation Counseling Bulletin,* 1971, *15*(2), 84–85.

Muthard, J. E. & Salomone, P. R. The Roles and Functions of the Rehabilitation Counselor. *Rehabilitation Counseling Bulletin,* 1969, *13* (1-SP).

National Rehabilitation Counseling Association."The History and Development of the Rehabilitation Counselor Certification Within the National Rehabilitation Counseling Association." Washington, D.C.: The Association, 1974.

Natress, L. Personal Communication, September, 1977.

Parker, R. M., A Survey of the NRCA Membership Regarding Rehabilitation Counselor Certification. *Journal of Applied Rehabilitation Counseling.* 1972, *3*(3), 173–177.

Thoreson, R. W. Certification: A Good Provisional Measure. *Rehabilitation Counseling Bulletin,* 1971, *15*(2), 80–83.

United States Department of Health, Education, and Welfare, Public Health Service, National Institute of Health. *Certification in the Allied Health Professions.* 1971 Conference Proceedings. Washington, D.C.: U.S. Government Printing Office, 1971.

Weber, W. F. An Item Analysis of the Performance of College Freshmen, Third Quarter Juniors, and Seniors on the July 18, 1975 Rehabilitation Counselor Certification Field Review. Unpublished doctoral dissertation, University of Northern Colorado, 1977.

RELATED REFERENCES

Bruyere, S. M., Certification Maintenance for Rehabilitation Counselors. *Rehabilitation Counseling Bulletin,* 1978, *22*(1), 2–4.

Engelkes, J. R. and Livingston, R. H., "Implications of the Commission on Rehabilitation Counselor Demographic Data for Rehabilitation Research Curricula." *Rehabilitation Counseling Bulletin,* 1977, *20*(4), 282-285.

Feinberg, L. B., Employment of the Certified Rehabilitation Counselor. *Journal of Rehabilitation,* 1977, *43*(5), 42–45.

Gianforte, G., Certification: A Challenge and a Choice. *Journal of Rehabilitation,* 1976, *42*(5), 15–17, 39.

Hansen, C. E. Rehabilitation Counselor Certification. In *Rehabilitation of the Severely Disabled,* W. Jenkins, et al. (Eds.), Dubuque; Kendall Hunt, 1976.

Hansen, C. E., The Question of Rehabilitation Counselor Certification. *Journal of Rehabilitation,* 1977, *43*(2), 2.

Hedgeman, B., Readers Response to Another Perspective on Certification. *Rehabilitation Counseling Bulletin,* 1979, *22*(4), 308–310.

Livingston, R. H., *A Time for Change?? Implications of the C.R.C.C. Demographic Data for Rehabilitation Curriculum.* Paper presented in a program entitled "A Challenge to Counselor Educators: New and Innovative Curriculum in Rehabilitation Counseling, presented at the APGA National Convention, Dallas, Texas, March, 1977.

Livingston, R. H., Certification Examination Performance and Training Needs of Certified Rehabilitation Counselors. Paper presented in a program entitled "Implications of the C.R.C.C. Demographic Data for Practicing Rehabilitation Counselors: New and Innovative Curriculum", presented at the National Rehabilitation Association National Convention, Washington, D.C., September, 1977.

Livingston, R. H., The Certified Rehabilitation Counselor. *Newsletter for Rehabilitation Facilities in Region VII.* Warrensburg, Missouri: Central Missouri State University, 1977, *3*(1), 5–6.

Livingston, R. H., Counselor Certification; Conflict and Controversy. *Rehabilitation Association of Nebraska Newsletter,* October, 1977.

Livingston, R. H., The History of Rehabilitation Counselor Certification: Past, Present, and Future Trends. Paper presented at the Rehabilitation Association of Nebraska Annual Convention, Kearney, Nebraska, October, 1977.

Lunz, M. E., Commission on Rehabilitation Counselor Certification. March, 1975, Field Review Report. *Journal of Applied Rehabilitation Counseling,* 1976, *6*(2), 67–72.

McAlees, D. C., Report on Certification Commission. *Journal of Applied Rehabilitation Counseling, 1973, 4(3).*

McAlees, D. C. and Shumacher, B., Toward a New Professionalism: Certification and Accreditation. *Rehabilitation Counseling Bulletin,* 1975, *18*(3), 160–165.

Salomone, P. R., Another Perspective on Certification. *Rehabilitation Counseling Bulletin,* 1978, *22*(1), 6–7.

Jim Messina, past president of AMHCA and currently chairperson of the board of the National Academy of Certified Clinical Mental Health Counselors, provides in this article the rationale for establishing the national academy. The rationale is based on HEW's studies and guidelines that resulted in the creation of the National Commission of Health Certifying Agencies. It is important to note that the national academy was developed following guidelines developed by the National Commission of Health Certifying Agencies.

[From: *American Mental Health Counselors Association Journal,* Vol. 1, No. 1]

Why Establish a Certification System for Professional Counselors? A Rationale

JAMES J. MESSINA

Since 1970 the Department of Health, Education, and Welfare has been investigating the entire field of certification and licensure of health-related professionals. A final report of their findings resulted in the creation of the National Commission of Health Certifying Agencies. HEW studies and the guidelines of the new commission are the background reviewed in this article, providing the rationale for the establishment of national certification procedures by AMHCA.

The American Mental Health Counselors Association has announced the implementation of a national certification program for professional counselors (AMHCA 1979). In establishing a Board of Certified Professional Counselors, the field of counseling has taken a giant step toward its own professionalization. But many counselors are confused. Some wonder what the advantages of certification are over those of licensure. Others are concerned that counselors might be following the lead of other mental health professionals in establishing a "clubby guild system" (Arbuckle 1977). Still others ask, why credential counselors at all? (Gross 1977). The intent of this article is to address some of these questions and to make a case for certification.

Since 1970, the U. S. Department of Health, Education, and Welfare has been investigating professional credentialing in health-related fields (HEW 1971). A final report of its findings (Cohen 1977) recommended instituting a voluntary network of certification. This recommendation has resulted in the establishment of the National Commission for Health Certifying Agencies (Piemme 1977). The research leading to the setting up of this commission and its guidelines for certification bodies (National Commission 1977) was the foundation on which

---

James J. Messina, the President of AMHCA, 1978-79, is an Associate Professor and Project Director at the Florida Mental Health Institute in Tampa.

the AMHCA credentialing effort is based. The following is a review of the literature related to these efforts. Before we can discuss professional certification, however, we must have a common understanding of *profession*.

WHAT IS A PROFESSION?

Peterson (1976) defined the conditions that any group must meet if it is truly to be a profession:

> 1. The objectives of professional work are definite and immediately practical.
> 2. Educationally communicable techniques for the attainment of these objectives are available.
> 3. Applications of techniques involve essentially intellectual operations and practitioners exercise responsible discretion in matching techniques to individual problems.
> 4. Techniques are related to a systematic discipline such as science, theology, or law whose substance is large and complex and hence ordinarily inaccessible to laymen.
> 5. Members of the profession are organized in some kind of society with rules for membership and exclusion based in part on professional competence.
> 6. The aims of the professional organization are at least in part altruistic rather than merely self-serving, and entail a code of ethics whose sanctions are also invoked, along with those of competence, in determining membership in the society and therefore legitimate practice of the profession. (Peterson 1976, p. 573)

Sweezy (1974) posited that a profession is characterized as resting on a systematic body of knowledge of substantial intellectual content, which involves the acquisition of skills for application of this knowledge to specific cases, and that it has standards of professional conduct that override goals of personal gain established with its means for the enforcement of standards and the advancement of knowledge.

Credentialing provides the instrument for enforcement of professional standards. Professional counseling has not defined itself as a profession with recognized and measurable competencies. Its efforts in the licensure and certification areas are an attempt to rectify the lack of credentialing procedures. Before this issue can be addressed, it will be necessary to share a common vocabulary.

DEFINITIONS OF TERMS

The following definitions are used by the AMHCA Certification Committee. These were developed by the HEW Subcommittee on Health Manpower Credentialing, chaired by Harris S. Cohen (Cohen 1977).

Credentialing, the accreditation of individuals, is the formal recognition of professional or technical competence. It is a generic term referring to both the process of certification and of licensure.

Licensure is the process by which an agency of government grants permission to persons to engage in a given profession or occupation by certifying that those licensed have obtained the minimal degree of competency necessary to ensure that the public health, safety, and welfare will be reasonably well protected.

Certification or registration is the process by which a nongovernmental agency or association grants recognition to an individual who has met certain predetermined qualifications specified by that agency or association. Such qualifications may include (a) graduation from an accredited or approved training program; (b) acceptable performance on a qualifying examination or series of examinations, and/or (c) completion of a given amount of work experience.

Cohen (1977) has discussed three possible forms of examination used in issuing credentials:

A certification examination (a licensing examination), which is developed and used under private auspices to determine the level of competence of practitioners in a specific occupation. These are, in essence, qualifying examinations concerned primarily with entry into the occupation.

A proficiency examination, which is used to determine the level of proficiency of practitioners, with opportunity for those whose competency is based primarily on on-the-job training and experience.

An equivalency examination, which is used to determine the value of experience in nonaccredited education in meeting education requirements under accredited programs.

There is a need for an equitable integration of all three forms of examinations with a certification or licensing process so as to avoid any discriminatory barriers. Now that terms are defined we need a historic perspective in which to place them.

CRITIQUE OF STATE-OF-THE-ART CREDENTIALING

John F. Adkinson (Bureau of Health Resources Development 1975, p. 28) stated:

> Health service without competence is basically no health service at all. There is only one way for assuring the general public of competence in the health field, whether referring to health professionals or related allied health personnel, and that is through credentialing or licensing of individual participants. Credentialing encompasses, among other things 1) formal education in an accredited institution, 2) examination by

a duly designated body be it governmental or private in nature, 3) internship, 4) continuing education, 5) renewal of credentials.

Tucker (1975, p. 3) summed up the three reasons for credentialing:

1. To protect the public and provide for quality health care delivery through regulation and control (the degree of which varies depending on the mode of credentialing) of the performance of the practitioners
2. To determine the qualifications for entrance into a profession and
3. To protect the profession and the professionals themselves

Goldberg (1974), however, stated that licensure was not fulfilling the function of protecting the public from unqualified practitioners. He saw it as imposing on health-related personnel unnecessarily difficult requirements, and curtailing the scope and function of such personnel. He concluded that meaningful standards for licensure are not necessarily set, which causes fragmentation of health careers by prohibiting the coordination of interrelated allied health personnel within career lines, and thus contributes to underuse of health manpower through narrow statuatory definitions of the scope of functions.

Conant and Hatch (1974) found that attention given to credentialing practices was a result of increased demands for health services, public concern regarding perceived manpower shortages, inefficient use of health manpower, questionable quality of services, and higher costs. Ballanger and Estes (1971) described the disadvantages of licensure. First, licensure provides no real guarantee of the quality or professional acceptance of the group licensed. It is questionable whether substantial quality control can be exerted by an administrative board that has only intermittent contact with the practitioners it licenses. Second, licensure requires a description of the activities and functions of the designated profession. If these are precisely delineated new tasks or responsibilities, they cannot be assumed without a change in the law, which may entail prolonged and costly delays. If they are loosely or vaguely defined, nonuniform interpretation of the bounds of the profession, with consequent legal uncertainties, results. Last, licensure can become a weapon with which a given profession, jealously guarding its boundaries against encroachment, can frustrate reasonable accretion of its preempted duties by other groups over time.

Forgotson and Raumer (1968) warned that professional licensure laws do not often recognize that development of new information renders a person's initial qualifications obsolete unless they are upgraded periodically by continuing education.

In the 1971 HEW report, states were urged to observe a two-year moratorium on the enactment of legislation. The states were also urged to adopt and fully use national examinations for those categories of health personnel for which examinations were available. At the close of the two-year moratorium, a second report (Cohen & Miike 1973) listed preliminary findings and conclusions since the initial report. As a result, HEW requested an additional two-year moratorium on the establishment of more licensure legislation.

In 1973 certain trends were identified that have a bearing on the national certification and licensure issues (Goldberg 1974). Most new legislation that year did not leave the approval of accreditation of schools up to the various boards. Instead, it deferred such decisions to the national organization of the occupation in question. Some states were concerned with making their educational requirements conform to standards set by professional associations and with the possibility of accepting national examinations in lieu of their own state examinations. Some legislation was proposed to replace the licensure requirement of the state board with certification by some national board or association. States were increasingly accepting national examinations and certification in place of their own work, and some legislation was passed providing for this substitution.

Mehringer's (1975) analysis of the 1974 licensure legislation pointed to a significant result of that year's legislation—Virginia's attempt to coordinate all licensure procedures. The Virginia legislature created a Commission for Professional Occupational Regulation. The Commission evaluates professions and occupations not currently regulated, and determines whether they should be regulated. Through such a commission, Virginia became one of the few states to establish the goal of consistency and cooperation among its regulating boards. (It should be noted that only Virginia allows counselors to be licensed as a result of a public law enacted in 1977.)

There has been no further analysis by the Department of Health, Education, and Welfare of manpower licensure legislation activities for the years since 1974; however, the early trends identified a need for closer coordination and consistency among the regulatory boards, and for the identification of national-level standards, especially in the examinations of such professions. Also recommended was research into alternate forms of credentialing other than licensure.

INSTITUTIONAL LICENSURE: AN ALTERNATIVE?

An alternate form of credentialing, institutional licensure, was investigated by Starrer, Rose, and Saltzberg (1976). In this process, the institution would establish a committee to define jobs within the institution, set standards required to fill those jobs, develop entry evaluation procedures, evaluate candidates for employment, develop performance evaluation procedures, set standards for maintenance of and promotions in job status, evaluate employees periodically, issue certificates of job status of employees, and establish educational and training requirements necessary to meet standards for entry, maintenance, and promotion. The committee created to fulfill these tasks could be adapted within existing institutional committee structure, but would include an expert (or a consultant to the committee) in functional task analysis, and would require necessary clerical staff to maintain records. The institution would submit its procedures and ratings to a state monitor composed of the state licensing board and representatives from various health disciplines. The duties of the state monitor would be to establish minimum standards for utility and validity of the processes for use by the committees, approve the processes adopted by each committee, issue certificates of process-approved-status to institutions that meet minimum standards, approve certificates of job status granted to individuals employed within the institution, and make recommendations to the department of education in regard to health-related formal education programs in the state.

The conclusion of the Starrer et al. report was, although it seemed feasible to employ institutional licensure, that the political realities were such that it would be impossible to recommend a national adoption of such a model. Tucker (1975) concurred in his report, where he stated, "Although theoretically feasible it was concluded that the numerous political, technical and social problems which are identified cannot be surmounted to make implementation of institutional licensure feasible" (p. iii). With this alternative discounted, another type of national initiative in credentialing was needed.

ADVANTAGE OF NATIONAL CERTIFICATION PROCESSES

Sweezy (1974) stated that a system of certification that is voluntary is compatible with three important philosophical premises:

1. Certification is a validation of individuals' capacities and must be consistent with the concepts of individual freedom embodied in our national tradition and law.
2. Egalitarian societies reached their necessary balance and control by successive undercontrolling the actions, rather than over controls applied by authoritarian societies. Voluntary action by associated citizens is always preferable to compulsary action if the public interest is adequately protected.
3. The classic law of conservation, which holds that the best solution to a problem is that which requires the least force. (Sweezy 1974, p. 28)

Certification provides evidence of a level of competence defined by the profession as a national standard for practitioners of occupations. Sweezy pointed out that "reliance upon educational records confuses evidence of scholastic performance with job skill. Scholastic credentials attest to performance of a number of separate units of education, but they are not necessarily evidence of an integrated mastery of a complex set of knowledges and skills," and that "the educational credential progressively loses its relevance as time elapses after graduation. It does not match certification and capability to attest to the maintenance of continuing competence after completion of formal accredited educational programs" (p. 31).

Sweezy found that licensure is limited in value in that it defines a minimum level of competence rather than the highest level of competence possessed by the licensed, and that it has been adopted in some occupations as a vehicle for restricting entry mobility to protect the economic interest of licensed resident practitioners. On the other hand, he observed that certification systems are capable of showing both the breadth and depth of competence, differing from the minimum levels established by a state as requirements for licensing. Certification is also capable of doing so without geographic limitations.

Movement from one locale to another for personal preference or labor market efficiency, which is essential in a free labor market, is restricted when prospective employers have no readily available means for establishing the type and level of occupational competence. The rigidity of licensure can impair the ability of the labor market to meet the changing demands of the health-care delivery system. Lack of uniform licensing requirements and the ever-present possibility of uncoordinated changes between states create a tenuous basis for acceptance of the licensure mode of credentialing as conducive to a free, open labor market. Sweezy (1974) concluded that a national certification system makes more uniform and credible information available to a prospective employer.

There is the danger of developing overqualifications for certification, which can operate to deny significant segments of our society access to a certified occupation. Excessive educational requirements are the most common type of qualification that can be discriminatory against socially and economically disadvantaged segments of our society (Sweezy 1974).

Another potentially undesirable effect would be the growth of an attitude among the professional groups that they have been somehow endowed with a higher status in the social system (Sweezy 1974). The assumption of a mystique or aura of this sort can destroy good working relationships within the health-care system. The real needs of individuals to advance in self-esteem and self-actualization can be met if a certification system emphasizes progressive growth of a person's command of a real body of special knowledge, skill, or art, and gears this recognition to career development and mobility.

Certification of professionals is affected by a number of influences arising from laws, regulations, and other functions of authority

(Sweezy 1974). These influences are liability for malpractice, eligibility for reimbursement of payment for services, corporate taxation of citizens under law, possible affects of antitrust statutes under the feasibility of a national voluntary system, and collective bargaining and rights of employees.

The liability of an institution for the actions of persons permitted to practice their occupation within its facilities was greatly extended by the decision of *Darling v. Charlestown Community Memorial Hospital* (Illinois) (Sweezy 1974). The doctrine adopted in this case has since been followed in some other state jurisdictions. The primary effect was to hold the institution accountable for the competent performance of all persons permitted to use its facilities in the treatment of patients. It can be strongly inferred, therefore, that the administrators and others employing or granting staff privileges to health-related personnel must be able to ascertain that professional employees do, in fact, have sufficient competence to perform the functions permitted or delegated to them. Certification on a national level makes this task much easier without restricting the geographic mobility of the professionals involved. Another landmark decision relevant to credentialing was handed down in the *Griggs v. Duke Electric Power Company* (Sweezy 1974). The key aspect of this decision was its requirement that test questions used in employment practices must be directly related to the duties of the position for which the test is being used, that is, "job-related." Otherwise, the test was ruled to be discriminatory. If this rule of fairness and relevance is applied to certification it would lead toward greater emphasis on specifically practical, as distinguished from generally intellectual, qualifying criterion standards. The issue of practical criteria and standards for certification leads to larger questions of training and testing for these standards.

A major philosophical question concerns the close ties between accreditation of training and certification. That is, is certification for initial entry into the occupation redundant and should certification be more appropriately used to attest to continuing competence?

There are individuals who, although they have not taken traditional academic training, have acquired the skills necessary to meet maximum standards of competency. Licensure has often acted as a professional roadblock to these individuals. This has been a concern for groups creating a national certification and has provided the impetus for the development of proficiency examinations (Selden 1971). A certification system must protect the interest of those in the society who cannot or do not follow a conventional pattern in obtaining their qualifying knowledge and skills. A practitioner who has achieved adequate levels of competency by nonconventional routes is entitled to the same opportunities for continued employment and updating of capabilities as one who has the more traditional background (Sweezy 1974). If the certification process is to operate as the public-spirited gatekeeper for a profession, it must have adequate mechanisms for recognizing and dealing with both conventionally and nonconventionally trained personnel.

A balanced assessment of the kinds of accountability, and the need to have a responsive organizational apparatus, leads to the conclusion that other interested parties, including the general public, must have more than token representation or a limited advisory role in the management of a national certification system (Sweezy 1974). Sweezy pointed out that organizations that accredit educational and training programs must not be permitted solely to perform the certification that practitioners can apply the knowledge and skills taught in those programs. Unless this separation is maintained, a definite conflict of interest is created. Such a conflict can be avoided by placing the certification process under the control of an organization or apparatus that can independently represent the public interest. This should be an organization not subject to domination by special interests of educational, economic, medical, or consumer groups. Many hold that the function of certification is to attest to the continued professional qualification of practitioners. Future procedures can validate or challenge certification standards and make it especially urgent that provisions for maintaining professional quality be incorporated into the certification process.

Possible threats to the effectiveness of certification detailed by Sweezy (1974) include, first, the jurisdictional disputes among certifying bodies applying different competence standards in the same occupational field and contesting the control of overlapping functions in emerging occupational roles; second, the pressure for state licensure; third, the potential use of proficiency examinations as a competing system to certification; and fourth, the number of noncertified persons working in the field. These problems must be addressed in the establishment of a national certification system so that it is clear to the professionals involved that there is not a desire to create conflict for their professional identity.

Sweezy found that role definition is still a major process underway in the community of health and manpower. Some factors evidencing this state of flux were competition between occupations, competition between spokespersons for the same occupation, competition with external forces for control of the occupational field, changes in techniques of health care, and changes in the structure of the health delivery organizations.

An advantage that certification has, in contrast to licensure, is one of flexibility. Certification can adapt more readily to changes in technology and delivery systems, and can redefine the knowledge and skills required accordingly. Licensure, on the other hand, is seen (Sweezy 1974) as freezing the professional's scope of duties in statute or regulation, and intruding the "heavy hand of government" into the credentialing process.

TOWARD A NATIONAL VOLUNTARY CERTIFICATION SYSTEM

The most recent HEW report (Cohen 1977), in reviewing previous studies, concluded that they demonstrated that state licensure of health-related occupations had evolved into a system of varying requirements, responsibilities, and controls that tended, in many instances, to impede effective use of health personnel, to inhibit geographic and career mobility, and to foster variable licensure standards and procedures in different regions of the country. Furthermore, licensing agencies often tended to emphasize formal education and other requirements for entry into a profession, but devoted less attention to assuring the continued competence of those who are licensed. In some cases, the involvement of a professional association in the activities of a licensure board raised questions about the independence and objectivity of the boards. In this regard, other studies had confirmed that formal disciplinary procedures available to boards are not often used except in cases of blatant misconduct. This 1977 HEW report pointed out that legislatures are frequently the setting for intense political battles over the issue of "to license or not to license" with decisions made—not on the basis of an objective assessment about whether an occupation should be licensed—on the basis of the relative political strengths of the participants. This report concluded that the certificate alternative should be further developed and that the institutional licensure approach, because of the intense controversy that it generated, should not receive their further consideration.

In this report (Cohen 1977), the U. S. Public Health Service endorsed the approach of a national certification system as a viable alternative to state licensure of allied health occupations not presently licensed by states. They also recommended that a National Commission for Health Certifying Agencies be developed to provide a forum for a new level of dialogue among professional organizations, certifying agencies, employers, consumer representatives, and governmental agencies (state and federal). By insuring the participation of a variety of interests, policy decisions would more adequately reflect the public interest and, therefore, promote public accountability in the certification process. It was hoped that the commission would convene ad hoc working groups to develop national standards for allied health personnel (Samuels 1976). The working groups would consist of functionally related clusters of health professionals whose responsibilities bring them into direct contact with one another. In this way, standards for a given health-related profession would be developed primarily by the profession itself with important contributions from related occupational categories.

The report recommended that national standards for the credentialing of selected health occupations be developed and continually evaluated. Standards should be uniformly applied, and therefore these standards should address not only examinations but training requirements for practice, continued competencies, recertification, and disciplinary functions. Moreover, these standards should be continually evaluated for validity and relevance. The report also pointed out that it is critical that the employer representatives participate fully in the process to ensure that the standards developed are practicable and responsive to the unique characteristics of certain regions or facilities without compromising quality services. The report states firmly that licensure is presently, and will continue to be, a function of the state government. What is recommended is the development of a set of uniform standards for health-related personnel, which would assist states in formulating compatible licensure programs where licensure is the appropriate mode of credentialing.

The HEW report (Cohen 1977) set up criteria for future state licensure decisions, and suggested how the public could be effectively protected by means other than licensure. A recommendation was to expand membership on boards to include effective representation of consumers and other functionally related health professionals.

A major recommendation of this report was that effective competency measures need to be promoted and adopted to determine the qualifications of health personnel. Special attention should be given to further development of proficiency and equivalency measures for appropriate categories of health personnel. The 1977 HEW report urged that individuals in the health-related fields be assessed by their actual competence as well as by their formal educational achievement.

The issues of what constitutes competence and of the testing and measurement of competence to perform in a given job setting are not simple or noncontroversial matters. Little can be done without a careful and systematic analysis of the relevant occupational role and the development of criterion measures (Boyd & Shimberg 1971). The use of proficiency and equivalency examinations offers a potentially important complementary mechanism to measure the qualifications of various health-related professions.

The Cohen (1977) report also recommended that additional study and training for the professional are the best mechanisms to ensure continued competence, and should be supported as high priority by professional associations. Certifying bodies should work closely with educators and institutions to develop appropriate programs to upgrade knowledge and skills of health-related personnel on a continuing basis. The key recommendations of the 1977 HEW report were:

1. A national voluntary system for allied health certification should be established.

2. National standards for the credentialing of health occupations should be developed and continually evaluated.

3. Criteria should be set up for future state licensure decisions.

4. Licensure procedures should be improved in the states.

5. Competency measurements should be developed.

6. Continued competency of the professionals should be encouraged and certified.

NATIONAL COMMISSION FOR HEALTH CERTIFYING AGENCIES

In 1977 the National Commission for Health Certifying Agencies was announced (Piemme 1977). This marked the formation of a group of 65 national organizations representing health certifying agencies, health professional associations, societies, and state licensing and regulatory bodies. It was a sign of a national initiative for the support of national certification efforts for health-related professionals. The purposes of this voluntary, nongovernmental organization are:

1. to promote public health and safety through the certification process
2. to develop and encourage high standards of professional conduct among certifying agencies
3. establish performance standards for existing certifying bodies and to monitor their implementation through the determinations of criteria, policies and roles for certifying systems which are responsive to the needs of the health care system
4. to advise on the need for standards and processes in the establishment of a new certifying system for both emerging and existing health occupations
5. to recommend methods for assuring competency after initial certification
6. to encourage voluntary participation of health related organizations in this commission
7. to maintain and publish a register of organizations which participate in and meet the current and continuing standards of the commission
8. to recognize certifying agencies for outstanding contribution to the certification process
9. to encourage and facilitate the development of common and/or collaborative examinations programs within a profession
10. to study test construction and validation practices
11. to investigate cost saving procedures to collect, analyze and disseminate information to the membership regarding certification technology and its effects on standards to be met by health personnel
12. to conduct educational programs designed to acquaint member organizations, educators, health professionals and the general public with issues relating to the certification process

13. to collect and disseminate information relative to the functions and accomplishments of the national commission on voluntary certification process. (Piemme 1977, p. 3)

It is this National Commission for Health Certifying Agencies to which any national-level board for certification must apply for membership if it hopes for its certification procedures to gain national recognition. This is a process of validating certification procedures and ensuring that they provide a professional service in the public interest.

The National Commission standards were the guidelines (National Commission 1977) followed in the development of the procedures for the certification of professional counselors. The American Mental Health Counselors Association Certification Committee made every effort to ensure that this newly established certification process would meet the approval of the new commission.

AMHCA'S EFFORTS

The Board of Directors of AMHCA decided in March 1978 (AMHCA 1978) that national certification of professional counselors was to be their top priority for the next two years. They chose certification over licensure because they were aware of the findings of the HEW-sponsored studies and of the perils of the state-by-state effort needed to license counselors. The Board recognized that certification, with a national standard of performance and a national examination, would also complement the efforts in states to assist counselors to be licensed.

The Board of Professional Counselors established by AMHCA will become an autonomous entity by January, 1982. This will help meet the guidelines of the National Commission for Health Certifying Agencies (1977), which require that all certifying agencies be separate from the organizations of the professionals they certify.

The formation of the Board and establishment of procedures for certification of professional counselors are major steps in the professionalization of the field of counseling, a field that will surely receive close scrutiny in the next decade.

REFERENCES

American Mental Health Counselors Association. Minutes of Board of Directors Meeting, 18–19 March 1978. Washington, D. C.: Author, 1978.
AMHCA Certification Committee. The Board of Certified Professional Counselors Procedures. *AMHCA Journal,* 1979, 1, 23-38.
Arbuckle, D. S. Counselor licensure: To be or not to be. *Personnel and Guidance Journal,* 1977, 55, 581-585.

Ballinger, M. D. & Estes, E. H. Licensure or responsible delegation. *New England Journal of Medicine,* 1971, *284,* 330-331.

Boyd, J. L., & Shimberg, B. *Handbook of performance testing. A practical guide for test makers.* Princeton, N. J.: Educational Testing Service, 1971.

Bureau of Health Resources Development. *Report of the meeting to discuss the feasibility of a national system of certification for allied health personnel.* Springfield, Va.: Author, 1975. (NTIS No. PB-248-860).

Christ-Janer, A. *Study of accreditation of selected health educational programs.* Washington, D. C.: ASAHP, 1971.

Cohen, H. S., & Miike, L. H. *Developments in health manpower licensure: A follow up to the 1971 report on licensure and related health personnel credentialing* (DHEW Publication No. (HRA) 74-3101). Washington, D. C.: Government Printing Office, 1973.

Cohen, H. S., & HEW Subcommittee on Health Manpower Credentialing. *Credentialing health manpower* (DHEW Publication No. (OS) 77-50057). Washington, D.C.: Government Printing Office, 1977.

Conant, R. M., & Hatch, T. D. Policies for the development of credentialing mechanisms for health personnel, a progress report—1974. *American Journal of Occupational Therapy,* 1974, *28,* 289.

Forgotson, E. H., & Roemer, R. Government licensure and voluntary standards for health personnel and facilities: Their power and limitations in assuring high quality health care. *Medical Care,* 1968, *6,* 346.

Goldberg, I.; Hurley, L.; & Mehringer, A. *Analysis of 1973 state health manpower licensure legislation.* Springfield, Va.: Aspen Systems Corp., 1974. (NTIS No. PB-237-816)

Gross, S. J. Professional disclosure: An alternative to licensing. *Personnel and Guidance Journal,* 1977, *55,* 586-588.

Mehringer, A.; Hershey, N.; & Kabinow, J. *Analysis of 1974 state health manpower licensure legislation.* Springfield, Va.: Aspen Systems Corp., 1975. (NTIS No. PB-240-665).

National Commission for Health Certifying Agencies. *Criteria for approval of certifying agencies.* Unpublished text, Washington. D. C., Author, 1977.

Peterson, D. R. Is psychology a profession. *American Psychologist,* 1976, *31,* 572-581.

Piemme, T. E. Statement to the press. Unpublished manuscript, Washington, D. C., National Commission for Health Certifying Agencies, 1977.

Samuels, W. M., Proceedings certification conference, Kansas City, Missouri, August 2-5, 1976. Washington, D. C.: National Commission for Health Certifying Agencies, 1976.

Selden, W. K. (Ed). *Part One: Working papers SASHEP, accreditation of health educational programs.* Washington, D. C.: ASAHP, 1971.

Starrer, R. L.; Rose, W. L.; & Saltzberg, E. J. *Alternate regulation of health personnel: Institutional licensure study.* Springfield, Va.: Hospital Educational and Research Foundation of Pennsylvania, July 1976. (NTIS No. PB-262-231).

Sweezy, E. E. *Feasibility study of a voluntary national certification system for allied health personnel.* Springfield, Va.: Institute of Public Administration, 1974. (NTIS No. HRP-0002053).

Tucker, W. R. *Credentialing health personnel by licensed hospitals: The report of a study of institutional licensure.* Springfield, Va.: Rush-Presbyterian-St. Luke's Medical Center, 1975. (NTIS No. PB-244-329).

U. S. Department of Health, Education, and Welfare. *Report on licensure and related health personnel credentialing* (DHEW Publication No. (HSM) 72-11). Washington, D. C.: Government Printing Office, 1971.

School counselor certification is the oldest and most widespread form of counselor credentialing. Standards vary widely from state to state, as do job descriptions and performance expectations. Certification procedures now are in a state of flux and are subject to much study and debate. This article describes efforts in Georgia to upgrade school certification standards and to approve accountability. While recognizing that this certification process is different from the certification process we have been discussing, the editors believe that this article is important because it could very well be a model for other states.

[From: *Counselor Education and Supervision*, Vol. 18, No. 4]

Toward Performance-Based Counselor Certification

STAN BERNKNOPF
JOHN L. SHULTZ
WILLIAM B. WARE

For the past four years the Georgia Department of Education has been involved in a statewide effort to establish standards and procedures for certification of educational personnel based on competency demonstration. As part of this effort, a project was commissioned to develop a performance-based system for the certification of school counselors. This article presents the premises, procedures, and products of the model which was developed.

During the past decade competency-based strategies have emerged as a means of certifying school personnel. Although the primary emphasis has been teacher certification, some states have attempted to develop competency-based guidelines aimed at certification procedures for school counselors. These attempts were most evident during the late 1960s when professional journals presented some of the concepts and rationale underlying such a certification procedure. Although the literature, in general, was highly encouraging, it was not until the early 1970s that a few operational programs began to appear in print. These initial attempts are characterized by the procedures developed by the State of Washington (Allen, Cady & Drummond, 1969; Brammer & Springer, 1971; Springer & Brammer, 1971).

In 1972 the Georgia State Board of Education authorized the staff of the Georgia Department of Education to prepare a proposal for establishing guidelines and standards for certification of professional personnel based on competency demonstration. These standards were to assure the development and maintenance of professional competency in educational personnel. During the academic year 1973–74, funds became available for a project to develop a competency-based system for the certification of school counselors in the state. This article makes a preliminary report on the model that is emerging from that project.

Stan Bernknopf is the coordinator of student assessment at the Georgia State Department of Education, Atlanta. John Shultz is the area representative in educational psychology at the Georgia Retardation Center, University of Georgia, Athens. William Ware is professor of education and chairperson, Department of Education, Bernau College, Gainesville, Georgia.

PREMISES OF THE PROJECT

Some of the earliest efforts of the project staff were directed towards developing a conceptual frame of reference. To a large degree, this procedure involved explicating the values or assumptions that underlie any attempt at developing a system for certifying school counselors. In effect, the question was, What important principles should be built into the certification process? A time frame was not set aside in which all personnel sat down and "clarified their values," rather, the values emerged quite naturally. As decisions were made about the nature and direction of the project, many values became self-evident and developed into premises for the project. These premises are presented below as follows:

Premise 1. *Guidance programs should be based on student needs.* Analysis of previous attempts at developing counselor training and/or certification programs indicated that many of them had begun by asking various groups of people what they considered to be appropriate guidance goals. As such, school administrators, teachers, counselors, and, in rare cases, people outside the school system (e.g., employers and parents) were contacted and questioned. Although this procedure provides an adequate beginning, it eliminates students (the direct consumers) from contributing to the development of goals for a program that, theoretically, should have considerable impact on them and the development of their own life goals. Therefore, it was decided to include samples of students in the groups of people questioned about student needs. Only then could programs be developed that would meet perceived student needs.

Premise 2. *Colleges and universities train, state departments certify.* On the surface, Premise 2 may seem a radical assumption. Actually, it is somewhat conservative. Consider the following: Traditionally, certification has been a joint effort between institutions of higher learning and state departments of education. Through the Approved Program concept, completion of prescribed course work was tantamount to certification. The state departments' role thus became one of approving institutional programs and verifying individual applicants' transcripts. Although this procedure was expedient (and, at times, efficient) it left unanswered many questions about the effectiveness of individual counselors; weaknesses do not often appear in a summation of courses, grades and credits. As a result, the project took the position that the certification process would be independent of the training process: Colleges and universities would be responsible for training and the state departments of education responsible for certification. Although procedures for certification are still open to question, the right of states to set certification requirements which includes establishing minimum standards has long been upheld in the courts (see, e.g. Dent v. West Virginia, 1889).

Premise 3. *Competency has both knowledge and performance dimensions.* Previous research, as well as our own experience, has consistently demonstrated that acquired knowledge does not guarantee adequate performance. As a result, this certification model considered the assessment of knowledge and performance competencies as if they were, if not mutually exclusive, at least relatively independent factors. This premise raised a number of interesting measurement problems; the assessment of knowledge competencies lends itself quite handily to paper-and-pencil testing, while assessment of performance competencies would have to be done through demonstrated on-the-job performance. Yet, it was believed the outcomes would be well worth the extra effort.

As an aside, the erudite reader will note that attitudes were not included in this definition of competency. A more detailed explanation of the rationale for the exclusion is published elsewhere (Ware, 1975). Suffice it here to say that (a) not only were attitudes considered impossible to define and measure with any degree of consistent reliability or validity, but (b) as presently measured attitudes were also believed to be essentially unrelated to performance.

Premise 4. *Certification requirements should be job-related.* In wording this assumption, using the word *must* rather than *should* was seriously considered. This is because recent court cases have established job-relatedness as an essential criterion for any assessment procedure. (*Chance* v. *Board of Examiners,* 1974; *Georgia Association of Educators, Inc., et al.* v. *Jack P. Nix,* 1976; *Griggs* v. *Duke Power Company,* 1971). The developers of this model are not lawyers (although there have been many times in the past four years when we wished we at least had some of their training), and this is not the place to describe all the court decisions that have caused a sensitivity to potential judicial appeals about certification decisions. We operated on the assumption, idealistic as it may sound, that if we did our best to establish the relatedness of the requirement to actual on-the-job performance, we would not have any trouble. The present model was based on the assumption that these kinds of assurances could be built in if we used the pooled judgments of persons who actually had knowledge of the school counselor's job. This jury was used in both the development of the competencies and the validation of all procedures used to assess these competencies. This pooled-judgment procedure is presently accepted by the Equal Employment Opportunity Commission (1976).

Premise 5. *Certification sets minimal standards of effectiveness.* This premise is based on the belief that the assurance of minimal competence is all that can be implied by the licensing or certifying procedure. Seeking and retaining the best counselor is, and should be, the function of the hiring agency. This seems to us most reasonable. When someone goes to a physician the only assurance the person has of the physician's competency is the fact that the physician has passed various and sundry boards and is licensed to practice in the community. The school system is in a similar position. When hiring professional counselors, the school system knows only that the counselor has met *minimal* requirements and is certified to practice counseling in that state. Further, it is up to the employer to assure that the counselor continues to demonstrate competence; if for no reason other than determining whether or not to continue employing that counselor.

Premise 6. *The counselor should have more than one opportunity to become certified.* This principle is particularly difficult to elucidate. What we are trying to communicate is that counselor trainees are in control of the certification process. They decide whether or not they want to enter the process, whether or not they want to lay their skills on the line. On receiving indication that they have been found wanting on some dimension, they have control over when, or, indeed, whether they choose to be reconsidered for certification.

The certification process is fully explained in another part of this article. Suffice it to say here that the certification process has been designed as one that does more than make judgments. To be sure, decisions are made as to the adequacy of the protocols being presented as representative of the applicant's competencies. If the applicant is deemed unprepared or inadequately prepared in certain areas, prescriptions are offered to correct observed deficiencies. In essence, the process is not interested in excluding candidates; rather, it is aimed at ensuring that only qualified candidates enter the profession. Given a motivated candidate, there should be minimal failure among applicants.

Premise 7. *Effective guidance requires a team approach.* The statement "Guidance requires a team approach" has been made so many times that it has almost become a cliché. The reality of our experience, however, is that, like most clichés, the above statement contains more than a grain of truth. In the latter part of the 20th century the responsibility for implementation of a guidance program can no longer be delegated solely to the counselor. Fulfillment of the guidance function actually does require a team approach involving not only the counselor, teachers, administrators, and other educational personnel, but parents as well.

PROCEDURES

To develop an entry certification model for school counselors in Georgia that would incorporate the above premises, a management system was designed. The purpose of the system was to identify the major tasks to be accomplished. This plan is summarized in Table 1 by major stages and the processes, purposes, and products contained in each stage.

TABLE 1
Stages in the Development of the Georgia Model for Counselor Certification

	Process	Purpose	Product
Stage 1	Needs assessment	Validate new and existing information regarding student needs	Hierarchical listing of guidance related student goals
Stage 2	Development of a school counseling model (conceptual framework)	To develop a process for meeting and/or moving students toward identified goals	A series of school programs with identified knowledge and performance competencies for counselors
Stage 3	Verification of programs and competencies	To ensure that the competencies were appropriate and needed for minimal competence	A refined and verified list of competencies (knowledge and performance)
Stage 4	Development of competency assessment procedures	To ensure valid and reliable methods of obtaining information relative to competence of prospective counselors	A. A criterion-referenced test designed to assess mastery of the knowledge competencies B. A set of observation instruments designed to assess mastery of the performance competencies
Stage 5	Development of training modules	To provide a series of alternative strategies for strengthening diagnosed weaknesses	Six individualized training modules which parallel the six performance competencies
Stage 6	Field test	To determine feasibility of procedures for assessment of performance competencies	A certification model

Stage 1

During the initial project year (stage 1) a comprehensive needs assessment was made. Student goals developed during this needs assessment became the basis for the entire project's development. The needs assessment involved three steps: (a) the development of a survey type instrument, (b) personal interviews with students, and (c) workshops with counselors, teachers, principals, and pupil personnel directors.

The purpose of the survey was to validate student guidance needs hypothesized in the existing literature as well as *Goals for Education in Georgia* (1970). This procedure also allowed respondents to have input into what they considered to be student needs. The decision to use personal interviews was prompted by the belief that many students below the 8th grade might not have the reading skills necessary to validly respond to the instrument. Interviews were also held with samples of students in the 9th grade and above. These interviews had as their purpose discovering concerns or needs of students not covered in the original questionnaire.

The use of workshops was an attempt to involve representatives of as many groups as possible in the development of the certification model. During two workshops, about 50 counselors, teachers, principals, and pupil personnel directors from the state were asked to identify and rank what they perceived to be guidance-related student needs. Data obtained from these procedures allowed the staff to develop consensual estimates of the importance of each goal, and to identify those goals generally considered most important. A total of 28 goals were identified.

Stage 2

Stage 2 of the project centered around the creation of a conceptual framework for meeting the previously identified needs of students. This framework provided a blueprint for guidance program development. In reality the blueprint yielded many programs, one for each of the 28 student goals. Each program contained the following components:

1. *Rationale.* A logical explanation of the importance of the goal and how it related to student needs.

2. *Personnel.* Members of the educational staff to have direct or indirect impact on the goal.

3. *Medium.* An existing or innovative activity of the school or community through which the goal might be attained.

4. *Content.* The cognitive, affective, and/or psychomotor elements prerequisite to goal attainment.

5. *Competencies.* The knowledge and skills required of personnel to facilitate the achievement of the goal.

Stage 3

The purpose of stage 3 was to develop procedures for verification of the competencies decided on in stage 2. This was done by first determining whether the school programs designed in stage two would, in fact, move students toward the identified goals. Descriptions of the programs were sent to five recognized experts in guidance and counseling located in the U.S. The experts were asked to respond to a detailed evaluation form and to participate in an evaluative interview.

In addition, procedures were carried out to determine whether or not the previously identified competencies were actually needed by school counselors for them to be considered "minimally competent." Minimally competent was defined as that level of performance necessary to be effective at the time of entry into the profession. This was done through what was essentially a content validation process. A jury of 20 counselors, counselor educators, pupil personnel directors, and graduate students (all from the state) was selected on the basis of their knowledge in the content areas and asked to rate the knowledge and performance competencies in terms of the degree to which they were needed for minimal competence. All competencies were then grouped into domains. Knowledge competencies were grouped on the basis of similarity of concepts. Performance competencies were grouped on the basis of skill involved. (A complete list of these competencies can be found in Bernknopf, 1978.) These procedures resulted in a list of knowledge and performance competencies falling into ten domains (four knowledge and six performance).

Stage 4

The purpose of stage 4 was to develop a set of procedures for assessment of these competencies. Because the initial plan called for certification to be based on two components—knowledge and performance—separate assessment procedures were designed for each component. Criterion-referenced tests were developed to assess mastery of the knowledge competencies. An item pool capable of producing several test forms was created and a qualifying score related to a minimal level of test performance was developed for each form.

The procedures associated with on-the-job performance were much more complicated than those associated with the assessment of the knowledge competencies. These procedures involved the identification of behavioral indicators for each competency and the development of rating scales. In addition to the development of the instruments, criteria for determining "acceptable" performance had to be derived. Finally, a training procedure had to be developed for data collectors. The data collectors had to be trained to observe counselors at a high level of interrater reliability. The training format required production of sets of protocol materials. Some nine videotapes, two audiotapes, and two planning and two information files were produced to show examples of acceptable and unacceptable performance.

Stage 5

Although the major purpose of the model is certification, a system of supportive supervision was believed to be of equal importance. As such, the goal of stage 5 was to develop six modules that could serve as a vehicle for professional development in the field. The modules were to be used by the individuals themselves or as part of a formal group staff development plan. After completing the module, the participant should be able to successfully demonstrate the skills needed to be certified as competent in the performance area covered by that module.

Stage 6

The sixth stage involved field testing the major components. The field test was designed to assess the model's effectiveness and efficiency. Specifically, answers were sought to three questions:

1. Could counselors be trained in the use of on-the-job rating scales?
2. What were the problems involved in collecting on-the-job performance data?
3. How valuable were the training modules in the development of counselor competencies?

Field testing lasted one year. First, two training workshops were held to train 30 data collectors. These data collectors in turn assessed other counselors to determine their colleagues' areas of deficiency. Training modules were then prescribed to correct the observed weakness. Finally, post-testing was carried out to assess the effectiveness of the training modules.

PROPOSED CERTIFICATION MODEL

A schematic that shows the proposed Georgia Counselor Certification system can be found in Figure 1. This system is consistent with the state's overall model for certification of educational personnel in that it provides a candidate for professional counselor certification the opportunity to demonstrate both knowledge and performance competencies.

Entry into the certification process will require that applicants are eligible for a baccalaureate level teaching certificate and have completed a state-approved fifth-year program in guidance and counseling. Candidates who meet this criterion become provisionally certified by successfully completing the Criterion-Referenced Exam. This certificate is valid for three years and is not renewable. During this period, the candidate has the responsibility for demonstrating minimal competence in the performance areas in an actual on-the-job work setting.

It is the responsibility of the candidate to obtain employment. Once employment has been secured, candidates initiate procedures necessary for demonstration of their performance competencies. By doing so, they enter into a three-stage cycle. In the first stage, data are collected on that area which the counselor seeks to demonstrate his/her competency. These data come from a variety of sources and are funneled through the data collector to the state department for the second stage of the cycle,

FIGURE 1
Proposed Certification Model for Georgia School Counselors

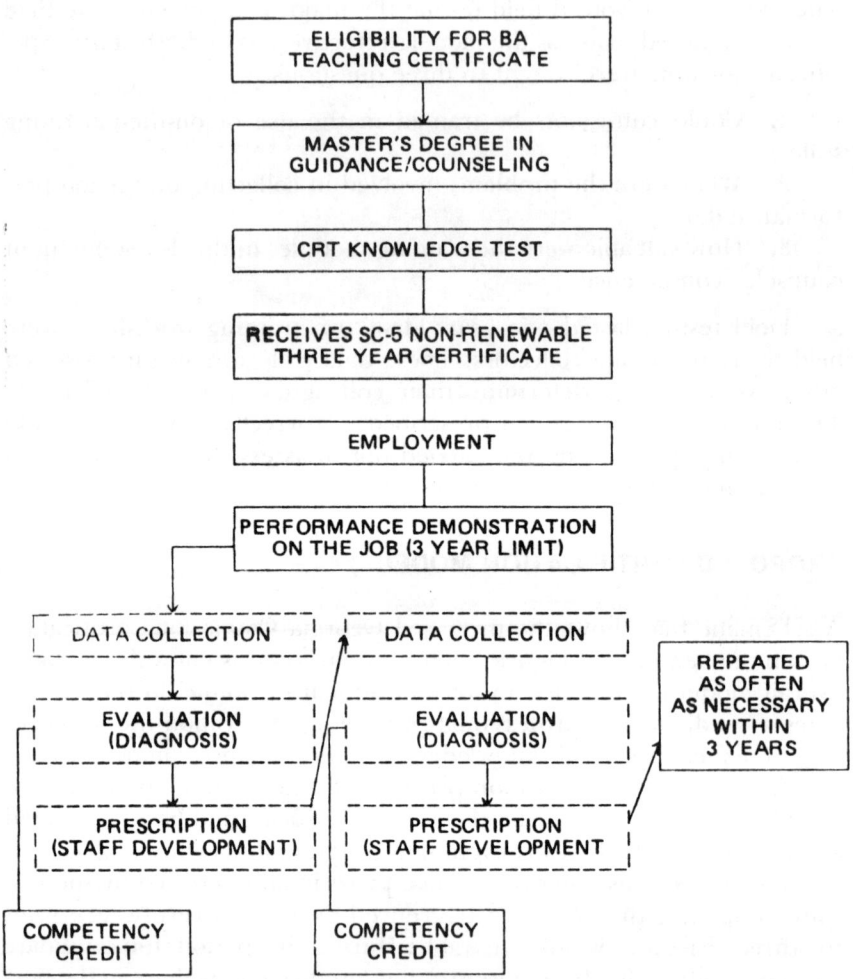

evaluation. State department personnel use predetermined criteria to compare counselor performance with statewide standards. When a candidate has been judged to have successfully demonstrated a performance competency or competencies, they receive competency credit(s). Where a candidate has been judged deficient a diagnosis and a prescription for remediation are provided. This prescription, which provides the candidate with detailed instruction for correcting diagnosed weaknesses, constitutes the third stage in the cycle. This cycle is repeated until the candidate masters all the performance competencies or until the three year period ends. After successfully demonstrating of all the performance competencies, the counselor receives a renewable professional certificate as a school counselor.

The implementation of this model dramatically affects the evaluation and certification of counselors. Evaluation of counselor performance is based on criterion-referenced instruments and techniques. Certification criteria are no longer based on the number of courses passed or grades achieved or general letters of recommendation, but are developed around the degree of performance mastery demonstrated in specific knowledge and skill areas of counseling. If a person is professionally certified, all will be informed as to his specific skills.

REFERENCES

Allen, W. C.; Cady, L. V.; & Drummond, W. H. Performance criteria for education personnel development. *Journal of Teacher Education,* 1969, *20,* 133–135.

Bernknopf, S. Performance based counselor certification. Presented at the annual meeting of the American Personnel and Guidance Association, Washington, D.C., March 1978.

Brammer, L. M., & Springer, H. C. A radical change in counselor education and certification. *The Personnel and Guidance Journal,* 1971, *49,* 803–808.

Chance v. *Board of Examiners.* 496 F. 2d 820 (2d CIR. 1974).

Dent v. *West Virginia* 129 U.S. 114 (1889).

Equal Employment Opportunity Coordinating Council, Staff Committee Draft. *Uniform guidelines on employee selection procedures.* 1974. Federal Register, Vol. 41, No. 136.

Georgia Association of Educators v. *Nix* 407 F. Supp. 1102 (1976).

Goals for Education in Georgia, Atlanta: Division of Planning, Research, and Evaluation, 1970.

Griggs v. *Duke Power* 401 U.S. 424 (1971).

Springer, H. C., & Brammer, L. M. A tentative model to identify elements of the counseling process and parameters of counselor behavior. *Counselor Education and Supervision,* 1971, *11,* 8–16.

Ware, W. B. *Critical issues for competency based education and performance based certification of school counselors: A position paper.* Cleveland, Ga.: Pioneer CESA Guidance Project, Pioneer Cooperative Educational Service Agency, 30528, 1975.

Janet K. Asher examines the interest that counselors have in licensure in private practice of the mental health care system. She also provides extensive discussion on the future role of counselors in a third party payment setting. The outlook seems bleak if counselors are not protected by licensure laws that do not exclude insurance payments for counselors. The article points to the need for a strong licensure movement coupled with a strong certification/registry program.

[From: *American Mental Health Counselors Association Journal,* Vol. 1, No. 1]

The Coming Exclusion of Counselors From the Mental Health Care System

JANET K. ASHER

It is argued that master's and doctoral level counselors face exclusion from the mental health care system because of the trend toward funding by health insurance. Organized psychology is moving to bar doctoral level counselors and counseling education graduates from participation in licensure. Counselors in organized care settings dependent on third-party payment are already losing their jobs to other master's level practitioners with insurance-eligible credentials. Even counselors working in community mental health centers may be affected if present trends in reimbursement policies are not reversed. The present interest in counselor licensure and private practice is examined within this context.

The future role of both master's and doctoral-level counselors in the mental health care system is in doubt. As that system shifts to third-party payments as its funding base, counselors are facing loss of their jobs. Those who have worked in private clinics dependent on health insurance payments have already felt the pinch. Those employed in exempt settings will be next, unless present trends are reversed.

Events are fast overtaking the counseling profession in mental health settings—so fast that it is difficult to remain sanguine about the prospects for success of counseling's eleventh-hour efforts at credentialing and licensure. At the doctoral level, these events signal a parting-of-the-ways between the professionals of counseling and psychology. This writer looks on this parting as an unfortunate, artificial, forced separation rooted in guildism, as both psychology and counseling share common literature, vocabulary, mentors, and treatment approaches.

For years, many doctoral-level counselors have been permitted to assume a dual identity as "back door" psychologists and participate as licensed or certified providers in the mental health care system. Until

---

The author is an Assistant Professor of Psychology and Director of the Rehabilitation Counseling Psychology Program at Towson State University in Baltimore, Maryland.

now, the definition of a psychology doctorate for purposes of licensure/certification has been left up to each individual state psychology board. Some states have been exclusionary, refusing to allow holders of counseling doctorates to sit for examinations. Others have taken a broader view, accepting at least those counseling doctorates that conformed to certain minimal standards. As a result of developments within the past year, however, the 51 state psychology licensing/certification boards are attempting to move toward a uniform exclusionary standard nationwide. The "back door" is closing.

As with so many things in professional life, the basic impetus behind this move to exclude seems to be an economic one. Mental health services are being increasingly covered by health insurance plans. Psychologists have naturally looked on this trend with great hope; it promises a stable funding base for their services. As the prospect of national health insurance has loomed ever nearer over the past few years, the profession has become increasingly preoccupied with pleasing the insurance industry.

Faced with the charge from that industry that psychology harbored a "bottomless pit" of questionable practitioners, the profession undertook a major house-cleaning over the past few years; only the chosen would be permitted to enter the promised land of reimbursement under National Health Insurance. First, organized psychology virtually disowned its master's graduates, refusing to accord them any recognition as qualified psychologists for purposes of licensure or reimbursement eligibility. Next, organized psychology created a National Register of Health Service Providers in Psychology to help the insurance carriers identify practitioners qualified for reimbursement. It was through this process that the psychological establishment became acutely aware of the large number of counseling and other nonpsychology doctoral graduates providing mental health services as licensed psychologists.

The psychological establishment has now turned its attention to examining that deliberately ambiguous phrase, a doctoral degree "primarily psychological" (Wellner 1978)—the educational prerequisite for admission to psychology licensure exams in most states. The American Psychological Association hosted a series of conferences on Education and Credentialing in Psychology (APA 1976, 1977b) with the intent of arriving at a standardized set of educational requirements for entrance into professional practice. Guidelines that emerged from the second of these conferences in June 1977 were in a large measure adopted by the American Association of State Psychology Boards in August 1977.

Before examining these guidelines, let us first consider the motives that underlie them. In a position paper prepared for the 1977 Credentialing Conference, the principal architect of this movement to standardize, and president of the American Association of State Psychology Boards (AASPB), Morton Berger, called for a purge of what he called "not-psychology" doctorates—degrees from training programs that he labeled "third-rate" (Berger 1977, p. 5). What is "not-psychology"? According to Berger, the difference between psychology and "not-psychology" is something akin to the difference between matter and antimatter in science fiction:

> Not-psychology programs come in various shapes, sizes and orientations. Some examples: counselor education, counseling, guidance, pupil personnel services, organizational behavior, human sexuality, . . . community mental health, behavioral science, psychotherapy, psychoanalysis, rehabilitation counseling, etc. etc. (Berger 1977, p. 4)

Berger stated that "somehow" these "not-psychology" doctorate-holders manage to pass a psychology licensing examination—"on the second or third try"—and then melt into the ranks of psychologists, working for employers who "may begin to notice that the caliber of psychologist coming to their agencies appears to be deteriorating of late" (Berger 1977, p. 5).

Berger accused colleges of education throughout the country of hiring a few psychologists and starting "not-psychology" graduate programs with easy admission standards, which hide their low quality under the label of being "innovative."

Berger added that there are "at least an equal number of not-psychologists competing with psychologists for jobs" (Berger 1977, p. 6), and argued that the market is being flooded with incompetent "not-psychologists " grabbing up jobs that should go to real, true-blue psychologists. It was ideas such as these that inspired the guidelines for credentialing of psychologists that the AASPB is now championing.

The guidelines state that a program designed to train professional psychologists must clearly identify itself as a psychology program. Programs in counseling, counselor education, and the like would not qualify unless they officially relabeled themselves "counseling psychology," an unlikely eventuality in universities that already have a counseling psychology program in a psychology department.

The guidelines, as adopted by the AASPB, also state that students must have a minimum of six or more graduate semester hours in the following four substantive content areas: (1) biological bases of behavior, (2) cognitive-affective bases of behavior, (3) social bases of behavior, and (4) individual differences (Wellner 1978, p. 31). Neither the social bases of behavior (e.g., group process, social psychology) nor the individual differences area (e.g., abnormal psychology, personality) would seem to pose problems for present counseling program graduates. Many, however, probably would wash out in the cognitive-affective bases of behavior area (e.g., motivation, emotion, and cognition), and certainly in the biological bases of behavior area (physiological psychology, comparative psychology, neuropsychology, and psychopharmacology).

While such guidelines may have merit in that they clear up much of the prevailing confusion about what constitutes a psychology doctorate, it must be remembered that these are guidelines with an exclusionary intent. In many states, if doctoral-level counselor education is found lacking, candidates are only permitted to take two courses postdoctorally to make up for deficits. If three courses are lacking, then there is nothing that can be done to ever be licensed, short of going through another doctoral program. Meanwhile, organized psychology has already promulgated standards for "retreading" experimentalists into clinicians.

For a document ostensibly addressed to the training of helping professionals, the new guidelines seem unduly preoccupied with tangentially related coursework. One can only suspect that licensure is being used not to protect the public but to secure the interests of the professional establishment.

Such good old-fashioned guildism might not be so reprehensible were the public not in great need of more trained professionals. National Institute of Mental Health biometricians (Regier, Goldberg, & Taube 1977) estimate that, over the course of a year, 15 percent of the population suffers from a bona fide mental disorder. They are not talking about "problems of living," which afflict up to 80 percent of us, but about serious neurosis, psychosis, depression, and so forth. While 32 million people obviously need help, according to the NIMH data, no more than about three percent of Americans, or about six and one-half million, are actually seen by mental health specialists each year. Acutely aware of the need for insurance-eligible providers, NIMH has proposed training primary care physicians and nurses to help fill this gaping hole in the mental health services system.

Meanwhile, organized psychology seems bent on curtailing the number of eligible providers. The numbers of young doctoral-level counseling professionals potentially excluded from psychology licensure by the new guidelines are substantial. According to the National Research Council (Harmon 1977), 693 counseling doctorates were awarded by schools of education in 1976, compared to only 266 in counseling psychology by psychology departments. Some portion of these 693 counseling doctorates would probably meet the guidelines criteria, but not very many. About half of the 20 or so programs accredited by the APA in counseling psychology are housed in schools of education. Perhaps they fit the adopted model. But simply by scanning *Graduate Study in Psychology 1977-78* (APA 1977a) one can find about two dozen other doctoral counseling programs that would not qualify on the basis of their titles alone.

What will be the fate of doctoral-level counselors not yet licensed or certified as psychologists? Events in California suggest one possible outcome (Duricka 1977). Until last summer, the wording of California psychology licensure law did not explicitly state that a doctorate in counseling qualified an applicant for admission to the exam. Rather, the law read "counseling psychology." The state board had promulgated guidelines based on a strict constructionist interpretation of "counseling psychology," excluding graduates of counseling programs. Yet prestigious universities in that state, such as the University of California at Berkeley and Stanford, offered doctorates in counseling. With backing from their departments, doctoral-level counselors engaged in political action for more than two years, writing letters to, and visiting legislators and members of the state psychology examining committee. Last summer these efforts paid off. Counselors succeeded in having an amendment passed that deleted the word "psychology" from "counseling psychology," thus explicitly mandating that counseling doctorates be considered.

Whatever course of action counselors chose, they should not expect any support from within organized psychology. APA's Division 17 (counseling psychology) met with the AASPB more than a year ago and agreed on a position statement identifying counseling psychology as a "substantive specialty area of practice distinguished from related disciplines such as counseling and guidance, counselor education and counseling." (APA 1977b, p. 10) A proposal, endorsed by the AASPB, to establish a National Commission for Education and Credentialing in Psychology, which would designate psychology training programs as set forth in the guidelines, is soon to be implemented.

For now, let us assume that the "back door" does close, and many young doctoral counselors are forced to cast their lot with their master's level colleagues and make a go of it on their own—as counselors. What are their prospects in the evolving mental health care system?

The long-term outlook seems bleak if present trends continue. Mental health services are moving inexorably toward funding by health insurance. Third-party payers have traditionally not reimbursed for the services of counselors (as counselors). The only exception is the marriage and family counseling benefit under CHAMPUS (Civilian Health and Medical Program of the Uniformed Services), and even that narrowly escaped being cut as "nonmedical" a few years ago. The newly proclaimed mental health counseling profession will have to buck a lot of precedent. It must somehow convince government and insurance carriers that counseling is suddenly not an education or social service field, but a bona fide health profession—and this at a time when spiraling health care costs are often cited as justification for limiting the pool of reimbursable health service providers.

Some counselors still take comfort in the belief that as long as they forego private practice and work in organized settings, such as community mental health centers, they will be safe from the insurance pinch. Indeed, the network of federally subsidized community mental health centers has become a job haven for thousands of counselors and other noncore professionals (National Institute of Mental Health 1977, p. 46). But what will happen when these centers are weaned from the federal teat and have to capture third-party payments to survive? If events follow the pattern we are now witnessing in private organized care systems, they will bode ill for counselors. Private mental health clinics and other agencies that depend on the health insurance dollar have been laying off counselors and hiring people with insurance-eligible credentials—usually Masters of Social Work. It isn't that counselors can't do the work; they simply can't bring in the bucks.

Insurance carriers reimburse for outpatient mental health care delivered in organized settings only through a licensed core professional. Services provided by anyone other than a fully credentialed psychiatrist, psychologist, psychiatric social worker, or psychiatric nurse are not covered.

The best hope in sight for counselors in organized settings is contained in a recommendation of the President's Commission on Mental Health report released in April (President's Commission on Mental Health 1978, p. 440). Counselors were recognized as an "other allied" mental health profession, a category that accounts for 12 percent of the full-time equivalent staff in mental health facilities.

The President's Commission proposed that organized care systems be reimbursed directly rather than through a professional, provided that all care is delivered "under the direct clinical supervision of a physician, psychologist, social worker or nurse" (President's Commission on Mental Health 1978, p. 30). This would open up insurance coverage for the services of noncore professionals. Outside of organized settings the commission recommended that only the four core professionals be reimbursed directly as private practitioners.

This scheme might not seem magnanimous in lumping doctoral and master's level counselors together with paraprofessionals and subordinating them to master's level social workers and nurses. But at least it would provide a funding base for counselors that existing reimbursement policies do not afford. The threat of total exclusion is the reality counselors must reckon with. Remember, the Commission's recommendation is just that—a proposal. Unfortunately, the track records of past mental health commission recommendations are not very encouraging.

An appreciation of the counselor's plight in organized care settings affords a sober view of the current interest in counselor licensure, certification, and private practice. The American Personnel and Guidance Association has published a series of *Licensure Commission Action Packets* (APGA 1977) designed to aid state associations in their licensing efforts. The definitions they contain for "the practice of counseling" and "counseling procedures" are broad and certainly cast counselors as mental health providers.

Similarly, the national certification effort of the American Mental Health Counselors Association embraces a broad definition of practice. Yet, while necessary, licensure or certification of counselors will not be sufficient to assure a firm funding base for counselors' services in the future mental health care system. Moreover, because gaining legal recognition involves politics and interprofessional turf wars, there is always the danger that important territory will be forfeited in the bargaining process.

Virginia has become the first state to license "personnel and guidance" counselors. An early draft of the licensure bill was full of "don'ts" for counselors, most of them demanded by organized psychology. The final draft also contains some "don'ts," such as prohibiting counselors from administering projective tests. Does the Virginia law set a worthy precedent for counseling to follow in other states? That depends on one's expectations. It does help the public identify a qualified practitioner by setting standards. It does legalize private practice. It probably improves the status of the profession. It has not, however, captured insurance payments for counselors.

What we are left with is a gut sense of injustice. Why should counselors, and, for that matter, master's level psychologists, be accorded lower status than master's level clinical social workers and nurses?

Despite historical allegiances to different models, which have long since blurred, each profession now does essentially the same kind of work in mental health settings. It boils down to a matter of political power. Historically, the younger guilds have won a piece of the mental health action only after years of skirmishing with the psychiatric establishment in state legislatures and in Congress.

Psychologists, the one-time underdogs, have turned their battle-hardened lobbying prowess against counselors, the new underdogs. To have a fighting chance, the mental health counseling movement will have to champion the cause of disenfranchised master's level psychologists as well as counselors and cast off the shroud of naivete that has blinded it to the financial realities of its existence.

REFERENCES

American Psychological Association. *Graduate study in psychology 1977-78*. Washington D. C.: Author, 1977a.

American Psychological Association. *Sourcebook II: Education & credentialing in psychology, June 4-5 1977*. Washington, D. C.: Author, 1977b.

American Psychological Association Committee on State Legislation. *A model for state legislation affecting the practice of psychology*. Washington D. C.: American Psychological Association, 1975.

Berger, M. The vital interests of academic psychology, professional psychology and state licensing boards: Are they in conflict? (Or whose ox is being gored?). In *Sourcebook II: Education & credentialing in psychology*. Washington D. C.: American Psychological Association, 1977.

Duricka, P. Licensure grievances will be aired. *Guidepost*, May 1977, pp. 2-3.

Harmon, L. Science Commission on Human Resources, National Research Council, National Academy of Sciences. Personal communication, January 1978.

Licensure Commission Action Packet. Washington D. C.: American Personnel and Guidance Association, 1977.

National Institute of Mental Health. *Community mental health centers: The federal investment*. Washington, D. C.: Department of Health, Education, and Welfare, November 1977.

President's Commission on Mental Health. *Report to the President, Vol. I*. Washington D. C.: Government Printing Office, 1978.

Regier, D. A.; Goldberg, I.; & Taube, C. The de facto U.S. mental health services system: A public health perspective. *American Journal of Psychiatry* (in press).

Wellner, A. (Ed.). *Education and credentialing in psychology*. Washington, D. C.: American Psychological Association, 1978.

APPENDIX A

Alabama, Arkansas, and Virginia Counselor Licensure Laws

Alabama Licensure Law

H. 347

Enrolled, An Act,

To regulate the private practice of counselors in Alabama; to create a Board of Examiners in Counseling; to prescribe the duties and powers of said Board; to provide for the licensure of counselors and the certification of counselor associates; to fix penalties for the violation of this Act; to impose licensure and certification fees and to provide for the use of funds received.

BE IT ENACTED BY THE LEGISLATURE OF ALABAMA:

Section 1. There is hereby created a Board to be known as the Alabama Board of Examiners in Counseling composed of seven (7) members, appointed by the Governor of this State within sixty (60) days after the effective date of this Act, in the manner and for the term of office as hereinafter provided. Said Board shall perform such duties and have such powers as the Act prescribes and confers upon it.

Section 2. As used in this Act, unless the context requires a different meaning:

(a) "Licensed Professional Counselor" shall mean any person who holds himself out to the public by any title or description of services incorporating the words "Licensed Professional Counselor" or "Licensed Counselor"; and who offers to render professional counseling services in private practice to individuals, groups, organizations, corporations, institutions, government agencies, or the general public for a fee, monetary or otherwise, implying that he is licensed and trained, experienced, or expert in counseling, and who holds a current, valid license to engage in the private practice of counseling, with the exception of those practitioners listed in Section 3 of this Act.

(b) "Counselor Associate" shall mean any person that has been certified by the Board to offer counseling services as defined in the Act while under the supervision of a licensed professional counselor.

(c) "Board" shall mean the Alabama Board of Examiners in Counseling.

(d) "Counseling Services" shall mean those acts and behaviors coming within the "Practice of Counseling" as defined in this Act.

(e) The "Private Practice of Counseling" shall mean rendering or offering to render to individuals, groups, organizations, or the general public counseling services, in private practice, for a fee, monetary or otherwise, involving the application of principles, methods, or procedures of the counseling profession which include, but are not restricted to:

1. "Counseling" which means assisting an individual, through the counseling relationship, to develop understanding of personal problems, to define goals, and to plan action reflecting his or her interests, abilities, aptitudes, and needs as these are related to personal-social concerns, education progress, and occupations and careers.

2. "Appraisal activities" which means selecting, administering, scoring, and interpreting instruments designed to assess an individual's aptitudes, attitudes, abilities, achievements, interests, and personal characteristics, but shall not include the use of projective techniques in the assessment of personality.

3. "Counseling, guidance and personnel consulting" which means interpreting or reporting upon scientific fact or theory in counseing, guidance, and personnel services to provide assistance in solving some current or potential problems of individuals, groups, or organizations.

4. "Referral activities" which means the evaluating of data to identify problems and to determine advisability of referral to other specialists.

5. "Research activities" which means the designing, conducting, and interpreting of research with human subjects.

Section 3. Nothing in this Act shall be construed to apply to:

(a) The activities, services, and use of an official title on the part of a person employed as a counselor or by any federal, state, county, or municipal agency; public or private educational institution; medical personnel in a clinic; law practice; or licensed private employment agencies, provided such persons are performing counseling or counseling-related activities within the scope of their employment.

(b) The activities and services of a student, intern, or trainee in counseling pursuing a course of study in counseling in a regionally accredited institution of higher learning or training institution, if these activities and services constitute a part of the supervised course of study, provided that such person be designated a "counselor intern."

(c) The activities and services of a nonresident person rendered not more than thirty (30) days during any year, provided such person is duly authorized to perform such activities and services under the laws of the state or county of his residence.

(d) The activities and services of qualified members of other professions, such as physicians, psychologists, psychoanalysts, registered nurses, social workers, or recognized religious practitioners performing counseling consistent with the laws of the state, their training, and any code of ethics of their professions, provided they do not represent themselves by any title or description in the manner prescribed in Section 2 of this Act.

(e) The activities, services, titles and descriptions of qualified members of the law profession.

(f) The activities, services, titles and descriptions of persons employed, as professionals or as volunteers, in the practice of counseling for public and private non-profit organizations or charities.

Nothing in this Act shall be construed as permitting counselors licensed under this act to administer or prescribe drugs, or in any manner engage in the practice of medicine as defined by the laws of this State.

Nothing in this Act shall be construed as permitting a counselor licensed under this Act to represent himself in any manner to the public as an attorney as defined by the laws of this State.

Nothing in this Act shall be construed as permitting a counselor licensed under this Act to represent himself in any manner to the public as a psychologist as defined by the laws of this State.

Lecturers from any school, college, agency or training institution may utilize an academic or research title when invited to present lectures to institutions or organizations.

Section 4. There is hereby created an Alabama Board of Examiners in Counseling hereinafter referred to as the Board to consist of seven (7) members who shall be appointed by the Governor under the conditions hereinafter set forth.

Within thirty (30) days from the effective date of this Act, the Executive Committee of the Alabama Personnel and Guidance Association shall submit to the Governor a list of qualified candidates for the Board; said list shall contain names of at least four (4) citizens from the general public; four (4) qualified counselor educators; and six (6) qualified practicing counselors from which the Governor, within sixty (60) days, will select the Board consisting of two (2) citizens from the general public; two (2) counselor educators; and three (3) counselors in private practice. A minimum of one of those counselors must be a marriage and family counselor certified by American Association of Marriage and Family Therapists.

The initial appointments to the Board shall be for the following terms: The term of two (2) members is one (1) year, the term of two (2) members is two (2) years, the term of three (3) members is three (3) years.

The professional membership of the Board authorized under this section shall be licensed under this Act, except that the initial professional members shall be members who have been rendering the private practice of counseling services for at least one (1) year, or who have been giving instruction in counseling in a regionally accredited institution of higher learning for at least three (3) years.

Said Board shall perform such duties and exercise such powers as this Act prescribes and confers upon it. No member of the Board shall be liable to civil action for any act performed in good faith for the performance of his duty as set forth in this act.

Board members shall be ineligible for reappointment for a period of three (3) years following completion of their terms. Subsequent appointments to the Board shall be made by the Governor in the following manner: Not later than October 1 of each year the Executive Committee of the Alabama Personnel and Guidance Association shall submit to the Governor the names of two (2) qualified candidates for the position on the Board to be vacated by reason of expiration of term of office. From the two (2) candidates the Governor shall appoint one (1) member not later than January 1 to serve on the Board for a term of five (5) years). Other vacancies occurring in the Board shall be filled for the unexpired term by appointment of the Governor from two (2) candidates for each such vacancy submitted within thirty (30) days after the vacancy occurs by the Executive Committee of the Alabama Personnel and Guidance Association. Such appointments shall be made within thirty (30) days after the candidates' names have been submitted. Any Board members may be removed by the Governor, after notice and hearing, for incompetence, neglect of duty, malfeasance in office, or moral turpitude. Composition of the Board shall always consist of two (2) citizens, two (2) counselor educators, and three (3) counselors in private practice. Appointments to the Board shall represent the difference in gender, racial, and ethnic origins and the different levels of graduate and professional degrees and specialty represented in the Alabama Personnel and Guidance Association, though not all such differences necessarily will be reflected at the same time in Board membership. A college or university shall have one representative, faculty or staff, as a member of the Board at any one time.

Immediately and before entering public duties of said office, the members of the Board shall take the Constitutional oath of office and shall file same in the office of the Governor, who upon receiving said oath of office shall issue to each member a certificate of appointment. The Board shall have available for the Governor or his representative detailed reports on proceedings and shall make annual reports in such form as required by the Governor.

Section 5. The Board shall elect annually a Chairman and a Vice Chairman. Each member shall receive all necessary expenses incident to holding meetings plus an honorarium approved by the Governor provided, however, that such expenses shall in no case exceed funds available to the Board. The Board shall hold at least one (1) regular meeting each year. Additional meetings may be held at the discretion of the Chairman or at the written request of any three (3) members of the Board. Said Board shall adopt a seal which must be affixed to all licenses and certificates issued by the Board. The Board shall from time to time adopt such rules, and regulations, as they may deem necessary for the performance of their duties. Four (4) members of the Board shall be empowered to accept grants from foundations and institutions to carry on its functions.

Section 6. All fees from applicants seeking licensing or certification for private practice under this Act, and all license, certificate, or renewal fees received under this Act shall be paid to said Board. No part of any fee shall be returnable under any conditions other than failure of the Board to hold examinations at the time originally announced, whereupon the entire fee may be returned at the option of the candidate. All fees collected in this manner plus renewal fees and all gifts or grants shall be deposited in the State Treasury to the credit of the Board. There is hereby appropriated from the Treasury funds to the credit of said Board to be used for printing, travel expenses of the Board, and for other necessary expenses such as are necessary to the carrying out of the provisions of this Act. Expenses shall be paid under the written direction of the Chairman of the Board in accordance with normal State procedure.

The Board is required to charge an application fee to be determined by the Board.

Every licensed professional counselor or certified counselor associate engaging in private practice in this state is required to pay biennially to the Board during the month of July a renewal fee to be determined by the Board. The Chairman thereupon shall issue a document renewing his license or certificate for a term of two (2) years. The license or certificate of any counselor who fails to have his license or certificate renewed biennially during the month of July shall lapse; the failure to renew said license or certificate, however, shall not deprive said counselor or counselor associate of the right of renewal thereafter. Such lapsed license or certificate may be renewed within a period of two (2) years after such upon payment of fees in arrears, or thereafter, upon payment of a renewal fee to be determined by the Board.

Section 7. The Board shall issue a license as a licensed professional counselor to each applicant who files an application upon a form and in such a manner as the Board prescribes, accompanied by such fee as is required in this Act, and who furnishes satisfactory evidence of the following to the Board:

(a) the applicant is at least nineteen (19) years of age;
(b) the applicant is a citizen of the United States or has declared his intention

to become a citizen. A statement by the applicant under oath that he is a citizen or that he intends to apply for citizenship when he becomes eligible to make such application, is sufficient proof of compliance with this requirement;

(c) the applicant is of good moral character;

(d) the applicant resides in the State of Alabama;

(e) the applicant is not in violation of any of the provisions of this Act and the rules and regulations adopted hereunder;

(f) the applicant has received a master's degree from a regionally accredited institution of higher learning which is primarily professional counseling in content based on not less than thirty (30) graduate semester hours, or the substantial equivalent in both subject matter and extent of training. The Board shall use the standards of nationally recognized professional counseling associations as guides in establishing the standards for counselor licensure.

(g) the applicant has three (3) years of supervised full-time experience in professional counseling acceptable to the Board, one (1) year of which may be obtained prior to the granting of the master's degree. An applicant may subtract one (1) year of the required professional experience for every fifteen (15) graduate semester hours obtained beyond the master's degree, provided that such hours are clearly related to the field of professional counseling and are acceptable to the Board. However, in no case may the applicant have less than one (1) year of required professional experience;

(h) the applicant demonstrates competence in professional counseling by passing an examination, written, oral, or situational, or all three (3), as the Board will prescribe. A specialty designation may be added upon demonstration to the Board that the applicant has met the recognized minimum standards as established by nationally recognized certification agencies. Upon successful passage of an examination, written, oral, or situational, or all three (3), and upon receipt of credentials from certifying agencies the Board may, by a majority of the Board members present and voting, consider such credentials adequate evidence of professional competence and recommend to the Chairman of the Board that a license with appropriate specialty designation, if any, be approved. A professional counselor cannot claim or advertise a counseling specialty unless the qualifications of that specialty have been met and have been approved by the Board.

Section 8. The Board shall issue a certificate as a counselor associate to each applicant who files an application upon a form and in such manner as the Board prescribes accompanied by such fees as are required by this Act, and who furnishes satisfactory evidence of the following to the Board:

(a) the applicant has complied with provisions outlined in Section 7(a), (b), (c), (d), and (e) of this Act;

(b) the applicant has received a master's degree from a regionally accredited institution of higher learning based on a program of studies which is primarily professional counseling in content, or the substantial equivalent in both subject matter and extent of training. The counselor associate may not practice without direct supervision by a licensed professional counselor. The plan for supervision of the counselor associate is to be approved by the Board prior to any actual performance of counseling on the part of the counselor associate;

(c) any certified counselor associate after meeting the requirements specified in Section 7(g) and 7(h) may petition the Board for licensure as a professional counselor.

Section 9. After investigation of the application and other evidence submitted, the Board shall not less than thirty (30) days prior to the examination, notify each applicant that the application and evidence submitted is satisfactory and accepted or unsatisfactory and rejected. If rejected, said notice shall state the reasons for such rejection.

Section 10. The place of examination shall be designated in advance by the Board, and such examination shall be given annually at such time and place and under the supervision as the Board may determine, and specifically at such other times as in the opinion of the Board the number of applicants warrants.

Section 11. The examination shall require that the applicant demonstrate his knowledge and application thereof in those areas deemed relevant to his specialty and those services he intends to offer to the public.

Section 12. The Board shall grade the examination and recommend to the Chairman action to be taken. To insure impartiality, written examination documents shall be identified by number, and no paper shall be marked in the name of any applicant but shall be anonymously graded by the Board. In the event an applicant fails to receive a passing grade on the entire examination, he may reapply and shall be allowed to take a subsequent examination. An applicant who has failed two (2) successive examinations may not reapply until after two (2) years from the date of the last examination, or has satisfactorily completed fifteen (15) graduate semester hours in the applicant's weakest portion of the examination.

Section 13. The Board is required to preserve examination materials and an accurate transcript of the questions and answers to an examination, and the grade assigned to each answer thereof, as part of its records for a period of two (2) years following the date of examination.

Section 14. Counselors licensed as a professional counselor or certified as a counselor associate by the Board shall be required to submit biennially at the time of renewal a license or certificate renewal fee to be established by the Board. No license or certificate shall be renewed unless the renewal request is accompanied by evidence satisfactory to the Board of the completion during the previous twenty-four (24) months of relevant professional and continued educational experience. The relevant experience required shall be sent in writing to all licensed and certified counselors one(1) year prior to the renewal dates.

If any professional counselor or counselor associate duly licensed or certified under this Act, by virtue of additional training and experience, is qualified to practice in a specialty other than that for which he was deemed competent at the time of initial licensing, or certification, and wishes to offer such service under the provisions of this Act, he is required to submit at the time of annual renewal of licenses or certificates, additional credentials and he is to be given the opportunity to demonstrate his knowledge and application thereof in areas deemed relevant to his specialty. This procedure is considered a necessary part of the renewal process. No charge in addition to the renewal fee is levied.

Section 15. Upon application accompanied by fee the Board is authorized to issue a license or certificate to any person who furnishes upon a form and in such manner as the Board prescribes, evidence satisfactory to the Board that he is licensed as a professional counselor or certified as a counselor associate by another state, territorial possession of the United States, District of Columbia or

Commonwealth of Puerto Rico if the requirements for such licensure or certification are substantially equivalent to those of this Act.

Section 16. The Board by a majority of the Board members present and voting is authorized to withhold, deny, revoke or suspend any license or certificate issued or applied for in accordance with the provisions of this Act or otherwise discipline a licensed professional counselor or certified counselor associate upon proof by proper hearing that the applicant, licensed professional counselor or certified counselor associate:

(a) has been convicted, within or without the jurisdiction of this state, of a felony or any offense involving moral turpitude, the record of conviction being conclusive evidence thereof;

(b) has violated the current code of ethics adopted by the Board;

(c) is using any narcotic or any alcoholic beverage to an extent or in a manner dangerous to any other person or the public, or to an extent that such impairs his ability to perform the work of a professional counselor or counselor associate with safety to the public;

(d) has impersonated another person holding a professional counselor license or counselor associate certificate or allowed another person to use his license or certificate;

(e) has used fraud or deception in applying for a license or certificate or in taking an examination provided for in this Act;

(f) has allowed his name or license or certificate issued under this Act to be used in connection with any person or persons who perform counseling services in private practice outside the area of their training, experience or competence;

(g) is legally adjudicated mentally incompetent, the record of such adjudication being conclusive evidence thereof; or

(h) has willfully or negligently violated any of the provisions of this Act.

Notice of denial, revocation, suspension, or disciplinary action is required to be sent by registered mail or personal service setting forth the particular reasons for the proposed action and fixing a date not less than thirty (30) days nor more than sixty (60) days from the date of such mailing or such service, at which time the applicant, licentiate or associate shall be given an opportunity for a prompt and fair hearing. The written notice shall be sent to the person's last known address, but the nonappearance of the person shall not prevent such a hearing. The hearing shall be conducted by the Board by means of sworn, recorded testimony. Parties have the right to be represented by counsel and to conduct cross-examination of witnesses.

On the basis of any hearing or upon default of applicant, licentiate, or associate, the Board shall make a determination specifying its findings of fact and conclusions of law. A copy of such determination shall be sent by registered mail or served personally upon the applicant, licentiate, or associate. The decision of the Board denying, revoking, or suspending the license or certificate shall become final thirty (30) days after so mailed or served unless within said period the applicant, licentiate, or associate appeals the decision to the courts of this State in the same manner and subject to the same powers and conditions as now provided by law in regard to rulings, orders and findings of other quasi-judicial bodies in Alabama, where not otherwise specifically provided. No such appeal while pending appropriate court action shall supersede such denial, revocation or suspension. All proceedings and evidence, together with exhibits presented at such hearings before the Board in the event of appeal, are admissible in evidence in said court.

Every order and judgment of the Board shall take effect immediately on its promulgation unless the Board in such order or judgment fixes a probationary period for applicant, licentiate, or associate. Such order and judgment shall continue in effect unless upon appeal the courts by proper order or decree terminate it earlier. The Board may make public its order and judgments in such manner and form as it deems proper.

The Board is authorized to suspend the license of a professional counselor or the certificate of a counselor associate for a period of not exceeding one (1) year. At the end of this period, the Board is required to reevaluate the suspension and may recommend to the Chairman the reinstatement of revocation of the license or certificate. A person whose license or certificate has been revoked under the provisions of this section may apply for reinstatement after a period of not less than three (3) years from the date such denial or revocation is legally effective. The Board may, upon favorable action by a majority of the Board members present and voting, recommend such reinstatement.

Section 17. When it shall appear to the Board that any person has engaged or is about to engage in any act or practice constituting a violation of any provision of this act or any rule or order hereunder, the Board in its discretion and in its own name may bring an action in any court of competent jurisdiction to enjoin such acts or practices, and to enforce compliance with this act or any rule or order hereunder, regardless of whether criminal proceedings have been or may be instituted. Upon a proper showing, a permanent or temporary injunction, restraining order, or writ of mandamus shall be granted.

Within one (1) year from the effective date of this Act, if any person shall hold himself out to the public as a licensed professional counselor or use any title or description, as prescribed in Section 2(a) and 2(b), or if any person for a fee, monetary or otherwise shall engage in the "Private Practice of Counseling," as prescribed in Section 2(e), subsections 1, 2, 3, 4, 5, and shall not then possess in full force and virtue a valid license to engage in private practice as a professional counselor under the provisions of this Act, he shall be fined not less than one hundred dollars ($100.00) nor more than five hundred dollars ($500.00).

The Board and its members shall assist prosecuting officers in the enforcement of this Act, and it shall be the duty of this Board and its members to furnish the proper prosecuting officers with such evidence as it or they may ascertain to assist them in the prosecution of any violation of this act, and the Board is authorized for such purposes to make such reasonable expenditures from the funds of the Board as it may deem necessary to ascertain and furnish such evidence. The Attorney General of the State shall be the attorney of the Board, but the Board may in its discretion employ other counsel. It shall be the duty of the district attorney of the judicial circuit wherein any offense is committed to prosecute violations of this Act.

The Alabama Board of Examiners in Counseling shall have authority to administer oaths, to summon witnesses, and to take testimony in all matters relating to its duties. Said Board shall be the sole agency in this state empowered to certify concerning competence in the private practice of counseling, and the sole Board empowered to license for the private practice of counseling.

The Alabama Board of Examiners in Counseling shall license to engage in private practice all persons who shall present satisfactory evidence of attainments and qualifications under provisions of this Act and the rules and regulations of the Board. Such licensure shall be signed by the Chairman of the Board of Examiners in Counseling under the Board's adopted seal.

Section 18. For the purpose of this Act, the confidential relations and communications between licensed professional counselor or certified counselor associate and client are placed upon the same basis as those provided by law between attorney and client, and nothing in this Act shall be construed to require any such privileged communication to be disclosed.

Section 19. The Alabama Board of Examiners in Counseling shall adopt a Code of Ethics to govern appropriate practice or behavior as referred to in Section 16 and Section 17 and shall file such code with the Secretary of State within thirty (30) days prior to effective date of such code.

Section 20. The provisions of this Act are severable. If any part of the Act is declared invalid or unconstitutional, such delcaration shall not affect the part which remains.

Section 21. All laws or parts of laws which conflict with this Act are hereby repealed.

Section 22. For a period of one year from the effective date of this Act the Board shall waive the requirements of Section 7(f), 7(g), and 7(h), and shall grant the appropriate license upon payment of the required fee to any person submitting an application for licensure to the Board who is qualified by experience to practice counseling, and who has engaged in such private practice of counseling as of the effective date of this Act.

Section 23. This Act shall become effective immediately upon its passage and approval by the Governor, or upon its otherwise becoming a law.

Speaker of the House of Representatives

President and Presiding Officer of the Senate

House of Representatives:

I hereby certifiy that the within Act originated in and was passed by the House June 14, 1979, as amended.

John W. Pemberton, Clerk

Senate:

Approved: July 18, 1979

Governor

Arkansas Licensure Law

ACT 593 of 1979

An act to provide for the regulation of the practice of counseling; to create a board of examiners in counseling and prescribe the powers and duties of the board; to provide for the examination and licensure of counselors; and for other purposes.

BE IT ENACTED BY THE GENERAL ASSEMBLY OF THE STATE OF ARKANSAS:

SECTION 1. Statement of Policy and Purpose. It is declared to be the policy of this State that activities of those persons who render service to the public in the counseling area and use the title Licensed Professional Counsel or Licensed Associate Counselor should be regulated for the protection of public health, safety, and welfare. Therefore, it is the purpose and intent of this Act to provide for the regulation of the practice of counseling in the State of Arkansas; to create a Board of Examiners in Counseling, and prescribe the duties and powers of said Board; to provide for the examination and licensure of counselors, fix penalties for the violation of this Act; and to impose license fees and provide for the use of funds derived therefrom. It is also the purpose of this Act to provide for the regulation of the use of the titles Licensed Professional Counselor and Licensed Associate Counselor for those who offer counseling services to the public.

SECTION 2. Board of Examiners in Counseling Created. There is hereby created a Board to be known as the Arkansas Board of Examiners in Counseling composed of seven (7) members, appointed by the Governor of this State within sixty (60) days after the effective date of this Act, in the manner and for the term of office as hereinafter provided. Said Board shall perform such duties and have such powers as the Act prescribed and confers upon it.

SECTION 3. Definitions. As used in this Act, unless the context requires a different meaning, these definitions apply:

(a) "Licensed Professional Counselor" shall mean any person who holds himself or herself out to the public by any title or description of services incorporating the words Licensed Professional Counselor; and who offers to render counseling services to individuals, groups, organizations, corporations, institutions, government agencies, or the general public for monetary remuneration or otherwise, implying that he or she is licensed, trained, experienced, and/or expert in counseling, and who holds a current, valid license to practice counseling, with the exception of those professions listed in Section 15 of this Act.

(b) "Licensed Associate Counselor" shall mean any person who holds himself or herself out to the public by any title or description of services incorporating the words Licensed Associate Counselor; and who offers to render counseling services to individuals, groups, organizations, corporations, institutions, government agencies, or the general public for monetary remuneration or otherwise implying that he or she is licensed, trained, experienced, and/or expert in counseling, and who holds a current, valid license to practice counseling, under the supervision of a duly licensed professional counselor. Nothing in this definition shall be construed to include those professions excluded by Section 15 of this Act.

(c) "Board" shall mean the Arkansas Board of Examiners in Counseling whose members shall be appointed by the Governor of the State of Arkansas in accordance with the provisions of Section 5 of this Act.

(d) "Counseling Services" shall mean those acts and behaviors coming within the "Practice of Counseling" as defined in this Act.

(e) "Practice of Counseling" shall mean rendering or offering to render to individuals, groups, organizations or the general public any service involving the application of principles, methods, or procedures of the counseling profession which include but are not restricted to:

(1) "Counseling" which means assisting an individual or groups, through the counseling relationship, to develop understandings of personal problems to define goals, and to plan action reflecting his or her interests, abilities, aptitudes, and needs as these are related to personal-social concerns, educational progress, and occupations and careers.

(2) "Appraisal activities" which means selecting, administering, scoring, and interpreting instruments designed to assess an individual's aptitudes, attitudes, abilities, achievements, interests, and personal characteristics, but shall not include the use of projective techniques in the assessment personality.

(3) "Consulting" which means interpreting or reporting scientific fact or theory to provide assistance in solving current or potential problems of individuals, groups, or organizations.

(4) "Referral activities" which means the evaluating of data to identify problems and to determine the advisability of referral to other specialists.

(5) "Research activities" which means reporting, designing, conducting, or consulting on research in counseling with human subjects.

SECTION 4. Professional Ethics. The Board of Examiners in Counseling of the State of Arkansas shall adopt the Code of Ethics of the American Personnel and Guidance Association and any revisions or additions deemed appropriate by this Board to govern appropriate practice or behavior referred to in this Act.

SECTION 5. The Establishment of the Board. There is hereby created a Board to be known as the Arkansas Board of Examiners in Counseling consisting of seven (7) members who shall be appointed by the Governor in the following manner:

(a) Within thirty (30) days from the effective date of this Act, the Executive Committee of the Arkansas Personnel and Guidance Association shall submit to the Governor a list of qualified candidates for the Board; the composition of said Board shall include six licensed or licensable counselors, three (3) who are practicing counselors and three (3) who are counselor educators or supervisors, and one (1) member from the general public who is not licensed or licensable. Appointments shall ensure that the Board consists of citizens of the United States, residents of Arkansas, at least one member of each sex, and at least one member of an ethnic minority.

(b) Board members shall be appointed for a three (3) year term. Initial appointment to the Board shall be for the following terms: Two (2) members for one (1) year, two (2) members for two (2) years, and three (3) members for three (3) years.

(c) Not later than November 1 of each year, the Executive Committee of the Arkansas Personnel and Guidance Association shall submit to the Governor the names of qualified candidates to fill the expired terms of the Board members. Other vacancies occurring in the Board shall be filled for the unexpired term by appointment of the Governor from candidates submitted within thirty (30) days of such vacancy by the Executive Committee of the Arkansas Personnel and Guidance Association. Such appointments shall be made within thirty (30) days after the candidate's names have been submitted.

(d) Any Board member may be removed by the Governor, after written notice and hearing, for incapacity, incompetence, neglect of duty, misfeasance or malfesance in office.

(e) Board members shall be ineligible for reappointment for a period of three (3) years following completion of their terms.

SECTION 6. The Organization of the Board. The Board of Examiners in Counseling shall organize within thirty (30) days following the appointment of any new members by the Governor on January 2 of each year. The Board shall elect a Chairman and Secretary from its members to serve for terms of one year. The members shall immediately and before performing public duties take the Constitutional Oath of Office, and shall file same in the Office of the Governor, who upon receiving said Oath of Office shall issue to each member a certificate of appointment. Each member shall receive all necessary expenses incident to holding meetings provided that such expenses shall in no case exceed funds available to the Board. The Board shall hold at least one (1) meeting each year. Additional meetings may be held at the discretion of the Chairman or upon the written request of any three (3) members of the Board. The Board shall adopt such rules, regulations and procedures as they deem necessary for the performance of their duties. Five (5) members of the Board shall at all times constitute a quorum. The Board shall adopt a seal which must be affixed to all licenses issued by the Board. The Board shall be empowered to accept grants from foundations and institutions to carry on its functions and to hire such assistants as are necessary to perform its activities. The Board is required to charge an application fee determined by the Board.

SECTION 7. Licensure Fees. All fees from applicants seeking licensure under this Act, and all license or renewal fees received shall be paid to said Board. No part of any fee shall be returnable under any condition other than failure of the Board to hold examinations at the time originally announced, whereupon the entire fee may be returned at the option of the applicant. All fees collected or gifts or grants shall be deposited in the State Treasury to the credit of the Board. There is hereby appropriated from the Treasury funds to the credit of the Board to be used for printing, travel expenses of the Board, and other necessary expenses to the carrying out of the provisions of this Act. Expenses shall be paid under written direction of the Chairman and Secretary of the Board in accordance with usual State procedures.

requirements of subsection (a) through (f) of Section 8 of this Act and further provided that the Board shall have the power to consider experience of the applicant prior to application for licensure as a waiver of all or part of the supervised experience requirement of Section 8 (g) and further provided that if the prior experience of the applicant does not meet all requirements of Section 8 (g) then the applicant will be issued the Licensed Associate Counselor license with acceptable experience credited toward the experience requirements of Section 8 (g) of this Act.

SECTION 11. Examination of Applicants. The place of examination shall be designated in advance by the Board, and such examination shall be given annually at such time and place and under the supervision as the Board may determine, and specifically at such other times as in the opinion of the Board the number of applicants warrants.

The examination shall require that the applicant demonstrate his or her knowledge and application thereof in those areas deemed relevant to his or her specialty and identify those services he or she intends to offer to the public.

The Board will report the results of the examination and recommend to the Chairman action to be taken. To insure impartiality, written examination documents shall be identified by number, and no paper shall be marked in the name of any applicant. In the event an applicant fails to pass the entire examination, he or she may reapply and shall be allowed to take a subsequent examination. An applicant who has filed two (2) successive examinations may not reapply for two (2) years from the date of the last examination.

The Board is required to preserve examination materials and an accurate transcript of the questions and answers to any examination, and the applicant's performance on each section, as part of its records for a period of two (2) years following the date of the examination.

SECTION 12. Renewal. Counselors licensed under this Act shall be required to submit biannually at the time of renewal, a license renewal fee to be established by the Board. No license shall be renewed unless the renewal request is accompanied by evidence satisfactory to the Board of the completion during the previous twenty-four (24) months of relevant professional or continued educational experience. Failure to pay the biannual renewal fee within the time stated shall automatically suspend the right of any licensee to practice while delinquent. Such lapsed license may be renewed within a period of one (1) year after payment of all fees in arrears.

If any Licensed Professional Counselor or Licensed Associate Counselor duly licensed under this Act, by virtue of additional training and experience, is qualified to practice in a specialty other than that for which he or she was deemed competent at the time of initial licensing and wishes to offer such service under the provisions of this Act, he or she is required to submit additional credentials and he or she is to be given the opportunity to demonstrate his or her knowledge and application thereof in areas deemed relevant to his or her specialty.

SECTION 13. Licensing Under Special Conditions. The Board may at its discretion waive formal examination requirements of a candidate, provided that such candidate is licensed or certified to practice counseling by a similar board in

SECTION 8. Requirements for Licensed Professional Counselor. The Board shall issue a license as a Licensed Professional Counselor to each applicant who files an application upon a form and in such a manner as the Board prescribes, accompanied by such fee as set by the Board, and who furnishes satisfactory evidence of the following to the Board that:

(a) the applicant is a major under the laws of Arkansas;

(b) the applicant is a citizen of the United States or has declared his intention to become a citizen;

(c) the applicant is highly regarded in personal character and professional ethics;

(d) the applicant is a resident of or is in the act of establishing residency in the State of Arkansas;

(e) the applicant is not in violation of any of the provisions of this Act and the rules and regulations adopted hereunder;

(f) the applicant has received a graduate degree from a regionally accredited institution of higher education which is primarily professional counseling in content and has accumulated at least thirty-six (36) graduate semester hours and which meets the academic and training content standard established by the Board (the Board shall use the standards for the preparation of counselors prepared by that special professional association nationally as a guide in establishing the standards for counseling);

(g) the applicant has three (3) years of supervised fulltime experience in professional counseling acceptable to the Board; one (1) year of experience may be gained for each thirty (30) graduate semester hours earned beyond the Master's degree, provided that such hours are clearly related to the field of counseling and are acceptable to the Board, provided that in no case the applicant has less than one (1) year of the professional experience; and

(h) the applicant will declare special competencies and demonstrate professional competence in specialty areas by passing an examination written and/or oral and/or situational, as the Board will prescribe. Upon examination of credentials the Board may, by a majority of the Board members present and voting, consider such credentials adequate evidence of professional competence and recommend to the Chairman of the Board that a license be approved in that specialty.

SECTION 9. Requirements for Licensed Associate Counselor. The Board shall issue a license of Licensed Associate Counselor to each applicant who meets the requirements established in Section 8 of this Act with the exception of subsection (g). The Licensed Associate Counselor may practice only under direct supervision of a Licensed Professional Counselor. The plan for supervision of the Licensed Associate Counselor must be approved by the Board prior to any actual performance of counseling on the part of the Licensed Associate Counselor. Any Licensed Associate Counselor may petition the Board for licensure review for the Licensed Professional Counselor provided that requirements of Section 8, subsection (g) have been completed.

SECTION 10. Interim Licensure. The Board will issue to any person upon application during the first six months following the effective date of this Act the license of Licensed Professional Counselor provided that the applicant meets the another state and, further provided, that in the opinion of the Board, the standards and qualifications required for the practice of counseling in the candidate's licensing state are at least equal to those required by this Act. The Board has the power to waive formal examination requirements only and does not have the power to waive any required period of supervision as provided in this Act.

SECTION 14. Privileged Communication. For the purpose of this Act the confidential relations and communications between a licensed counselor and client are placed upon the same basis as those provided by statute between an attorney and client. Nothing in this Act shall be construed to require any such privileged communication be disclosed.

SECTION 15. Practice Without License Prohibited—Penalty. Any person who shall hold himself or herself out to a public as being engaged in the practice of counseling as defined in Section 3 of this Act or represents himself or herself by the title Licensed Professional Counselor or Licensed Associate Counselor and shall not then possess in full force and virtue a valid license to practice counseling as provided in this Act shall be deemed guilty of a class A misdemeanor and upon conviction thereof shall be punished by a fine of not less than Five Hundred Dollars ($500.00) nor more than One Thousand Dollars ($1,000.00) and may be imprisoned for a term not exceeding one (1) year. Each violation and conviction shall be deemed a separate offense. Notwithstanding the limits imposed for a class A misdemeanor, if the defendant has derived pecuniary gain in the form of client fees received for services in violation of this Act, such fees will be refunded.

Nothing in this Section shall be construed to limit the professional pursuits of administrators, teachers, and school counselors certified by the State Department of Education within the scope of their duties in recognized public and private schools; non-resident persons engaged in consulting or research activities in counseling for a period not greater than thirty (30) days in a calendar year; clergymen; practitioners of medicine; psychologists; social workers; <u>listed Christian Science practitioners; or individuals offering volunteer services who are approved by the organization or agency for whom the service is rendered</u>; persons in the employ of the federal, state, or local government or accredited institutions of higher education, insofar as such activities and services are a part of the official duties in salaried positions; or other professionals; provided that such persons hold a valid license, certificate, or registration in the State of Arkansas and operating within the scope of their professional duties; provided that the title Licensed Professional Counselor or Licensed Associate Counselor is not used. Students engaged in counselor training programs and other persons preparing for the profession of licensed counselor may perform as part of their training the functions specified in Section 3 of this Act provided that such functions are performed only under supervision of a Licensed Professional Counselor.

No firm, partnership, or corporation may offer to the public or other firms, partnerships, or corporations any counseling services as specified in Section 3 hereof unless such services are performed or supervised by individuals fully and validly licensed under this Act.

SECTION 16. Power to Petition for Injunctions. The courts of this State are hereby vested with the jurisdiction and power to enjoin the unlawful practice of counseling and/or false representation as a licensed counselor in any proceeding brought by the Arkansas Board of Examiners in Counseling or by any member thereof or by any citizen of this State.

SECTION 17. Suspension or Revocation of License. The Board shall have the power to suspend or revoke the license of any person licensed by the Board and found guilty in violating any ethical or professional standard. The sanction of suspension upon order of the Board shall not be for a period greater than six (6) months and any licensee thereby sanctioned shall not be allowed to practice counseling in this State until the termination of the suspension period and subsequent timely review by the Board.

SECTION 18. This Act shall not apply to persons whose counseling activities are confined to the area of alcohol and drug abuse.

Virginia Licensure Law

CHAPTER

An Act to amend the reenact §§ 54-102.17 and 54-864 as amended, of the Code of Virginia;
to amend the Code of Virginia by adding in Title 54 a chapter numbered 28, consisting of sections numbered 54-923 through 54-948; and to repeal Chapter 5.1 of Title 54, containing sections numbered 54-102.1, 54-102.2, 54-102.3 and 54-102.14, as severally amended, and Chapter 18.1 of Title 54, containing sections numbered 54-775.2, 54-775.3, 54-775.4 and 54-775.7, as amended, of the Code of Virginia; and to amend the second enactment of Chapter 648 of the 1975 Acts of Assembly, the amended, added and repealed section relating to the regulation of behavioral science professions.

[H 378]

Approved

Be it enacted by the General Assembly of Virginia:

1. That §§ 54-102.17 and 54-864 as amended, of the Code of Virginia are amended and reenacted, and that the Code of Virginia is amended by adding in Title 54 a chapter numbered 28, consisting of sections numbered 54-923 through 54-948, as follows:

§ 54-102.17. Certification of persons entitled to practice; advertising prohibited.—A. Any person having at least a masters degree in guidance, counseling, personnel services, or educational counseling or an equivalent degree, and who has at least four years of experience in guidance and personnel counseling as herein defined and described shall be entitled to practice guidance and personnel counseling as defined in this chapter upon receipt of a certificate from the Department of Professional and Occupational Regulation. Practice of guidance and personnel counseling without a certificate is hereby prohibited.

B. Application for a certificate to practice guidance and personnel counseling shall be in writing to the Director, Department of Professional and Occupational Regulation, and shall include his name, age, residence and business or employment address, names of two character references, and documentary evidence as to having satisfied the above-stated degree requirement and an affidavit with regard to the experience requirement above set forth.

C. Upon verification that the above-stated academic and experience requirements are met, unless there is evidence that the applicant is not of good moral character, the Director of the Department of Professional and Occupational Regulation shall issue the applicant an appropriate certificate, which shall evidence his right to perform the services defined and described and as limited by this chapter. The Director of the Department of Professional and Occupational Regulation shall have the authority to establish criteria and procedures for determining whether an applicant for a certificate meets the educational and experience requirements of § 54-102.17.

D. No person certified under this chapter shall advertise, directly or indirectly, as a psychologist or a clinical psychologist.

E. All certificates issued in accordance herewith shall be null and void and of no effect after January one, nineteen hundred seventy-seven and shall contain the expiration date thereon.

§ 54-864. Administration; certain powers and duties of Director with respect to boards.—It shall be the duty of the Director to perform the administrative duties of the following boards and agencies of the Commonwealth: (1) the State Board of Accountancy; (2) the State Board of Architects, Professional Engineers and Land Surveyors; (3) [. . .] (4) the State Board of the Certification of Librarians; (5) the Board of Examiners of Mines, created by Chapter 150 of the Acts of the General Assembly of nineteen hundred forty; (6) the Board of Commissioners to Examine Pilots; (7) the Virginia Real Estate Commission; (8) the Board of Veterinary Examiners; (9) the Board of Barber Examiners; (10) the Virginia State Board of Opticians; (11) the Virginia State Board of Registered Professional Hairdressers; (12) [. . .] (13) the Virginia Board of Hearing Aid Dealers and Fitters; (14) Board for Certification of Operators of Water and Wastewater Works; (15) the State Board of Sanitarian Examiners; (16) the State Board of Examiners for Nursing Home Administrators; (17) the Virginia Board of Examiners for Audiology and Speech Pathology; and (18) the Virginia Board of Behavioral Science.

Each of the boards designated in this section and § 54-865 is hereby transferred to the Department of Professional and Occupational Regulation, and each shall be a separate board within said Department. All of the administrative functions of the boards designated in this section shall be under the direction and supervision of the Director, and it shall be the duty of the members of each of the several boards designated in this section to cooperate with the Director to the end that his powers of direction and supervision of the administration function of each board shall not be impaired.

In the performance and discharge of his duties hereunder with respect to the boards designated in this section only, the Director shall (1) be the secretary of each board; (2) maintain all records for each board; (3) collect and account for all fees prescribed to be paid into each board and account for and deposit the moneys so collected into a special fund from which the expenses of the Commission, regulatory boards and Department shall be paid; (4) make and file annually with the Governor a consolidated report with respect to each board; (5) employ such personnel and assistance as may be required for the operation of said boards; (6) enforce all regulations promulgated by said boards; (7) exercise such other powers as may be necessary to function as the sole administrative officer and director of each of said boards; and (8) perform such additional administrative functions as may be prescribed by the Virginia Commission for Professional and Occupational Regulation.

Chapter 28.
Behavioral Science Professions.
Article 1.
Behavioral Science Board and
Professional Boards and Certification
Committees Generally.

§ 54-923. Statement of policy; intention.—It is declared to be the policy of the Commonwealth of Virginia that the Activities of those persons who render services to the public in the behavioral science area be regulated to ensure the protection of the public health, safety and welfare. The Commonwealth also recognizes the fact that the many professions offering these services overlap and intertwine to a substantial degree. This fact results in the need for these professions to work in close harmony with each other to maintain quality service to the citizens and to prevent infringement on the rights of practitioners to engage in their lawful professions, which infringements may harm the public. The system of regulation established herein is intended to provide professional responsibility for the public and harmony among the professions.

§ 54-924. Definitions: As used in this chapter the following terms shall have the following meanings unless the context clearly indicates otherwise:

a. "Board" means the Virginia Board of Behavioral Science.

b. "Department" means the Department of Professional and Occupational Regulation.

c. "Commission" means the Commission for Professional and Occupational Regulation.

d. "Professional board" means any board having membership on the Virginia Board of Behavioral Science.

e. "Certification committee" is a specialty committee serving as part of a professional board.

§ 54-925. Virginia Board of Behavioral Science created; membership; removal.—There is hereby created the Virginia Board of Behavioral Science which shall consist of two citizen members appointed by the Governor and two members from and selected by each professional board operating under this chapter. The citizen members of the Board shall be appointed for five-year terms; provided, however, that the initial term of one of the first citizen members appointed shall be three years. Appointments to fill vacancies created by death, resignation or removal shall be for the remainder of the unexpired term; and no member may serve more than two full terms.

The Governor may remove any member of the Board for cause, and the Governor shall be the sole judge of the sufficiency of the cause of removal.

§ 54-926. Quorum of the Board.—A quorum of the Behavioral Science Board shall be a majority of the Board which includes at least one member of each professional board and one citizen member.

§ 54-927. Powers and duties of the Board.—The Board shall have the following powers and duties:

a. To promulgate qualifications of applicants for licensing or certification developed by each professional board provided that all such qualifications shall be necessary to ensure either competence or integrity to engage in such profession or occupation, and provided further, that each professional board shall have sole power to determine qualifications for licensure or certification within the profession regulated by such professional board.

b. To license or certify qualified applicants as practitioners of the particular behavioral science profession regulated. The Board of Behavioral Science shall certify or issue a license to practice the particular behavioral science profession to every applicant who is recommended to the Board by the appropriate professional board, who complies with the requirements of this chapter, the rules of the Board, and the rules of such professional board.

c. To levy and collect fees for certification or licensing and renewal thereof that are sufficient to cover all expenses for the administration of this chapter and a proper proportion of all expenses for the administration and operation of both the Department and the Commission.

d. To promulgate regulations necessary to administer effectively the regulatory system administered by the Board; provided that such regulations shall not be in conflict with the purposes and intent of Chapter 1.1, Title 54 and the regulations of each professional board.

e. To ensure that inspections are conducted by each professional board relating to the practice of each practitioner in conducting his practice in a competent manner and within the lawful regulations promulgated by the Board and such professional board.

f. To review the investigative action taken by each professional board.

g. To revoke, suspend or fail to renew a certificate or license which it has the authority to issue for just causes as are enumerated in regulations of the Board and of the appropriate professional board.

h. To meet with the Commission annually to review the activities of the regulatory systems of the Board prior to the report by the Commission to the General Assembly of Virginia.

i. To recommend to the Commission the creation of related professional boards, if deemed necessary and in the best interest of the public.

j. To promulgate a canon of ethics under which the professional activities of persons regulated shall be conducted.

§ 54-928. Membership of professional boards and certification committee; terms; removal.—The professional board and certification committees operating under this chapter shall consist of those members appointed by the Governor and, where appropriate, selected by certification committees as provided in this chapter. Appointments to fill vacancies created by death, resignation or removal shall be for the remainder of the unexpired term; and no member may serve for more than two full terms. The Governor may remove any member of any board or certification committee for cause, and the Governor shall be the sole judge of the sufficiency of the cause for removal.

§ 54-929. Powers and duties of professional boards.—Each professional board operating under this chapter shall have the following powers and duties:

a. To promulgate regulations necessary to administer effectively the regulatory system administered by the professional board.

b. To develop and forward to the Board, for promulgation, qualifications necessary for licensure certification, or designation under this chapter.

c. To evaluate the qualifications of individuals applying to it for licensing based upon the regulations promulgated by the Board. Such evaluation may include the preparation and administration of examinations.

d. To hire independent examiners and/or to establish examining committees.

e. To recommend to the Board for licensing certification or designation of all persons who successfully meet the qualifications developed by the appropriate professional board or certification committee. Only a majority vote of the appropriate professional board shall be necessary for such recommendation.

f. To investigate complaints concerning the conduct of any person whose activities are regulated by the professional board.

g. To hold hearings and recommend to the Board revocation, suspension or nonrenewal of a license or certificate.

h. To establish a canon of ethics consistent with the canon of ethics of the Board.

i. To cooperate with and maintain a close liaison with the Board, the other professional boards and the community to ensure that regulatory systems stay abreast of community and professional needs.

j. To select two of its members to serve on the Board.

§ 54-930. Powers and duties of certification committees.—Each certification committee operating under this chapter shall have the following powers and duties:

a. To develop and forward to the appropriate professional board, qualifications necessary for certification. Such standards as they propose shall be approved by the professional board.

b. To evaluate the qualifications of individual applicants for certification by that particular certification committee based on the regulations promulgated by the Board. Such evaluation may include the preparation and administration of examinations.

c. To recommend for certification to the professional board all persons who have successfully met the qualifications developed by that certification committee. Only a majority vote of the appropriate certification committee shall be necessary for such recommendation.

d. To establish a canon of ethics consistent with the canon of ethics of the professional board and the Board.

§ 54-931. Designation of specialties.—The professional boards operating under this chapter may provide for the designation of specialties within their professional fields.

Article 2.
Professional Counselors; Certified Alcoholism and Drug Counselors; Virginia Board of Professional Counselors; Certification Committees; License without Examination.

§ 54-932. Definitions.—As used in this article:

a. "Professional counselor" shall mean a person trained in counseling and guidance services with emphasis on individual and group guidance and counseling designed to assist individuals in achieving more effective personal, social, educational and career development and adjustment.

b. "Certified alcoholism counselor" shall mean a person certified to provide alcoholism counseling in a State approved public or private alcoholism program and/or facility.

c. "Certified drug counselor" shall mean a person certified to provide drug counseling in a State-approved public or private drug program and/or facility.

d. "Practice of counseling" shall mean rendering or offering to render to individuals, groups, organizations, or the general public any service involving the application of principles, methods or procedures of the counseling profession, to include:

(1) "Counseling" which means assisting an individual, through the counseling relationship, to develop understanding of personal problems, to define goals, and to plan action reflecting his interest, abilities, aptitudes, and needs as these are related to educational progress, occupations and careers, and personal-social concerns.

(2) "Appraisal activities" which mean selecting, administering, scoring and interpreting instruments designed to assess an individual's aptitudes, attitudes, abilities, achievements and interests, and shall not include the use of projective techniques in the assessment of personality.

(3) "Counseling, guidance and personnel consulting" which mean interpreting or reporting upon scientific fact or theory in counseling, guidance and personnel service to provide assistance in solving some current or potential problems of individuals, groups, or organizations.

(4) "Referral activities" which mean the evaluating of data to identify problems and to determine advisability of referral to other specialists.

§ 54-933. Virginia Board of Professional Counselors created; membership.—There is hereby created the Virginia Board of Professional Counselors which shall have such powers and duties as are granted it under this chapter for the purpose of regulating the practice of counseling.

The Virginia Board of Professional Counselors shall consist of seven members, five appointed by the Governor directly and two selected pursuant to § 54-934, as follows: one faculty member from an accredited college or university in this State and actively engaged in teaching counseling, and one member, respectively, from an actively engaged in each of the fields of (i) educational counseling, (ii) rehabilitation counseling, (iii) marriage-family counseling, (iv) pastoral counseling, (v) alcohol counseling and (vi) drug counseling.

The professional board members initially shall be persons who are eligible for licensure or certification hereunder; and subsequent appointees shall be licensed or certified counselors, as the case may be.

The terms of the members of the board shall be four years; provided, however, that of the initial board, one member shall be appointed for one year, two members for two years each, two members for three years each, and two members for four years each.

§ 54-934. Drug and Alcoholism Counselor Certification Committees.—The Drug and Alcoholism Certification Committees shall be composed of five members, each appointed by the Governor, who are eligible for certification as certified drug or alcoholism counselors, or who have direct responsibility for drug or alcoholism certification programs. The separate committees shall each elect a chairman and shall each elect a member to serve as a member of the Virginia Board of Professional Counselors.

§ 54-935. License without Examination.—Any person certified or qualified for certification as a Guidance and Personnel Counselor under Chapter 5.2, Title 54 (§ 54-102.15, et seq.,) shall upon proper application made prior to January one, nineteen hundred seventy-seven, be licensed to practice as a Professional Counselor.

Article 3.
Psychologists, School Psychologists, Clinical Psychologists, etc. Virginia Board of Psychology; Licenses.

§ 54-936. Definitions.—As used in this article:

a. "Psychologists" shall mean a person trained in the application of established principles of learning, motivation, perception, thinking and emotional relationships to problems of personality evaluation, group relations, and behavior adjustment.

b. "School psychologist" shall mean a person who specializes in problems manifested in and associated with educational systems and who utilizes psychological concepts and methods in programs or actions which attempt to improve learning conditions for students or who is employed in this capacity by a public or nonprofit educational institution or who offers to render such services to the public whether or not employed by such an institution.

c. "Clinical psychologist" shall mean a psychologist who is competent to apply the principles and techniques of psychological evaluation and psychotherapy to individual clients for the purpose of ameliorating or attenuating problems of behavioral and/or emotional maladjustment.

d. "Practice of psychology" shall mean the rendering or offering to render to individuals, groups, organizations, or the general public any service involving the application of principles, methods or procedures of the science and profession of psychology, and which includes, but is not limited to:

(1) "Measuring and testing," which consists of the psychological assessment and evaluation of abilities, attitudes, aptitudes, achievements, adjustments, motives, personality dynamics or other psychological attributes of individuals, or groups of individuals by means of standardized measurements or other methods, techniques or procedures recognized by the science and profession of psychology.

(2) "Counseling and psychotherapy," which consists of the application of principles of learning and motivation in an interpersonal situation with the objectives of modification of perception and adjustment; consisting of high developed skills, techniques, and methods of altering through learning processes, attitudes, feelings, values, self-concept, personal goals and adaptive patterns.

(3) "Psychological consulting," which consists of interpreting or reporting upon scientific fact or theory in psychology, rendering expert psychological opinion, psychological evaluation, or engaging in applied psychological research.

e. The "practice of school psychology" shall mean the rendering or offering to render to individuals, groups, organizations, government agents or the public any of the following services:

(1) "Testing and measuring" which consists of psychological assessment, evaluation and diagnosis relative to the assessment of intellectual ability, ap-

titudes, achievement, adjustment, motivation, personality or any other psychological attribute of persons as individuals or in groups that directly relates to learning or behavioral problems in an educational setting.

(2) "Counseling" which consists of professional advisement and interpretive services with children or adults for amelioration or prevention of educationally related problems.

(a) Counseling services relative to the practice of school psychology include but are not limited to the procedures of verbal interaction, interviewing, behavior modification, environmental manipulation and group processes.

(b) Counseling services relative to the practice of school psychology are short-term and are situation oriented.

(3) "Consultation" which consists of educational or vocational consultation or direct educational services to schools, agencies, organizations or individuals. Consultation as herein defined is directly related to learning problems and related adjustments.

(4) Development of programs such as designing more efficient and psychologically sound classroom situations and acting as a catalyst for teacher involvement in adaptations and innovations.

f. The "practice of clinical psychology" shall mean the offering by an individual of his services to the public as a clinical psychologist.

§ 54-937. Virginia Board of Psychology; membership.—The Virginia Board of Psychologists Examiners heretofore appointed pursuant to § 54-102.2 is hereby continued, and shall hereafter be known as the Virginia Board of Psychology with such powers and duties granted it under this chapter for the purpose of regulating the practice of psychology and school psychology. The membership of such professional board shall be representative of the practices of psychology and shall consist of three persons who are members of the faculty of an accredited college or university in this State, who are actively engaged in teaching psychology and who are licensed or qualified to be licensed as a psychologist, one person licensed or qualified to be licensed as a clinical psychologist, and one person licensed or qualified to be licensed as a school psychologist.

§ 54-938. Licenses and certificates continued.—All licenses and certificates heretofore issued under the provisions of Chapter 5.1 of Title 54 (§ 54-102.1 et seq.) shall continue in effect.

§ 54-939. License as clinical psychologist.—The candidate for licensure as clinical psychologist shall be recommended by the Virginia Board of Psychology to the State Board of Medicine from which all instructions regarding the administration of such license will thereafter be secured.

Article 4.
Social Workers; Virginia Board of
Social Workers; Licenses and Certificates.

§54-941. Definitions.—As used in this article:

a. "Social worker" means a person trained to provide service and action to effect changes in human behavior, emotional responses, and the social conditions by the application of the values, principles, methods, and procedures of the profession of social work.

b. "Clinical social worker" shall mean a social worker who, by education and experience, is professionally qualified at the autonomous practice level to provide direct diagnostic, preventive and treatment services where functioning, in threatened or affected by social and psychological stress of health impairment.

c. The "practice of social work" means rendering or offering to render to individuals, families, groups, organizations, governmental units, or the general public service which is guided by special knowledge of social resources, social systems, human capabilities, and the part conscious and unconscious motivation play in determining behavior. The disciplined application of social work values, principles and methods includes but is not restricted to the following:

(1) "Counseling and psycho-social treatment" shall mean helping individuals, families and groups in their personal, family and group adjustment; explaining and interpreting the psycho-social aspects of a situation to individuals, families, groups, or those persons in other settings, such as health care facilities.

(2) "Community organization" shall mean helping organizations and communities analyze social problems and human needs and providing human services, assisting organizations and communities in organizing for general neighborhood improvement or community development, and improving social conditions through the application of social planning, advocacy and social policy formulations.

(3) "Supportive services" shall mean providing general assistance, information referral sources, and other supportive services such as administration, consultation, research and teaching; and assisting in problem-solving activities.

§ 54-942. Virginia Board of Social Workers; membership.—The Virginia Board of Registration of Social Workers heretofore appointed pursuant to § 54-775.2 is hereby continued, and shall hereafter be known as the Virginia Board of Social Workers with such powers and duties granted it under this chapter for the purpose of regulating the practice of social work.

Each of the members of the board shall be residents of Virginia, shall be licensed and shall have been in active practice of social work for not less than five years prior to appointment.

§ 54-943. Licenses and certificates continued.—All licenses and certificates heretofore issued under the provisions of Chapter 18.1 of Title 54 (§ 54-775.1 et seq.) shall continue in effect, and be renewable under this chapter.

Article 5.
Exemptions; Drugs; Delayed Compliance;

Mental Health Service Providers; Hardship.

§54-944. Exemptions.—The requirements for licensure or certification provided for in this chapter shall not be applicable to:

(a) Persons who render services that are like or similar to those falling within the scope of the classifications or categories provided for in this chapter, so long as the recipients or beneficiaries of such services are not subject to any charge or fee, or any financial requirement, actual or implied, and provided that the person rendering such service is not held out, by himself or otherwise, as a licensed or certified practitioner.

(b) The activities or services of a student pursuing a course of study in counseling, psychology, school psychology or social work in an institution accredited by a regional accrediting agency approved by the State Board of Education or under the supervision of a practitioner licensed or certified under this chapter; provided that such activities or services constitute a part of his or her course of study and are adequately supervised.

(c) The activities of rabbis, priests, ministers or clergymen of any religious denomination or sect when such activities are within the scope of the performance of their regular or specialized ministerial duties, and for which no separate charge is made or when such activities are performed, whether with or without charge, for or under auspices or sponsorship, individually or in conjunction with others, of an established and legally cognizable church, denomination or sect, and when the person rendering service remains accountable to the established authority thereof.

(d) Persons employed as salaried employees or volunteers of the Federal government, the Commonwealth, a locality, or of any agency established or funded, in whole or part, by any such governmental entity or of a private, non-profit organization or agency sponsored or funded, in whole or part, by a community based citizen group or organization.

(e) Persons regularly employed by private business firms as personnel managers, deputies or assistants so long as their counseling activities relate only to employees of their employer and in respect to their employment.

§ 54-945. Prescribing drugs not permitted.—Nothing in this chapter shall be construed as permitting the administration or prescribing of drugs or in any way infringing upon the practice of medicine as defined in Chapter 12 (§ 54-273 et seq.) of this title.

§ 54-946. Delay of requirements for newly regulated occupations.—Those persons whose occupations were not previously either eligible or required to be licensed or certified and who now fall under the purview of this chapter will have until January one, nineteen hundred seventy-eight to comply with the appropriate provisions of this chapter.

§ 54-948. If the Board shall determine that enforcement of the provisions of this chapter will result in undue hardship to any person otherwise entitled to carry on an established activity that, in the opinion of the Board, does not constitute a substantial risk to the public, the Board may issue a temporary permit for the conducting of such activity; provided such permit shall not be for a period longer than one year, nor renewed more than once.

2. That Chapter 5.1 of Title 54, containing sections numbered 54-102.1, 54-102.2, 54-102.3, and 54-102.14, as severally amended, and Chapter 18.1 of Title 54, containing sections numbered 54-775.2, 54-775.3, 54-775.4 and 54-775.7, as amended, are repealed.

3. That this act shall become effective on January one, nineteen hundred seventy-seven, except those sections and parts thereof necessary for the appointment of the members of the various boards and for the establishment of rules, regulations, requirements and qualifications by the various boards, such sections and parts thereof to become effective on July one, nineteen hundred seventy-six.

4. That the regulations of those professional boards continued under this act, where not inconsistent with the provisions of this act, shall be adopted by such professional boards and in so doing such professional board shall not be bound

by the provisions of the Administrative Process Act (Chapter 1.1:1 of Title 9).
5. That the second enactment of Chapter 648 of the nineteen hundred seventy-five Acts of Assembly is amended to provide that the act shall expire and be of no effect after January one, nineteen hundred seventy-seven.

_____
President of the Senate

_____
Speaker of the House of Delegates

Approved:

_____
Governor

SAMPLE OF A "BRIEF"
(Used in Virginia, 1975)

AN APPEAL TO RESTORE THE CONSTITUTIONAL RIGHT
OF PROFESSIONAL COUNSELORS, GUIDANCE AND
PERSONNEL WORKERS
TO PRACTICE THEIR LAWFUL PROFESSION
AND TO
FACILITATE PROVIDING THESE PROFESSIONAL SERVICES
TO THE CITIZENS OF THE COMMONWEALTH OF VIRGINIA.

The 1,110 professional members of the Virginia Personnel and Guidance Association are clearly denied the constitutional right to engage in the practice of their lawful profession. Section 54-102.10, 102.11, and 102.14 of the Code of Virginia 1950 as amended effectuates the denial of this right and provides penalties for violations thereof. However, Section 54-1.3 states:

> The Virginia General Assembly finds that the right of every person to engage in any lawful profession, trade or occupation of his choice is clearly protected by both the Constitution of the United States and the Constitution of the Commonwealth of Virginia.

In spite of this affirmation, the Board of Psychologists Examiners, Department of Professional and Occupational Regulation, ruled against a counseling, guidance and personnel practitioner on March 23, 1972, stating:

> ... that the practice in personnel and guidance counseling, without the standards and regulations of a regulatory board established by Virginia Law, would not entitle the practitioner to an exemption from the psychologist licensure requirement as a member of another recognized profession. (Herein that of counseling, guidance and personnel work.)

Since this opinion the Board of Psychologists Examiners has refused to let qualified counseling, guidance and personnel workers holding even doctoral degrees from accredited universities take the examination, stating to one such applicant, for example, in a letter dated November 21, 1973:

> After reviewing your credentials, it is the opinion of the Virginia Board of Psychologists Examiners that you are a member of the profession of guidance and counseling rather than of psychology and that it must, therefore, deny your application for licensure.

This and similar actions have effectuated the denial of the applicants' constitutional right to practice their lawful profession.

The Honorable Douglas M. Smith, Judge, Corporation Court, Newport News, Virginia on October 4, 1972, ruling on one applicant (appellant) stated:

APPEAL

> ... I further feel that the profession of personnel and guidance counseling is a separate profession (from Psychology) and should be so recognized. However, I further feel that this profession does utilize the tools of the psychologist as does many other professions and consequently it would be necessary for him (appellant) to be exempt under Section 54-102.14(3)
>
> It appears now that the General Assembly has said that even if it is true that you are in another profession which uses to some degree the tools of psychology that there must be a regulatory body to govern the profession.

There is no provision for such regulation within the Department of Professional and Occupational Regulation for trained professionals in counseling, guidance and personnel work! The Board of Psychologists Examiners, while systematically denying doctoral level applicants permission to take the examination so that they might exercise their constitutional right to practice their lawful profession, stated to an applicant for licensure:

> The Virginia Personnel and Guidance Association is in the process of preparing for submission to the legislature a bill which would provide for the licensing of just such eminently qualified professionals as yourself.

The Chairman of the Board of Psychologists Examiners wrote on April 4, 1973:

> The Legislature seems to desire that a wide range of services be available to the public. The boards might include Personnel and Guidance . . .

The American Psychological Association affirmed:

> Psychology therefore, does not favor narrowly restrictive legislation, which provides that only psychologists . . . may engage in certain applications of psychological knowledge and techniques.

In spite of the above and similar public statements the Board of Psychologists Examiners has fought, "behind the scenes," at every opportunity against the establishment of such a board or regulation which could right the present injustice. This denies a free and open market place for the public, which, if available, would inevitably lower the costs of these professional counseling services to our citizens.

The legislative proposal attached hereto will provide temporary relief. Further details will be worked out between the Department of Professional and Occupational Regulation and the Virginia Personnel and Guidance Association during the coming year.

APPEAL

It is apparent from numerous meetings with professionals and others from all walks of life throughout Virginia that a great public need today is for well qualified counselors. Over one hundred (100) persons appeared at the open hearing held by the Department of Professional and Occupational Regulation this fall in Arlington in support of counseling, guidance and personnel worker regulation. Over twenty five (25) openly testified for this cause with only four (4) appearing in opposition!

The Commonwealth of Virginia itself has fully recognized this need for professional counselor in financially supporting counseling, guidance and personnel worker graduate school training programs in nine (9) state supported colleges and universities, including:

- The College of William and Mary
- Longwood College
- Madison College
- Old Dominion University
- Radford College
- The University of Virginia
- Virginia Commonwealth University
- Virginia Polytechnic Institute and State University
- Virginia State College

In spite of this clear evidence of a public need for professional counseling services the Department wants to procrastinate for yet another year, thereby denying counselors their constitutional right to practice their profession and denying the public access to their services!

The vast majority of our citizens either do not have counseling services available to them or do not have them at fees they can afford. Today's economic situation demands that the public be given this break. Permitting well qualified counselors the right to practice their profession through this proposed certification legislation will reduce the cost of these services to the public. Further, the citizens of Virginia are entitled to choose the professionals which might be of most help to them.

You can make this possible! You can return to professional counselors, guidance and personnel workers their constitutional right to practice their profession by becoming co-patrons of this legislation to be submitted at the 1975 session of the Virginia General Assembly by Senator Herbert H. Bateman and others.

CARL D. SWANSON

APPENDIX B

Chronological Bibliography of Certification, Credentialing, and Registry

by
Sylvia Nisenoff

REGISTERS

American Association of Marriage and Family Counselors. *Register of members.* Claremont, Calif.: Author, 1978.

American Association of Sex Educators, Counselors and Therapists. *1978 national register. Certified sex educators and certified sex therapists.* Washington, D.C.: Author 1978.

American Psychological Association, Council for the National Register of Health Service Providers in Psychology. *National register of health service providers in psychology.* Washington, D.C.: Author, 1975.

Commission on Rehabilitation Counselor Certification. *Registry of certified rehabilitation counselors.* Chicago: Author, 1976.

National Association of Social Workers. *NASW register of clinical social workers.* Washington, D.C.: Author, 1978.

1979

Accreditation moves forward. *Guidepost,* October 11, 1979, p. 2.

American Mental Health Counselors Association. *Application forms to certification committee work forms, procedure forms, plan for national registry, schedule of plans for Board of Certified professional counselors.* Temple Terrace, Florida: Author, 1979. (Folder cc)

American Mental Health Counselors Association. *National certification for clinical mental health counselors.* Washington, D.C.: American Personnel and Guidance Association (Brochure)

AMHCA credentialing of professional counselors. *AMHCA News,* February 1979, p. 2.

AMHCA Certification Committee. The board of certified professional counselors procedures. *AMHCA Journal,* 1979, *1,* 23–38.

American Psychological Association. *Background-the practice of psychology.* Washington, D.C.: Author, September 1979. (News release) (Folder cc)

Anderson, Janet. Mental health counselors launch certification. *APA Monitor,* July/August 1979, p. 4.

APGA Registry Committee meets. *Guidepost,* March 1979, pp. 1; 6.

Bernknopf, S.; Shultz, J. L.; & Ware, W. B. Toward performance-based counselor certification. *Counselor Education and Supervision,* 1979, *18,* 294–303.

A call to action for AMHCA members. *AMHCA News,* April 1979, p. 3.

Certification update. *AMHCA News,* June 1979, p. 3.

Certifying the certifiers. *APA Monitor,* August 1979, pp. 8; 45.

Counselors respond to association issues. *Guidepost,* September 27, 1979, Election supplement C.

Hutt, M. L. Letter to the editor. *APA Monitor,* September/October 1979, pp. 35; 42.

Lesser, L. Implications for mental health counselors . . . an editorial reply. *AMHCA News,* August 1979, p. 1.

Mental health counselors woo MA's. *APA Monitor,* August 1979, pp. 8; 45.

Messina, J. *AMHCA action alert.* March 15, 1979. (Located in folder with *AMHCA News*)

Messina, J. Why establish a certification system for professional counselors? A rationale. *AMHCA Journal,* 1979, *1,* 9–22.

National Commission for Health Certifying Agencies. *Members category A, category B.* Washington, D.C.: Author, 1979. (Folder)

New board to certify. *Guidepost,* March 1, 1979, p. 1.

Randolph, D. L. CMHC requisites for employment of master's level psychologists/counselors. *AMHCA Journal,* 1979, *1,* 64–68.

Recertification eyed. *Guidepost,* October 11, 1979, p. 8.

Standards up for debate. *APA Monitor,* August 1979, p. 45.

Update: Mental health counselor certification effort. *AMHCA News,* April 1979, p. 2.

Weisfeld, N. Staff surveys certification, licensure under federal authority. Commission reports. *Newsletter of the National Commission for Health Certifying Agencies,* July/August 1979, p. 5. (Folder)

Woellner, E. H. *Requirements for certification: Teachers, counselors, librarians, administrators, for elementary schools, secondary schools, junior colleges, 1979–80* (also 1978–79, 1974–75, 1961–62, 1953–54). Chicago: University of Chicago Press, 1979. (APGA has)

1978

AMHCA board seeks input on certification procedures. *AMHCA News,* August 1978, pp. 1; 3–4.

American Psychological Association, Office of Professional Affairs. *Psychology licensing (1) or certification (c) law summary.* May 1978. (Folder cc)

Certification set for 1980. *AMHCA News,* June 1978, p. 3.

Credentialing panel gives report to board. *Guidepost,* March 2, 1978, p. 3.

Forster, J. Counselor credentialing revisited. *Personnel and Guidance Journal,* 1978, *56,* 593–8.

Licensure and certification. *APA Monitor,* November 1978, p. 17.

Lindenberg, S. Why certification instead of licensure? *AMHCA News,* August 1978, p. 2.

Olsen, L. Reflections on credentialing. *APA Monitor,* December 1978, p. 3; 20.

Sex discrimination in certification? *AMHCA News,* December 1978, p. 3.

National Commission for Health Certifying Agencies. *Bylaws of the national commission for health certifying agencies.* Washington, D.C.: Author, 1978. (Folder)

National Commission for Health Certifying Agencies. *Criteria for approval of certifying agencies.* Washington, D.C.: Author, 1978. (Folder)

Sweeney, T. J. Counselor credentialing: Promises and pitfalls. *Viewpoints in Teaching and Learning,* 1978, *54;* 56–63. (APGA doesn't have)

Witmer, J. M. Professional disclosure in licensure. *Counselor Education and Supervision,* 1978, *18,* 71–73.

1977

Association for Counselor Education and Supervision, Commission on Standards and Accreditation. Standards for the preparation of counselors and other personnel services specialists. *Personnel and Guidance Journal,* 1977, *55,* 596–601.

American Personnel and Guidance Association. *Final report. APGA Special Committee for Credentialing* (November 4, 1977. Washington, D.C.: Author, 1977. (Folder PosP)

California Association for Counselor Education and Supervision. *Standards for accreditation and counselor certification.* n.p. given: Author, 1977. (Not in APGA)

Cohen, H. S., & U.S. Department of Health, Education, and Welfare Subcommittee on Health Manpower Credentialing. *Credentialing health manpower* (DHEW Publication No. (OS) 77-50057). Washington, D.C.: U.S. Government Printing Office, 1977. (Not in APGA)

Commission on Rehabilitation Counselor Certification. *Some commonly asked questions about rehabilitation counselor certification.* Chicago: Author, 1977. (Mimeograph)

Commission on Rehabilitation Counselor Certification. *Content areas needed for certification.* Chicago: Author 1977. (Mimeograph; folder)

Council for the National Register of Health Service Providers in Psychology. *Application form.* Washington, D.C.: Author, 1977. (APGA has)

Duricka, P. Guidelines for credentialing set. *Guidepost,* September 22, 1977, pp. 1; 12.
Forster, J. R. Introduction to the special feature on credentialing. *Personnel and Guidance Journal,* 1977, *55,* 571–572.
Forster, J. R. (Ed.). Licensure/certification for counseling psychologists and counselors: Symposium. *Personnel and Guidance Journal,* 1977, *55,* 570–9+; 1978, *56,* 573–576.
Forster, J. R. What shall we do about credentialing? *Personnel and Guidance Journal,* 1977, *55,* 570.
Gazda, G. M. An APGA progress report: Licensure/certification for counseling psychologists and counselors. *Personnel and Guidance Journal,* 1977, *55,* 570.
Goates, J. S., & Goates, W. A. Special reports. Increasing third-party coverage of speech-language pathology and audiology services. *Asha,* 1977, *19,* 887–889. (Folder licensure)
Guidelines for credentialing set. *Guidepost,* September 22, 1977, pp. 1; 12.
Livingston R. H., & Engelkes, J. R. Certified rehabilitation counselors: A new era. *Journal of Applied Rehabilitation Counseling,* 1977, *8,* 228–232. (Folder rehabilitation)
Massachusetts School Counselor's Association. Certification update. *Counselor's Notebook,* *13*(6), 1; 5; 7; 9; 11–14. (Folder cc)
Moracco, J. Another look at the national survey: The problem won't go away. *Counselor Education and Supervision,* 1977, *17,* 150–3.
National Commission for Health Certifying Agencies. *Criteria for approval of certifying agencies.* Unpublished manuscript, Washington, D.C., 1977. (Not in APGA)
Performance based counselor certification: An overview. Atlanta, Ga.: Georgia Department of Education, 1977. (Folder cc)
Piemme, T. E. *Statement to the press.* Unpublished manuscript, National Commission for Health Certifying Agencies, Washington, D.C., 1977. (Not in APGA)
Revised ethical standards of psychologists. *APA Monitor,* March 1977, pp. 22–23.
Seay, Tom. Counselor licensure: Some considerations. *Pennsylvania Personnel and Guidance Association Journal,* 1977, *5,* 25–31. (Folder licensure)
States which require teacher education, teaching experience or both as required for certification of counselors. Compiled in mimeograph form from E. Woellner (Ed.), *Requirements for certification for elementary schools, secondary schools, jr. colleges, 1977–78.* Chicago: University of Chicago Press, 1979. (Folder cc)
Sweeney, T. J., & Witmer, M. Who says you're a counselor? *Personnel and Guidance Journal,* 1977, *55,* 589–591.
Wachowiak, D. Counseling inside/out. *Personnel and Guidance Journal,* 1977, *55,* 222–4.
Yenawine, G. D. Certification: A small dose of ambivalence and a large dose of doubt. *Journal of College Placement,* 1977, *37,* 25–26. (APGA has)

1976

Commission on Rehabilitation Counselor Certification. *Proposed plan for certification maintenance.* Chicago: Author, 1976. (Folder rehabilitation)
Corcoran, J. P. Certification: One vote against; career and placement counselors. *Journal of College Placement,* 1976, *37* 34–35. (APGA has)
Cottingham, H. F., & Swanson, C. D. Recent licensure developments: Implications for counselor education. *Counselor Education and Supervision,* 1976, *16,* 84–97.
Jones, L. K. National survey of the program and enrollment characteristics of counselor education programs. *Counselor Education and Supervision,* 1976, *15,* 166–176.
Lewis, C. Memorandum to Adelaide Siegel concerning a national registry. January 13, 1976. (Folder cc)
Lindenberg, S. *Pilot study of licensure and national registry complete.* News release, University of Georgia, Athens, 1976. (Folder cc)

Lindenberg, S.; Stassin, D.; & Howard, M. *Licensing, registry, and the graduate student: A pilot study.* Athens: University of Georgia, Department of Counseling and Human Development Services, n.d. [1976]. (Folder cc)

Lindenberg, S. P. Attention students: Be advised . . . *Personnel and Guidance Journal,* 1976, *55,* 34-36.

Miller, J. N., & Engin, A. W. Tomorrow's counselor: Competent or unemployed? *Personnel and Guidance Journal,* 1976, *54,* 262-266.

National Association of Alcoholism Counselors, Inc. *What is the Association of Alcoholism Counselors, Inc.?* Arlington, Vir.: Author, n.d. (Mimeograph, folder cc)

Rosenbaum, J. Memorandum concerning a conversation with Ray Fowler, Executive Director of American Association of Marriage and Family Counselors. November 18, 1976. (Folder lic)

Samuels, W. M. *Proceedings certification conference, Kansas City, Missouri, August 2-5, 1976.* Washington, D.C.: National Commission for Health Certifying Agencies, 1976. (Not in APGA)

Shoemaker, J. T., & Splitter, J. L. Competency-based model for counselor certification. *Counselor Education and Supervision,* 1976, *15,* 267-274.

Siegel, Adelaide. *Memorandum to Dr. Charles Lewis* concerning a national registry. January 16, 1976. (Folder cc)

Standards committee discharged. *APA Monitor,* March 1976, p. 8.

U.S. Department of Health, Education, and Welfare. *A proposal for credentialing health manpower.* Washington, D.C.: Author, 1976. (Not in APGA)

1975

American Psychological Association, Division 17. The licensing and certification of psychologists. A position statement by the Division of Counseling Psychology of the APA. *Counseling Psychologist,* 1975, *5,* 135.

Asher, J. First edition of National Register due; 7000 psychologists to be included. *APA Monitor,* May 1975, pp. 1; 11. (Not in APGA)

Asher, J. Soaring medical costs endanger psychologists. *APA Monitor,* December 1975, pp 1; 12-13. (Folder)

Bureau of Health Resources Development. *Report of the meeting to discuss the feasibility of a national system of certification for allied health personnel.* Springfield, Vir.: Author, 1975 (NTIS No. PB-248-860). (Not in APGA)

Lune, M. E. Commission on rehabilitation counselor certification-March 1975 field review report. *Journal of Applied Rehabilitation Counseling,* 1975, *6,* 67-72. (Folder cc)

McAlees, D. C., & Schumacher, B. Toward a new professionalism: Certification and accreditation. *Rehabilitation Counseling Bulletin,* 1975, *18,* 160-165.

Menges, R. J. Assessing readiness for professional practice. *Review of Educational Research,* 1975, *45,* 173-207. (APGA has)

Notice (of registry being in preparation). *NRCA News,* April 1976, p. 3. (Folder cc)

Report of the Commission on Rehabilitation Counselor Certification, June 13, 1975. *NRCA News,* June 1975, pp. 3-4. (Folder rehabilitation)

1974

American Rehabilitation Counseling Association. *Revision of a statement of policy on the professional preperation of rehabilitation counselors.* Washington, D.C.: American Personnel and Guidance Association, 1974. (Unpublished mimeograph)

Center for Applied Linguistics. *Guidelines for the preparation and certification of teachers of bilingual/bicultural education.* Arlington, Vir.: Author 1974. (Folder cc)

Certification requirement for dormitory counselors. *American Annals of the Deaf,* 1974, *119,* 70. (Not in APGA)

Conant, R. M., & Hatch, T. D. Policies for the development of credentialing mechanisms for health personnel, a progress report—1974. *American Journal of Occupational Therapy,* 1974, *28,* 289. (Not in APGA)

Counselor certification commission report. *NRCA News,* June 1974, pp. 1-4. (Folder rehab)

Counselor certification program begins. *NRCA News,* April 1974, pp. 1-2.

Huff, S. Credentialing by tests or by degrees: Title VII of the Civil Rights Act and Griggs *v.* Duke Power Company. *Harvard Education Review,* 1974, *44,* 246-269. (APGA has)

Moll, K. L. Special Reports. Issues facing us—licensure and certification. *Asha,* 1974, *16,* 488. (Folder lic)

National registry plan nearing implementation. *APA Monitor,* January 1974, p. 1. (Not in APGA)

Penn, J. R. Professional accreditation: A key to excellence. *Journal of College Student Personnel,* 1974, *15,* 257-259.

Roy Littlejohn Associates, Inc. *Proposed national standard for alcoholism counselors. Final report.* Arlington, Vir.: NAAC, 1974. (Mimeograph; folder cc)

Sex educators propose professional standards. *Guidepost,* May 3, 1974, p. 6.

Special issue on certification and accreditation by the Association for Educational Communications and Technology. *Audiovisual Instruction,* 1974, *19* (9). (Not in APGA)

Sweezy, E. E. *Feasibility study of a voluntary national certification system for allied health personnel.* Springfield, Vir.: Institute of Public Administration, 1974. (NTIS No. HRP-0002053). (Not in APGA)

Wittmer, J., & Lister, J. Actual and preferred activities among certified counselors with and without teaching experience. *SPATE,* 1974, *13,* 8-17.

1973

Association for Counselor Education and Supervision. *Standards for the preparation of counselors and other personnel services specialists* (for membership consideration). Washington, D.C.: American Personnel and Guidance Association 1973. (Folder PosP)

ASCA explores certification. *Guidepost,* April 6, 1973, p. 1.

Certification commission meets. *NRCA News,* August 1973, p. 5.

Commission on Rehabilitation Counselor Certification. *Standards and criteria for rehabilitation counselor certification adopted by the National Commission on Rehabilitation Counselor Certification* (and an application form). Chicago: Author, December 1973. (Folder cc)

McAlees, D. C. Report on certification commission. *Journal of Applied Rehabilitation Counseling,* 1973, *4,* 131-132. (Folder rehabilitation)

Menges, R. J. *Assessing readiness for professional practice* (The Center for the Teaching Professions, Occasional Paper No. 1). Evanston, Ill.: Northwestern University, 1973. (Not in APGA).

Roth, R. A. Certifying teachers: An overhaul is underway. *The Clearing House,* 1973, *47,* 287-291. (APGA has)

States moving to recertification (of teachers). *Guidepost,* October 12, 1973, p. 5.

West Virginia Personnel and Guidance Association. *Ad Hoc Committee on Certification. Competency-based certification.* Huntington, W. Va.: Author 1973. (Mimeograph; folder cc)

1972

Accreditation, licensure, certification and public accountability. Clinic session no. 9. A report of the sixth annual meeting of the Education Commission of the States. *Compact,* 1972, *6* (4), 31. (APGA has)

ARCA-NRCA certification committee meets. *NRCA News,* August 1972, p. 6 (Folder cc)

Boller, J. D. Counselor certification: Who still needs teaching experience? *Personnel and Guidance Journal,* 1972, *50,* 388-391.

Carnes, G. D. Certification, philosophy, and conclusions. *Journal of Applied Rehabilitation Counseling,* 1972, *3,* 19-26. (Not in APGA)

NRCA adopts certification of rehabilitation counselors. *NRCA News,* October 1972, p. 5. (Folder rehabilitation)

Selden, W. K. Factors related to certification of rehabilitation counselors. *Journal of Applied Rehabilitation Counseling,* 1972, *3,* 37-42. (Folder rehabilitation)

Who's qualified in health fields? *Guidepost,* September 29, 1972, p. 7.

1971

American Personnel and Guidance Association, Professional Preparations and Standards Committee. *Report of meeting of PPS Committee held on April 5, 1971 on standards for elementary school counselors.* (Mimeograph, 1 sheet; folder cc)

Brammer, L. M., & Springer, H. C. A radical change in counselor education and certification. *Personnel and Guidance Journal,* 1971, *49,* 803-808.

Bruno, L. *Guidelines and standards for the development and approval of programs of preparation leading to the certification of school professional personnel.* Olympia, Wash.: State Department of Public Instruction, 1971. (Not in APGA)

Carnes, G. D. The certification of rehabilitation counselors. *Rehabilitation Counseling Bulletin,* 1971, *15,* 72-79.

Carnes, G. D. *Recertification of rehabilitation counselors.* Austin: University of Texas, n.d. [c. 1971]. (Mimeograph; folder cc)

Duncan, C. W. Private practice and the counselor educator. *Counselor Education and Supervision,* 1971, *11,* 156-160.

Miller, L. A. A reaction to the certification of rehabilitation counselors. *Rehabilitation Counseling Bulletin,* 1971, *15,* 84-85.

Patterson, C. H. Comment on "The certification of rehabilitation counselors." *Rehabilitation Counseling Bulletin,* 1971, *15,* 86-7.

Thoreson, Richard W. Certification: A good provisional measure. *Rehabilitation Counseling Bulletin,* 1971, *15,* 80-83.

Thorsen, Jack. *Counselor certification 1971.* Washington, D.C.: American Personnel and Guidance Association, 1971. (Mimeograph; folder cc)

1970

Dudley, G., & Ruff, E. E. School counselor certification: A study of current requirements. *School Counselor,* 1970, *17,* 304-311.

National Council for Accreditation of Teacher Education. *Standards for accreditation of teacher education: The accreditation of basic and advanced preparation programs for professional school personnel.* Washington, D.C.: Author, 1970. (Not in APGA)

Wehrly, B. L. Elementary school counselor preparation programs in the United States. *Elementary School Guidance and Counseling,* 1970, *4,* 203-210.

1969

Humes, C. W. Teaching experience a must for counselors? *The Clearing House,* 1969, *44,* 245-248. (Folder)

Ohlsen, M. M. Evaluation of education for the professions. *Counselor Education and Supervision,* 1969, *9,* 30-40.

1968

American Rehabilitation Counseling Association. The professional preparation of rehabilitation counselors. A statement of policy, August 1968. *Rehabilitation Counseling Bulletin,* 1968, *12,* 29–35. (Folder cc)

Bruno, L. *Statement of standards for preparation of school professional personnel leading to certification* (4th draft). Olympia, Wash.: Superintendent of Public Instruction, 1968.

Special Issue: Up-grading guidance practice through improved preparation of guidance workers. *Counselor Education and Supervision,* 1968, 7 (3SP).

1967

The professional preparation of rehabilitation counselors. *Rehabilitation Counseling Bulletin,* 1967, *10,* 163–167.

Stinnett, T. M. *A manual on certification requirements for school personnel in the United States.* Washington, D.C.: National Education Association, 1967. (There is a 1970 edition) (APGA has, 1967)

1966

Houghton, H. W. *Certification requirements for school pupil personnel workers.* Washington, D.C.: U.S. Department of Health, Education, and Welfare, Office of Education, 1966. (APGA has)

1965

Fitzgerald, P. W. Counseling: A growing profession. *School Counselor,* 1965, *12* 250–253.

Keppers, G. L. National certification of counselors. *Counselor Education and Supervision,* 1965, *4,* 202–207.

Noble, F. C. The two–year graduate program in counselor education: A re–examination. *Counselor Education and Supervision,* 1965, *4,* 160–162.

1964

American School Counselor Association. *Statement of policy for secondary school counselors.* Washington, D.C.: Author, 1964.

Porter, M. E., & Collison, B. B. *The elementary school guidance counselor . . . implications for establishing his training, certification and role.* (Speech given at 15th annual conference of counselors and administrators, Emporia, September 25 & 26, 1964). Moravia, N.Y.: Chronicle Guidance Publications, 1964–65.

1963

The counselor, professional preparation and role. *Personnel and Guidance Journal,* 1963, *41,* 480.

Dugan, W. E. Guidance in the 1970's. *School Counselor,* 1963, *10,* 96–100.

Hoyt, K. B. Should school counselors have taught? A research proposal. *Counselor Education and Supervision,* 1953, *2,* 126–129.

Rossberg, R. H. To teach or not to teach: Is that the question? *Counselor Education and Supervision,* 1963, *2,* 121–125.

Voice your opinion regarding professional preparation and standards, *SPATE*, 1963, *2*, 28.

1962

Association for Counselor Education and Supervision. *Report of the research committee.* Washington, D.C.: Author, 1962. (Mimeograph; folder cc)
Counselor and counselor trainer attitudes toward counselor certification in the United States. *Personnel and Guidance Journal,* 1962, *40,* 791–798.
Counselor education—a progress report on standards—discussion, reaction, and related papers. Washington, D.C.: Association for Counselor Education and Supervision & American School Counselor Association, 1962. (APGA has)
Hutson, P. W. Another 'position' paper. *Counselor Education and Supervision,* 1962, *2,* 40–44.
Patterson, C. H. Trends in vocational rehabilitation counseling. *Rehabilitation Counseling Bulletin,* 1962, *5,* 59–67.

1961

Cohen, N. K. Must teaching be a prerequisite of guidance? *Counselor Education and Supervision,* 1961, *1,* 69–71.
McClary, D. Report of the committee on counselor preparation and standards, *School Counselor,* 1961, *8,* 82–84.
McCully, C. H. A rationale for counselor certification. *Counselor Education and Supervision,* 1961, *1,* 3–9.

1960

Hill, G. E., & Green D. The selection, preparation, and professionalization of guidance and personnel workers. *Review of Educational Research,* 1960, *30,* 115–130. (APGA has)
Lloyd, D. O. *An evaluative study of guidance counselor certification in the United States.* Unpublished doctoral dissertation, final chapter, Arizona State University, Tempe, May 1960. (Folder)
Reynolds, J. P. The basic purpose of certification. *The Education of Teachers: Certification,* Report of the San Diego TEPS Conference, 1960. Washington, D.C.: National Education Association, 1960. (Not in APGA)
Woodring, P. Principles on criteria of certification programs. *The Education of Teachers: Certification,* Report of the San Diego TEPS Conference, 1960. Washington, D.C.: National Education Association, 1960. (Not in APGA)

1959

Farwell, G., & Vekich, A. M. Status and certification of counselors in Ohio high schools. *Personnel and Guidance Journal,* 1959, *38,* 285–289.
Mueller, K. H. Criteria for evaluating professional status. *Personnel and Guidance Journal,* 1959, *37,* 410–417.

1958

American Personnel and Guidance Association. Professional training, licensing and certification. *Personnel and Guidance Journal,* 1958, *37,* 162–166.

Williamson, E. G. Professional preparation of student personnel workers. *School and Society*, 1958, *1*, 3–5. (Not in APGA)

1957

Stoughton, R. W. The preparation of counselors and personnel workers. *Review of Educational Research*, 1957, *27*, 174–185. (APGA has)

1955

APGA committee reports on professional training, licensing, and certification. *Personnel and Guidance Journal*, 1955, *33*, 356–357.

Puryear, M. T. Child centering the certification program. *Vocational Guidance Quarterly*, 1954–55, *3*, 51–52.

RECENT PUBLICATIONS—REGISTER

The National Academy of Certified Clinical Mental Health Counselors. *Register of the NACCMHC, 1979–1980*. Tampa, Fla.: Author, 1979.

The National Academy of Certified Clinical Mental Health Counselors. *Register of the NACCMHC, 1980–1981*. Tampa, Fla.: Author. 1980.